EDUCATIONAL REFORM AND THE TRANSFORMATION OF SOUTHERN AFRICA

SOUTHERN AFRICA

Educational Reform and the Transformation of Southern Africa

DICKSON A. MUNGAZI
and
L. KAY WALKER

Westport, Connecticut
London

Library of Congress Cataloging-in-Publication Data

Mungazi, Dickson A.
    Educational reform and the transformation of southern Africa /
Dickson A. Mungazi and L. Kay Walker.
       p.   cm.
    Includes bibliographical references and index.
    ISBN 0–275–95746–2 (alk. paper)
    1. Educational change—Africa, Southern. 2. School management and
organization—Africa, Southern. 3. Education—Social aspects—
Africa, Southern. I. Walker, L. Kay, 1943– .
    LA1501.M82 1997
    370′.968—dc21   96–47620

British Library Cataloguing in Publication Data is available.

Library of Congress Catalog Card Number: 96–47620
ISBN: 0–275–95746–2

First published in 1997

Praeger Publishers, 88 Post Road West, Westport, CT 06881
An imprint of Greenwood Publishing Group, Inc.

Printed in the United States of America

The paper used in this book complies with the
Permanent Paper Standard issued by the National
Information Standards Organization (Z39.48–1984).

10 9 8 7 6 5 4 3 2 1

Africa needs change to ensure its development. Reform in education must be the starting point towards meaningful social change.

Julius Nyerere, 1974

When unemployment occurs between graduation from school and the first attempt to secure employment, it is often misinterpreted as inefficiency of the school itself.

George Psacharopoulos, World Bank, 1980

To the memory of Erwin H. Goldenstein, teacher, scholar, and friend, whose advice made a difference.

Contents

Preface

The purpose of this study is to furnish evidence supporting the conclusion that the thrust for the transformation of southern Africa, that region of Africa south of the equator, cannot be initiated without responding to the need for fundamental educational reform. In this study, transformation is defined as basic change in the structure of national institutions to allow the individual a maximum opportunity to ensure his advancement, without any restrictions in terms of socioeconomic development and political freedom to participate in the national purpose.

National purpose itself must be structured around the importance of the role of the individual in shaping the character of society. This development gives the individual the ability he needs to establish his own goals and to participate in a national endeavor to help him attain his own concept and ideals of self. Reform is defined as basic and purposeful change, not for change's sake, but to improve the effectiveness of the system of delivery.

In presenting this evidence, the study seeks to answer the following questions: What conditions exist in southern Africa today that must be addressed through fundamental educational reform? What should be considered in recognizing the need for that reform? What are some theoretical imperatives of educational reform? What is the purpose of educational reform in this critical region of Africa? What are some prerequisites of educational reform and national transformation? What approaches can nations of southern Africa employ to ensure successful reform? What are some results of educational reform? What problems can impede both educational reform and national transformation, and how can these problems be resolved?

The focus of this study is to show that the educational advancement of the individual is the best way to ensure national transformation that promotes development. But the educational development of the individual is possible only when education is reformed to make it possible for the educational process to allow students freedom of choice for a course of study. This process leads to educational reform through national transformation, which will ensure the development of the country.

The freedom the individual has in engaging in a purposeful educational pursuit generates confidence for the future. This confidence, in turn, generates a set of purposeful activities to fulfill defined objectives. This cannot occur in a climate that inhibits both the student's freedom and his aspiration for self-fulfillment. The evidence used to substantiate this conclusion was obtained during study trips to several countries of southern Africa between 1983 and 1996. This evidence consists of original materials and documents that we were able to secure.

In presenting this evidence, we reached the following conclusions: the thrust for educational reform to ensure national transformation must be initiated in the context of socioeconomic development. This requires individual political freedom to participate in all national endeavors. This national endeavor creates a climate that makes educational reform possible. Once educational reform takes place, it combines with socioeconomic and political factors to create essential elements of national transformation as a prerequisite of national development. The nations of southern Africa, like those of other regions of Africa, are experiencing enormous socioeconomic and political problems that can be resolved by introducing fundamental reform in the educational system. Reform and transformation cannot be separated, they are intertwined.

The reality that the nations of southern Africa have not been able to grasp is that their failure to initiate successful educational reform invariably leads to failure in initiating successful national transformation. The nations of southern Africa recognize the fact that there are major problems in this kind of social environment that must be resolved fully. They will continue to endure the agony of conflict, underdevelopment, and underachievement until national transformation begins.

Acknowledgments

In the process of writing a book that discusses highly critical aspects of a critical region, great care needs to be exercised in obtaining original materials and documents that enable one to interpret events and policies in an accurate manner and a logical fashion. For this reason, we wish to express our profound gratitude and appreciation to the embassies of the countries of southern Africa in the United States and the various departments of government in the countries of southern Africa itself for allowing us access to some of these materials. We also wish to thank individuals in the countries of southern Africa for their willingness to offer some important insights into the problems that are being experienced by the countries of this region.

We particularly wish to express our appreciation to the Zimbabwe National Archives, the Ministry of Information, and the Ministry of Education and Culture for allowing us access to original documents and materials.

We also wish to record our special appreciation to Betty Russell and Ed Bulinski of the Center for Excellence in Education at Northern Arizona University for their assistance in programming the computer so that the manuscript could be produced more efficiently. In a similar fashion, we wish to thank our colleagues at Northern Arizona University for their support and encouragement. Finally, we wish to express our appreciation to Candace Wheeler of the Center for Excellence in Education, Northern Arizona University, for the design of the map of southern Africa included in the study, and to Charlene Wingo and Margo Gay, also of the Center for Excellence in Education, for assisting in the production of the manuscript.

Introduction

THE CONCEPT OF NATIONAL DEVELOPMENT

This is a study of the effect of educational reform on national development in southern Africa, that part of Africa south of the equator. The term *reform* means change, not simply for the sake of change, but to ensure improvement. Therefore, educational reform calls for change in the educational system to improve it for the purpose of initiating change in the social system. The thrust for educational reform in southern Africa must be seen in the context of the enormous political and economic problems that this critical region of Africa is experiencing and from the point of view that change in the conditions that control human existence is imperative to the development of society itself.

Two questions are critically important to this study. The first is: Why is it important for the nations of southern Africa to initiate educational reform? The second question is: What does successful educational reform involve? The answers to these questions lie in the character of southern Africa itself. Before discussing that character, we must define the expression *national development*. Although the expression *national development* is not fully understood by the leaders and most of the people of the nations of southern Africa, it carries the definitive meaning of embracing a program of action designed to improve the essential features of national institutions. These institutions include efforts to ensure fundamental freedoms of the people, such as self-expression and the rights to be safe and secure, to participate in national politics, to earn a decent income, to have social associations, and to exercise freedom of religion. A nation that denies its citizens these basic freedoms cannot be regarded as progressive, and any thrust for its own definition of national development is void of any real meaning.

In the context of contemporary terminology, national development also means affording all the citizens basic freedoms to pursue goals and objectives that are consistent with their interests and purposes. These include the right to pursue careers without restrictions, to participate in the political process, to run for public office, to exercise freedom of choice, to own property, to criticize the government without reprisal, to belong to a political party of one's choice, and to earn a decent living and live where one wishes. In short, national development means setting goals that citizens can pursue to improve the conditions that control their lives so that they are better off than they were in the past. This process allows citizens to identify themselves with national purposes. These are the elements that combine to create a national social climate that brings happiness and security to the citizens. National development has its basis in this climate.

EDUCATIONAL REFORM AND NATIONAL DEVELOPMENT

An answer to the first question, why it is important for the nations of southern Africa to initiate educational reform, must be provided. The character of southern Africa itself demands that nations initiate educational reform because that is one viable way of finding solutions to the problems of national development. The release of Nelson Mandela on February 10, 1990, from life imprisonment, following his 1964 conviction on charges of attempting to overthrow the government of South Africa, was a dramatic turn of tragic events that began to unfold with the victory of the Nationalist Party led by Daniel Malan in the elections of 1948. Can one define Mandela's release as an element of national development without making an effort to dismantle apartheid? The answer is no, because apartheid did not allow the components previously identified to combine and operate in the manner that would translate subsequent events into a thrust for national development.

The enactment of the infamous Bantu Education Act in 1953 was an event that set South Africa on a course to deadly national conflict. When Malan retired from active politics in 1958, he was succeeded by Hendrik Verwoerd, a man of uncompromising belief in the supremacy of apartheid, the superiority of Afrikaners, and the assumed inferiority of Africans. As the director of the Bantu administration in the Malan government, Verwoerd became the principal architect of apartheid as he systematically applied it to reduce Africans to the status of bare existence. To accomplish this objective, Verwoerd used provisions of the Bantu Education Act to elevate Afrikaners to the pedestal of absolute political supremacy, enshrined in their presumed invincibility and infallibility.

Verwoerd's assassination in 1966 brought John Vorster to the seat of power from which he directed apartheid to new unprecedented heights. The decision of Vorster's government to enforce new provisions of the Bantu Education Act created a national climate that led to the explosion that was heard around the world from Soweto in June 1976. Facing a barrage of outcry and criticism from the international community, Vorster decided to resign in 1978 on grounds of poor health, rather than face the reality that apartheid was setting South Africa on a course of self-destruction. Indeed, apartheid was rolling with a vengeance.

Vorster's successor, Pieter Botha, approached the problems created by apartheid in all of southern Africa, not just in South Africa. With a new determination to ignore the outcry from the international community, his efforts were to make apartheid a sacred shrine that both Afrikaners and Africans must worship with total supplication. The intensification of the armed struggle, spearheaded by the African National Congress (ANC), along with a series of bomb explosions throughout South Africa, killing many and injuring many more, and the imposition of economic sanctions by the international community combined to force Botha to urge his fellow die-hard Afrikaners to *adapt or die*. However, Botha did not have the courage to face up to the reality that apartheid had gone too far. Instead, he warned the world, "Don't push us too far." When Frederick W. de Klerk succeeded Botha in 1987, he recognized the critical nature of the South African society, in its entirety, as a victim of apartheid. This is why, in 1990, de Klerk began to call for change. The release of Nelson Mandela was de Klerk's call for that change.

It is not surprising that Mandela's response to de Klerk's action was his own call to reform the system of education based on initiating nothing less than action to dismantle apartheid to transform the character of the South African society. F. W. de Klerk and his fellow Afrikaners were forced to the realization that the political status quo could not be maintained forever, and that it was an equally elusive task to institute change in the social system without initiating the thrust of educational reform. Therefore, the challenge to de Klerk was to respond to the call to end apartheid by changing the system of education so that a thrust for national development could be made based on principles requiring the nation's educational transformation.

Such an approach is the only way solutions to the problems of national development in any country can be found. This is why Africans persistently demanded an end to the policy of apartheid as a condition of that development. Bringing the people of South Africa, both black and white, closer to understanding and tolerating each other would benefit their country. This is what Mandela saw when he said on February 13, 1990, that education under apartheid was a crime against humanity. The recognition of this truth constitutes a prerequisite to meeting the challenge of educational reform in South Africa. Africans did not vote in national elections until 1994. They were also not allowed to run for national public office because they were not regarded as citizens of South Africa. These were, indeed, forms of the ultimate crime against humanity that the policy of apartheid perpetuated.

The first order of business for de Klerk and his government should have been to dismantle the Bantu Education Act of 1953 to convince Africans that he and his government meant well. Because they did not do this, serious doubt arose about their sincere intention to bring about genuine change. The action that was taken by the South African parliament on June 5, 1991, to repeal provisions of the apartheid law did not constitute the final act to remove the last vestiges of an oppressive system. Black people were still regarded as second-class citizens and foreigners in the land of their birth. The action taken by some Afrikaner parents at Potgietersburg in January 1996 in trying to deny registration of some African students in an all-white school came as a painful reminder of a system that was condemned by the entire international community.

The character of other countries in southern Africa also shows that educational reform is critical to reshaping their societies. In Mozambique, a country with a literacy rate of 14 percent in 1987, and in Angola with 30 percent, brutal civil wars have left the people without hope for the future and without purpose or direction. The plundering and brutality with which Jonas Savimbi's UNITA in Angola and Afonzo Dhlamini's Renamo in Mozambique have waged the struggle for their respective causes lead to the conclusion that educational reform would help the warring parties to understand the destructive nature of the conflict that these two former Portuguese colonies have endured since they gained independence in 1975.

Conventional wisdom suggests that investing in educational reform would make it possible for Mozambique, Angola, and Namibia to recognize the critical nature of national unity for purposes of initiating the transformation of their society for the benefit of all people. Once people are educated sufficiently, they understand the need to restructure national programs to ensure the happiness and security of all. This cannot be done successfully in the context of existing education conditions. Without adequate educational reform, it is not possible to recognize this reality.

Instead of directing their resources toward the destruction of each other, the people of these countries would be wise to direct them toward the development of dynamic societies with a potential for greatness. Observers have concluded that the economic, physical, and psychological damage that the people of these countries have endured will take years to repair. If there is a need to make a new thrust for educational reform anywhere in Africa, that need is greater in these countries than anywhere else on the continent.

Following a bitter fifteen-year war that led to independence in April 1980, Zimbabwe, the former British colony of Southern Rhodesia, recognized that the first priority in its efforts to rebuild the devastated country was to make a fresh start in education. The leaders realized that education was crucial to other aspects of their national endeavors. Therefore, as soon as it was instituted, the new government of Zimbabwe accepted the challenge of national development by initiating a new thrust in educational reform.

In 1980, however, the conflict between the government and dissident elements culminated in the government's announcement of its intent to turn Zimbabwe into a one-party state. This announcement derailed the educational program that the government had put in place, and it has seen the general decline of the economy along with a lack of confidence in the future among the people and the periodic waves of violence that have marked most of Zimbabwe's first decade of independence. When a new conflict broke out in 1989 between the government and university students over the question of corruption by some government officials, there was a widespread feeling that the government itself had become the problem, because in its desire to institute a one-party system, it had lost sight of the national objectives that it had identified at its inception in 1980.

The efforts that Zimbabwe had made since independence in initiating educational reform to improve its literacy rate of 40 percent in 1983 had, by 1991, been recognized as having a stabilizing influence in shaping the course of national development. By 1988, that rate had increased to 50 percent. If Zimbabwe could overcome the temptation to turn the country into a one-party state, then it could stand on the verge of becoming great, enshrined in the priceless potential that has been acknowledged as the basis of a truly happy and progressive nation. The road to this greatness lies in Zimbabwe's ability to meet the challenge of economic and educational reform within a national climate of political freedom and individual liberty.

In 1992, the system of universal and free primary education that Zimbabwe had introduced in 1980 came to a halt, causing despondency and alarm among the people. In 1996, the decline in the economy further hurt the efforts that the people were making to ensure a better future. Education for children was no longer free.

Attempts to initiate educational reform in other countries have been lost in the political milieu. The granting of independence to Malawi and Zambia in

Some Facts About Southern Africa 1996

	Angola	Botswana	Mozambique	Namibia	South Africa	Tanzania	Zaire	Zambia	Zimbabwe
Pop.	10,069,500	1,392,400	18,115,250	1,651,540	45,095,459	28,701,077	44,060,636	9,445,723	11,139,960
Area in Sq.Mile	481,353	231,804	308,261	318,261	435,868	364,886	905,063	290,586	150,873
Date of Col.	1575	1889	1575	1885	1835	1885	1885	1891	1890
Col. Nation	Portugal	Britain	Portugal	Germany	Britain	Germany	Belgium	Britain	Britain
Capital City	Luanda	Gaberone	Maputo	Windhoek	Cape Town	Dar es Salaam	Kinshasa	Lusaka	Harare
Curre.	Kwanza K35.1=US$1	Pula P100=US$1	Metical M403=US$1	Dollar $3.7=US$1	Rand R3.9=US$1	Shilling S550=US$1	Zaire Z9.50=US$1	Kwacha K8.20=US$1	Dollar $9.10=US$1
GNP in B$	5.7	2.2	1.6	2.4	6.0	7.20	6.50	7.40	5.30
Literacy Rate	40%	64%	33%	36%	75%	86%	55%	54%	55%
Type of Govt.	Socialist	Multi-party Democracy	Multi-party Democracy	Multi-party Democracy	Multi-party Democracy	One-party	One-party	Multi-party Democracy	Multi-party Democracy
Current Leader	Edwardo de Santos,1979	Quett Masire, 1980	Joachim Chissano,1986	Sam Nujoma, 1990	Nelson Mandela, 1994	Benjamin Mkapa, 1995	Sese Seko, 1965	Frederick Chiluba, 1994	R. Mugabe, 1980
Official Lang.	Portuguese	English	Portuguese	English	Afrikaans and English	English	French	English	English
% of GNP spent on Ed.	4.1	4.1	3.8	3.4	3.9	3.1	3.0	2.5	3.1
Date of Indep.	1975	1966	1975	1990	1910	1962	1960	1964	1980

October 1964 was an occasion that raised new hopes among the Africans of these countries for a better future. But, when Hastings Kamuzu Banda of Malawi and Kenneth Kaunda of Zambia converted their countries to one-party systems of government, the euphoria of a brighter future turned into an abyss of despair. The efforts that these two countries made in changing the educational system to reflect the needs of the people for a hopeful future fell into the background, as every activity by their national leaders focused on strengthening the notion of one-party rule.

In 1992, Kaunda was defeated in his bid for reelection in Zambia and Banda was also defeated in 1994. In that year, it was revealed that Banda was implicated in the death of three political opponents and he stood trial for his crime. Although he was acquitted of the charges in 1996, Banda apologized for his role in the death of those three men.

These developments were a sequel to the political events that have impacted the educational and economical developments in these countries. In 1990, Malawi had a literacy rate of 25 percent and Zambia's rate was 54 percent. Indeed, during the years that both Kaunda and Banda were in office, both countries endured an unprecedented agony of underdevelopment as a result of the action of these two leaders.

This pattern of one-party government has been persistent in southern Africa. When Mobuto Sese Seko staged a military coup in Zaire on November 25, 1965, it was the beginning of the road to a military dictatorship that has entrenched itself more deeply than in 1965. Seko has shown no mercy toward those who hold political views different from his own concerning the direction that Zaire must take. Over the years, Seko has been reported to have a personal fortune estimated in billions of dollars, while the people have been enduring grinding poverty. Instead of directing his efforts toward the development of the people through educational reform and genuine social change, Seko designed a strategy to keep himself in office for life, just as Banda and Kaunda did. The literacy rate of 55 percent in Zaire in 1989 could have been better if national resources had been directed toward the educational development of the people. Instead, by 1996 the literacy rate was declining.

Botswana is the only country in southern Africa whose government and people seem to understand and appreciate the importance of casting the educational process in a national framework of democratic principles. Although its literacy rate of 37 percent out of the total population of 1.2 million in 1996 is comparatively low, its people are among the happiest in all of southern Africa because they enjoy all the fundamental freedoms that are essential to national endeavors as we have defined them in this study. While we were in southern Africa in 1989, 1995, and 1996, we were pleased to see that a multi-party democracy is alive and well in Botswana. There was no government control of the media, no restrictions on the people's right to belong to the political party of their choice, and no massive nationalization of major industries.

The National Commission on Education of 1977 seemed to understand the importance of accepting the challenge of initiating educational reform to sustain these democratic values and practices. This study discusses its findings and the implications of its recommendations.

Since Botswana achieved political independence from Britain on September 30, 1966, under the leadership of Seretse Khama, it has never wavered in its commitment to democracy. When Quett Masire assumed the office of president on July 13, 1980, following Khama's death, there was no fear that the democratic principles that were established at the inception of independence would be in danger. The people and their government fully cooperated in a new endeavor to ensure national development based on a new thrust for educational reform. Botswana's efforts in this national thrust are also discussed in this study as an example of what the nations of southern Africa can do to promote national development through educational reform.

The problems that these examples show are the reasons why the nations of southern Africa, more than other countries of the *Dark Continent* with the possible exception of the *Horn of Africa*, must initiate educational reform. Conventional wisdom suggests that problems of national development cannot be resolved in isolation from those in education. Because change in education is necessary to initiate change in society, the concept of reform becomes an imperative to resolve other problems. Reform in education requires the ability to collectively resolve problems.

THE INITIATIVE FOR EDUCATIONAL REFORM

Now, the second question, what educational reform involves, must be answered. What has been discussed concerning the national character of the countries of southern Africa leads to the conclusion that the thrust for educational reform involves two basic components. The first component is to ensure the development of the individual to help make national development possible through basic understanding and agreement. The second component is to consider the outcome of educational reform. This will help the nations of southern Africa focus on why such reform is important. To discuss the importance of educational reform in southern Africa, this study begins by discussing its influence on the structure of society itself. In doing so, it underscores the need for reform in general and suggests its structure, purpose, and outcome. It also discusses the problems that have placed this region at a crossroads.

The study discusses the need for educational reform from the perspective of its role in helping shape the character of society during the colonial period. The discussion of the educational objectives, educational policy, and educational process during the colonial period leads to the conclusion that the need for educational innovation is an imperative to the growth and development of political independence. It is time to break away from past systems that were designed to serve the interests of colonial society. After establishing in the first chapter that the educational system during the colonial period was designed to serve the interests of the colonial society, the study moves on to discuss in subsequent chapters how educational innovation can help solve the problems left behind by the colonial governments. The study also relates to the conditions of education and the fullest opportunities for all students to plan their future in a manner unrestricted by financial and political restraints. This suggests the conclusion that a nation enjoys a greater degree of freedom as a result of educational reform. These components are summarized in Chapter 8.

CONCLUSIONS AND IMPLICATIONS

The nations of southern Africa must remember that as critically important as it is, educational reform must be initiated within the environment of fundamental change that must take place in the social system. This means that the political system has to change to embrace the general concept of change itself. The elections held in Namibia in November 1989 to pave the way for independence targeted for March 21, 1990; the elections held in South Africa in April 1994 to end apartheid; and the change of the socioeconomic system in Mozambique announced by President Joaquim Chissano in August 1989 did set the environment to initiate fundamental change in these three countries. Efforts were made toward a negotiated settlement between the warring parties in Angola, and de Klerk did make peace overtures toward ANC, and other formerly outlawed political parties. These factors combine to create a climate of regional peace so desperately needed to place southern Africa on the road to a new society and prosperity.

Initiating change is an enormous task, but it is a task that must be accomplished because while the risk of failure is there, the consequences of not trying are devastating. A relationship must exist between social transformation and educational reform because these are the two pillars of development the nations of southern Africa need to ensure the successful cooperation of national development.

For that cooperation to come about, South Africa had first to recognize from an apartheid point of view that a new nonracial society would be created.

Meaningful educational reform could take place only in this kind of setting. Because South Africa went through that process of change in 1994, it can be concluded that the elements of the transformation of southern Africa as a region are in place and beginning to operate. The extent of change that took place in South Africa now presents an opportunity to all the nations of the region to initiate a thrust for educational reform as a strategy for their transformation. This is the call that all nations of southern Africa must answer without delay and without fear of investing in their greatest national resources—the minds, bodies, and spirits of the youth.

Southern Africa in Crisis: A Region in Need of Reform

> I write as one of the victims of Zambia's injustice and oppression, especially the draconian laws on detention without trial that the government has introduced.
>
> Henry Kalenga, 1990

THE PANORAMA OF SOUTHERN AFRICA

Of all the regions of Africa none has experienced the agony of social change more than southern Africa.[1] In 1996, the brutal civil war in Angola and Mozambique was reaching a critical level. The political conflict caused by the decline of the economy and the fear of the introduction of a one-party system of government in Zimbabwe was causing uncertainty about the future. The continuing scourge of conflict following the 1994 installation of a black government in South Africa created new fear about the shift of political responsibilities. The political transformation of Namibia from the grip of apartheid to democracy in 1990 raised serious questions about the future of a democratic country. And finally the defeat of Kenneth Kaunda of Zambia and Kamuzu Hastings Banda in Malawi in 1994 added to the political uncertainty in those countries. All of these events have placed this critical region of Africa at the crossroads. From these events one is led to the conclusion that the problems of southern Africa are so complex and interrelated to the extent that, to find solutions, a major effort must be made on a regional basis.

To understand these complex problems one needs to understand the characteristics that make southern Africa unique. Africa is a huge continent second in size only to Asia, and more than three times the size of the United States. It covers an area of 11,677,239 square miles compared to 3,536,855 square miles for the United States. It stretches some five thousand miles from the Mediterranean Sea in the north to the Cape of Good Hope in the south. Africa's land mass is one third of the world land mass. Indeed, Africa, more than any other continent, is a land of great contrasts. Variation in the landscape of Africa is seen in the Great Sahara Desert stretching across the north and the heavy rain forests of the equatorial region. One sees snowy peaks, rolling sand dunes and the expansive savanna. Diversity also abounds in the human landscape. There are the impoverished and starving masses in East Africa compared to the white millionaires of South Africa. Both brutal military dictatorships and freedom-loving democratic states are found on this continent of panoramic contrasts. The human and physical diversity is as rich as the diversity of wildlife on the continent. Africa has it all.

These contrasts invariably distract the nations of Africa from focusing on the many problems they all face in common. One can also see that the dysfunctional nature of the political system is on a direct collision course with individual freedom. The human impulsive urge for freedom and the struggle for national development cannot be sustained in a politically oppressive environment. This situation combines with other factors to ravage the natural beauty of Africa. As they struggle to retain a sense of self, Africans seem to draw their aspirations from the majesty of the land forms, geographical features, and the cultural values, arts, and traditions that make this region unique.

Some spectacular landforms are found in southern Africa. This adds a panoramic sense of its importance to the rest of the world. The famous Drakensberg Mountains are about seven hundred miles long and the highest peak towers to eleven thousand feet. The legendary Ruwenzori Mountains, known among the Africans of the region as the "Mountains of the Moon," are found on the border between Uganda and Zaire, and reach a towering height of sixteen thousand feet, an example of the majestic beauty of the land forms characteristic of southern Africa. The famous Kilimanjaro Mountain in Tanzania reaches a staggering height of 19,340 feet, whereas Mount Kenya, the inspiration of Jomo Kenyatta, reaches a height of seventeen thousand feet.

Both of these mountains lie on the equator and add something unique to the charm and glory with which the Africans regard them. Both are so high that they are always covered with ice, snow, or mist. This adds to the majesty with which the Africans blend and live in perfect harmony with the greatness of nature's creation. In addition to these geographical features, some of the greatest rivers in the world are found in southern Africa. The historic and sacred Nile River, the longest in the world, begins its journey to the Mediterranean

Sea and starts its life-giving mission to the Sudan and Egypt in Uganda, a country that has been torn apart by political strife and ravaged by the civil war and by the dictatorship of Idi Amin Dada. From these rivers and mountains come the rich mineral and natural resources that attracted the interest of the European colonial adventurers.

In Uganda, the White Nile begins its course from the Kagera River and flows into Lake Victoria. The Blue Nile begins its turbulent journey from the deep gorges of Lake Tana, high in the mountain ranges of Ethiopia, a nation that has captured international news headlines because of its brutal civil war, starving masses, and frequent drought. The irony of it all is that the origin of a powerful life-giving river begins in a drought-ridden country. The Blue Nile and the White Nile merge at Khartoum, the capital city of the troubled Sudan, and their combined waters flow down through a vast territory depositing fertile silt that partially converts the desert lands into a productive agricultural stretch so vital to the economy of both the Sudan and Egypt.

The Zaire River is about three thousand miles long and drains a basin of nearly 1.5 million square miles. Its many tributaries have their origin in the region of heavy rainfall, nearly sixty inches per year. The Zambezi River starts its journey to the Indian Ocean from near Lubumbashi in southern Zaire and cuts its way through Zambia, forming a natural boundary between it and Zimbabwe. The impressive Victoria Falls attracts hundreds of tourists every year. The Africans of the area called it Mosi-oa-Tunya (the Smoke that Thunders).

David Livingstone (1813–1873), who is believed to have been the first white man to see the famous falls in 1855, named it the Victoria Falls in honor of Queen Victoria (1837–1901) of Britain. It never occurred to him that an African name would have endeared him to the Africans. However, on November 16, 1855, Livingstone was so impressed with the majesty of the falls that he was moved to remark, "Scenes so lovely must have been gazed upon by angels in their radiant flight." The breath-taking spectacle about the Victoria Falls is that a huge curtain of falling water roars in a continuous and thundering motion and a panoramic rising spray. Today, a huge bronze statue of the venerable Livingstone gazes east along the line of the majestic falls, reminding the tourists of the days of the glory and grandeur of the British Empire in Africa.

In 1956, the Kariba Hydroelectric Dam was constructed east of the falls to provide electricity to the then Federation of Rhodesia and Nyasaland, which lasted from 1953 to 1963. The Orange and Limpopo Rivers begin their journeys to the Atlantic and Indian Oceans, respectively, in the Drakensberg Mountains of eastern South Africa. The Limpopo enters the Indian Ocean at the Zambezi delta about halfway between Quelimane and Beira in Mozambique, and the Orange River ends its journey to the Atlantic at Alexander Bay, about halfway between Cape Town and Walvis Bay. All along the waterways, the indigenous art reflects the interaction of the people with the physical landforms. The diversity of the people and their art, artifacts, and livelihood are, like all people, dictated by their placement on the globe.

One of the most fascinating features of southern Africa is the diversity of its people.[2] The earliest known inhabitants of this critical region are the Khoi, known among Westerners as Hottentots and the Bushmen, some of whom still live in Botswana,[3] Namibia, and South Africa. In 1980, the South African government heavily recruited the Khoi into its army for its expanding war against guerrillas of the Southwest Africa People's Organization (SWAPO) in Namibia. But only about six hundred actually enlisted.

The Khoi live in the desert areas, the Mbuti, known among the Africans as Children of the Forest and by whites as pygmies, live in the equatorial forests of Zaire. The Khoi and the Mbuti have several things in common. Both average a height of 4.5 feet. That both have resisted all efforts to persuade them to accept "modern life" suggests not an inability to comprehend the need for their advancement, but a recognition of the dangers inherent in accepting Western culture. Both live a simple but happy life. Both hunt with bows and arrows. The Khoi have left evidence to suggest that they were accomplished artists. Many of their paintings and other forms of art can still be seen in many parts of southern Africa.

The Bantu people range widely in cultural practices and the diversity of their languages is an enrichment of their cultural heritage, and this cultural and linguistic diversity make it hard for Africans to promote national unity. Among the leading Bantu groups of southern Africa are the Masai of Tanzania, the Zulus and Xhosa of South Africa, the Bemba and Lozi of Zambia, and the Shona and Ndebele of Zimbabwe. The whites, or "Europeans" as they are called in southern Africa, include the Dutch or Afrikaners, as they are known today. They also include the British, the Germans, and the Portuguese. That European countries from which they came had extensive colonial empires in the region explains their presence. The effect of their creating colonies there is the subject of this study.

In 1996 there were about 120 million people in southern Africa, immensely diverse in physical appearance, cultural traditions, and languages. Indeed, the world sees the people of southern Africa, both black and white, as belonging to a strange world and has cast them into stereotypes of either blatant political dictators imposing a brutal and cruel yoke of oppression or as simple and primitive children of nature beating the drums of a life-style unaffected by any call to advancement and completely surrounded by an impenetrable veil of ignorance.

The outside world also sees southern Africa as being ruled either by the die-hard Afrikaner oppressive extremists and bigots who, until 1994, were totally unable to comprehend the need to end apartheid or by a band of black dictators who seek to serve their own political interests by equally oppressing their own people. While the policy of apartheid came to an end in 1994, conflict in South Africa has taken new dimensions. It is, however, true that the political and economic exploitation of the masses by elite groups and corruption by some government officials have created enormous problems for southern Africa, setting a stage for a major confrontation between the conflicting forces that exist in the region. This is the reason why fundamental social change and transformation has to come about based on a carefully designed approach to educational reform.

It is a sad truth that until recently it was not the search for solutions to the problems of social injustice in southern Africa that attracted the attention of the world, but its mineral wealth. High-quality gold, cobalt, diamonds, chromium, uranium, manganese, and copper have profoundly influenced the policies of Western nations toward southern Africa. In the world production figures of 1983, southern Africa accounted for the following percentages: diamonds 90 percent, gold 67 percent, manganese 24 percent, and cobalt 83 percent. But in the same year the literacy of the following countries was: Angola 12 percent, Botswana 30 percent, Mozambique 20 percent, Namibia 15 percent, South Africa 55 percent, Tanzania 60 percent, Zaire 40 percent, Zambia 50 percent, and Zimbabwe 30 percent.[4] This situation suggests that the vast resources of southern Africa have been utilized to benefit not the African people, but rather, those Western nations who have invested heavily in the exploitation of the mineral wealth. We discuss later how the establishment of colonial paradigms made this possible.

Discussing the geographical and social characteristics of southern Africa leads to three basic conclusions. The first conclusion is that the chronic racial, political, and social problems that exist there have placed the people of the region at a crossroads, just as has happened in the Middle East and Northern Ireland. However, change is imminent amid the great contrasts that exist in the traditional life-style. With the bulldozer, the soaring skyscraper, the tribal leader, the modern politician, the illiterate, the scholar, the black, and the white, the people of southern Africa have one thing in common—their struggle to maintain their own distinctive identity in an extremely hostile cultural and social environment. The struggle for social change or transformation must, therefore, be seen in this context. It is a struggle that carries meaning only if it is cast in the national and regional endeavor to reform education.

The second conclusion is that the problems of southern Africa can be traced to the inception of the colonial systems beginning with the Portuguese colonization of Angola and Mozambique in 1575 and their strengthening in the nineteenth century, which predisposed southern Africa to further colonization by other European countries. Indeed, colonization was effected at a great price. Bitterness and resentment among the Africans were a direct result of the naked force that Europeans used to subject them to colonial rule. Once this paradigm of social and racial relationship was established, it remained a permanent modus operandi.

The third conclusion is that from the inception of the colonial systems, the leaders fully entrenched themselves in promoting the exclusive political power of the whites as a means of ensuring their socioeconomic power, and the development of good human relationships based on mutual respect was pushed lower on the list of national priorities. Although the colonial systems survived on this practice, it sowed the seeds of a major conflict with the Africans in the future. After the Second World War it was not possible for the colonial governments to sustain themselves without resorting to extreme force to subdue the Africans. But in doing so, they raised in the Africans a determination to bring about the kind of change that the colonial governments did not envisage as an outcome of the war.

THE NATURE OF THE CRISIS

In 1994, southern Africa was going through a period of unprecedented crisis that had been unfolding since Nelson Mandela of South Africa was released unconditionally in 1990 after serving twenty-seven years in prison for opposing apartheid. Additionally, there were massive demonstrations that were staged in July 1990 in Lusaka, Zambia. There was discontent about the behavior of Kamuzu Hastings Banda in Malawi. There was a continuing saga of internal conflict in Angola and Mozambique. These five examples of crises carried four serious messages for all of southern Africa that could no longer ignored. The first message was that the region's old guard had controlled the socioeconomic and political system far too long and that it was time for change in national leadership.

The second message was that the one-party system of government that had been in place in most countries of this critical region of Africa must give way to a multi-party democratic system as a prerequisite of social transformation and the thrust for regional and national development. The third message was that mismanagement and corruption by government officials[5] and their unwillingness and the inability to see the need for fundamental social change combined to constitute an environment that produced a social cancer that was destroying the vital tissue of national life in the whole region.

The fourth message was that basic reform in education must become a major influential factor of political, social, and economic change in the region so that social transformation would occur to ensure regional and national development. Philip H. Coombs discusses the imperative nature of this approach for developing nations, saying, "Changes in educational growth trends in developing countries during the 1970s, compared to the 1960s, were not as clear-cut, and the picture differed greatly from region to region and country to country."[6] Coombs goes on to suggest that social transformation must, by its very nature, be related to educational reform to give coherence to national programs and regional cooperation.[7] To accomplish this objective, however, the nations of southern Africa must recognize the seriousness of the present problems and that they are similar to problems of the past.

THE EFFECT OF APARTHEID

There is no doubt that in 1994 every country in southern Africa was going through a very difficult period. As a result of popular action, there emerged a demand for fundamental social change and a better opportunity for education as prior conditions of an improved standard of living. This demand underscores the need for both social transformation and educational reform cast in an environment of emerging conditions. At present, the problems of southern Africa are many and varied, ranging from the one-party system of government to corruption and economic decline as well as a lack of confidence among the people for the future.

It is inconceivable for any national leader to assume that if left alone these problems would disappear. Yet, that is exactly what some leaders appear to believe. It is an equally tragic reality that the oppression of apartheid in South Africa has now been substituted for by the oppression of ethnic violence that threatens to disintegrate the fabric of the society. In this study, we make some suggestions on how the thrust for social transformation and educational reform, when properly understood and applied, can help set a stage for the resolution of these problems.

From its official inception in 1948[8] to its end in 1994, a "noble reign" for nearly a half century, the policy of apartheid in South Africa became recognized as a major problem in all of southern Africa. Every other problem, whether political, economic, or social, was believed to be directly related to the application of the policy of apartheid. This is why President Robert Mugabe of Zimbabwe used unprecedented emphasis to present a sad portrait of how apartheid caused major problems in all of southern Africa. Speaking to the summit conference of the Organization of African Unity (OAU) that was held in Freetown, Sierra Leone, on July 2, 1980, on the problems of national and regional development in all of southern Africa, Mugabe fully supported the position of the international community, which concluded that apartheid had become a major problem in the region.

Mugabe stated,

Apartheid is on the rampage in all of southern Africa in immoral defense of itself. In Mozambique, it is actively sponsoring acts of sabotage. In Zambia, it is not only deploying its own troops in open attacks upon that country, but it is also promoting the Mshala gang. In Angola, it has been committing mass murders of civilians, financing UNITA and directing numerous acts of sabotage. In Swaziland and Lesotho, it has conducted incursions. In Zimbabwe it has attempted to disrupt independence celebrations and has recruited some five thousand persons for military training to defend itself in Namibia.[9]

But the end of apartheid in South Africa in 1994 proved to be a temporary truce as the ethnic violence broke out in 1995. The conflict between the Inkatha Freedom Party and supporters of the African National Congress (ANC) shattered the emerging image of a nation that had just come out of an unprecedented seven decades of oppression. In this new wave of self-betrayal, the people of South Africa and those of southern Africa as a whole could no longer blame apartheid for the carnage that they were bringing on themselves. Indeed, it is true that, with the possible exception of the Horn of Africa, no region of Africa has experienced so great an agony of conflict between efforts to maintain the social and political status quo and endeavors to initiate meaningful change. While it is equally true that the existence of major problems in southern Africa prior to 1994 could be traced to the imposition of the policy of apartheid, by 1995 it was obvious that blame had to be spread beyond the policy and the government. The attitude of apartheid had become woven into the political and socioeconomic fabric of the region.

From its inception unofficially in 1652 and officially in 1948, apartheid inflicted an incalculable harm on the people of southern Africa, both black and white. All the people of this region were its victims. But it was now up to the people to make an examination of themselves to chart new directions in the struggle for development. On May 4, 1990, Nelson Mandela recognized the harmful effect of apartheid when he said, "When I went to prison [in 1964] I could not vote. Twenty-seven years later, I still cannot vote. We are all victims of apartheid."[10] Blacks were not allowed to vote in South Africa until 1994.

By 1995, the policy of apartheid was in the past. However, for the people of southern Africa to continue to live in the shadows of apartheid was to deny themselves an opportunity to forge a new future conceived in new ideals. Educational reform can illuminate the shadows of apartheid and shed new light on old problems. Although apartheid was a major problem in all of southern Africa, one must see it in the context of the array of other problems it created. These are the problems that pose a general threat to the security and development of the countries of the region in their struggle for meaningful social change through educational reform.

One of these problems is how to make education relevant to the conditions of the times. One must also understand that educational reform helps to determine the direction that nations take in their struggle for development. The fact of the matter is that educational reform, to serve its intended purpose of national development, must be related to other national aspects of social transformation, such as political and socioeconomic development.

The application of apartheid made it virtually impossible to initiate such change. This suggests the conclusion that if apartheid had been dismantled earlier than in 1994, it is quite possible that other problems could have been resolved sooner. The continuing saga of ethnic violence in South Africa and the claim made by the government of F. W. de Klerk in 1993 that it was unable to stop it set the stage for the failure of Mandela's government to stop it. This continuing ethnic violence undercut the very essence of an emerging nation. It casts doubt over the new governments' ability to act. This creates unrest among the people and threatens to destroy the fabric of national life that the government is trying to build.

THE PURPOSE OF THIS STUDY

To fully understand the nature and extent of the problems that southern Africa of 1994 faced, one needs to understand how, over many years, the colonial systems created an economic system that forced Africans in all the countries of the region to depend on what was imposed on them. The purpose of this study is to present some critical factors that show that educational reform is critical to the transformation of southern Africa as a prerequisite of both national and regional development. Without educational reform, any effort to initiate change in the national and regional character to meet the needs of all the people becomes elusive.

The study will also show that without fully understanding the nature of educational reform, the nations of southern Africa will always be handicapped by underdevelopment. In presenting the evidence to substantiate this conclusion, the study examines a number of critical factors that are related to educational reform in this critical region of Africa. For example, it offers some theoretical considerations of educational reform as well as the forces that influence it.

THE EXTENT OF THE PROBLEMS

In discussing the factors surrounding the need for reforming education in southern Africa, one must have a complete comprehension of the extent of the problems that exist in the region. Past practices forced southern Africa to experience serious social, economic, and political problems similar to the problems created by apartheid. These problems must be resolved if the future is to be made more meaningful for all people. As we change the political knowledge base to include the true principles of democracy, we will begin to unravel the complexities of the apartheid aftershock.

This study takes the position that among the viable methods of seeking resolution to these problems is initiating basic educational reform. Since the conclusion of the Berlin conference in February 1885, the economic system and the system of education were two major institutional structures that the colonial governments created to sustain their own position of political power at the expense of the development of the Africans. A brief discussion of national factors will be presented from a historical, educational, and political perspective as they affect the transformation of southern Africa.

POLITICAL SITUATION

From 1978 to 1996 all the countries in southern Africa have been experiencing serious social, economic, and political problems that require an immediate solution to avoid national disaster. Mozambique gained political independence from colonial rule in 1975. The following year a brutal civil war began inflicting an incalculable loss of human life and damage on national institutional programs.[11] In 1976, the Mozambique National Resistance (Renamo), which was led by Afonzo Dhlamini, began engaging in rebel and terrorist activities whose destruction and plunder defy comprehension. Renamo did not define its objectives in launching a campaign of destruction and killing. This suggests the tragic nature of the political situation that pervades southern Africa today. Renamo utilized the military assistance it received from South Africa[12] to carry out raids into Mozambique and Zimbabwe, killing at least 100,000 and maiming many more in 1989 alone.[13] This was an attempt by black nationalists to destabilize the new African government as part of South Africa's strategy to maintain apartheid in Mozambique.

This national tragedy led to an obvious question: How long would Mozambique continue to endure this political agony and self-destruction without losing the vital human resources that it needed to ensure its national development? In 1995, Mozambique's fifteen million people were yearning for an answer to the question so that they could redirect their efforts toward the reconstruction and development of their country. The knowledge that the political crisis in Mozambique posed serious developmental problems for the region of southern Africa as a whole is why, in August 1989, the Organization of African Unity appointed President Daniel Moi of Kenya[14] and President Robert Mugabe of Zimbabwe cochairmen of a continental commission charged with the responsibility of finding solutions to the political problems that Mozambique was experiencing as a nation.

It is not surprising that the two leaders fully shared OAU's commitment to educational reform as a solution. This would place Mozambique on the road to national reconstruction and development. All concerned recognized the fact that while this educational reform carried long-term outcomes, there was no viable short-term solution short of seeking a cease-fire. In a communiqué issued in Nairobi on August 8, 1989, the OAU stated,

The aim of the mission is to put an end to this inhuman situation. The first action is to stop all terrorist action. The acceptance of these principles could lead to a dialogue for ending the violence that has destroyed Mozambique and to establish peace for normal life so that national developmental programs can be reinitiated. Unless the scourge of violence is terminated, all other forms of national development cannot take place.[15]

While Mugabe was on a mission to find a formula for peace in Mozambique, political events in his own country suggested a potential for a major national crisis. Elements of a political crisis began to unfold in 1988. In that year Edgar Tekere, a leading member of the ruling ZANU-PF Party, resigned in protest against the possibility of the introduction of a one-party state. Following Mugabe's election in 1980, Mugabe stated that his government would prefer a one-party government rather than the multi-party system that was currently in operation and that had put him in office. Britain had stipulated the existence of a multi-party political system as a condition of independence. Tekere was also protesting against what he said was widespread corruption among top government officials. Indeed, in April 1989, a commission of inquiry appointed by the government under the chairmanship of Justice Sandura uncovered widespread corruption by six senior government officials.[16] The aftermath of this inquiry resulted in fines, resignations, and one suicide. In this environment, Zimbabwe was poised for the most serious political crisis it had experienced since it gained independence on April 18, 1980.

Prior to these events, the *Parade News Magazine* reported that, "The students called for academic freedom and their inalienable rights and demanded the university administration to lift its tacit ban on the student magazine, *Focus*."[17] Relations between the university and the government were becoming strained. Students were calling for the same educational reform that Mugabe had proposed for Mozambique. The irony in Zimbabwe is that the president is also the chancellor of the university.

Displeased with the efforts the government was making to restore the confidence of the public, students at the university engaged in a variety of activities that the government considered defiance of the law. On August 9, Joshua Nkomo, senior government minister, and Faye Chung,[18] the minister of education, went to the university in an effort to diffuse the situation. They held a meeting with the students and tried to establish dialogue. In an impassioned and emotional appeal, Nkomo pleaded with the students, saying, "We do not want a confrontation with our children. We have gone gray because we have a heritage to protect, and that heritage is yourself. Therefore, dialogue must be started. You cannot solve problems by shouting. Knowledge is not just shouting. Some of your behavior is not Zimbabwean."[19]

About two thousand students responded by demanding that Nkomo give them assurances that the government would not turn the country into a one-party state. They also demanded that the Zimbabwe Unity Movement (ZUM), which had been recently formed under the leadership of Edgar Tekere, be allowed a platform to express its political views. Chung's patience ran out as she responded: "Senior Minister Nkomo has been invited here not to be insulted. If this is what we call our future leaders, then I must say that this university is full of rubbish, and the government will not waste money on rubbish."[20] This exchange of views created a situation that posed a new potential for a confrontation leading to an explosive outcome and a halt in the educational process.

Historically, the political crisis in southern Africa has led to economic problems. In Zambia, the violent clashes that erupted between demonstrators and the police in June 1990 were a result of Kenneth Kaunda's government decision to raise the price of cornmeal, the staple diet of the people, from $0.05 to $0.12 per pound. This was done as part of the austerity measures introduced to halt further decline of the economy. For Zambians, whose average monthly income was $20.00, the rise imposed severe economic difficulties that the people were unable to bear. Demonstrations against the government led to riots, which in turn led to clashes with the police, causing forty-five deaths and 153 serious injuries.[21]

Kaunda faced other problems. Charges of corruption by government officials, the mismanagement of the government itself, a decline in the price of copper, and the strengthening of a one-party system that had been in place since 1972 caused an erosion in public confidence in the government by 1990. This is why the people demanded the resignation of the government and the restoration of a multi-party system. Kaunda promised to hold a national referendum in October 1990 to determine whether to restore the multi-party system of government that had been abolished in 1972. No referendum was held, and relations between the people and the government were damaged beyond repair.

Kaunda was elected to the office of president in a multi-party election at the inception of independence from Britain on October 24, 1964. In 1972, Kaunda abolished the multi-party system which had put him in office. By 1990, he was at a loss to understand why Zambians were in a state of rebellion against his government. Like many other African leaders, he could not understand the political implications that one-party rule brought about. Indeed, like other countries of southern Africa, Zambia was poised for a major national conflict unless changes were made in the political, social, and economic system. Change in education was imminent, and it was quite clear that the days of Kaunda's government were numbered.

In 1994, facing a general uprising unless a multi-party system of government was restored, Kaunda agreed to hold elections, still believing that the people would return him to power. When the results of the presidential elections were released, Kaunda was stunned and the people were elated to learn that Frederick Chiluba had been elected president. Chiluba's first official action was to restore the democratic system of government that Kaunda had eliminated in 1972. It is ironic that on January 4, 1996, eight opposition parties, including Kaunda representing the United National Independence Party (UNIP) which he led beginning in 1962, decided to form a coalition to oppose Chiluba's government in the elections that were due to be held in October.[22] Kaunda hoped that his party would nominate him to oppose Chiluba in the presidential election. One wonders what Kaunda would have said or done if Chiluba had maintained the one-party system of government that Kaunda imposed in 1972.

In Namibia, the odyssey of political conflict began with the inception of the German colonial system following the conclusion of the Berlin Conference in February 1885. The lack of interest among German colonial officials in the educational development of Africans shows that the Africans were at the mercy of their colonial masters. Over the years, the lack of educational reform that would have given them a degree of confidence in the future, as a prerequisite of national development, sentenced them to decades of underdevelopment.

When the United Nations (UN) was drafting its charter in San Francisco in 1945, South Africa again vigorously sought UN approval to incorporate Namibia into its own territory and went on to argue,

For twenty-five years, the Union of South Africa has governed and administered the territory as an integral part of its own territory and has promoted to the utmost the material and moral well-being and social progress of the inhabitants. There is no prospect of the territory ever existing as a separate state and the ultimate objective of the principle of the mandate is therefore impossible to achieve.[23]

However, the United Nations rejected this argument.

When, on September 29, 1981, the Security Council adopted Resolution 385 asking South Africa to withdraw from Namibia, there were related events that showed that South Africa must accept the UN's policy or face increased isolation. In 1989, a delicate agreement was reached to hold elections in Namibia as the first step toward achieving sovereign independence on March 21, 1990, seventy-four years after South Africa had occupied it. This was a new day for all Namibians. "Despite a hard-fought campaign and major ideological differences, the seven parties represented in the 72-member national assembly worked out compromises quickly after beginning negotiations on November 21, 1989"[24] to spare the country the agony that Angola was experiencing in the struggle for power.

Although SWAPO won forty-one seats, it fell short of a two-thirds majority of forty-eight seats needed to carry out its programs without forming a coalition with any other party. The Democratic Turnhalle Alliance, a multiracial coalition that favored an economic system similar to that of South Africa, won twenty-one seats, with the remaining five parties occupying a total of ten seats. The problems of reconstruction in Namibia seemed enormous, and Sam Nujoma's task as the first president must be understood as a complex one. Because he did not win an absolute majority, Nujoma teetered with uncertainty as he pondered the problems ahead. The light at the end of the tunnel showed the extent of the problems that Namibia has since encountered in the task of initiating a social transformation by trying to meet the challenge of educational reform to ensure national development.

In Angola, the bloody civil war that broke out at the time of independence in 1975 has destroyed national institutions and human life beyond repair. Hospitals, factories, schools, bridges, railroads, roads, and homes have been laid to waste. Thousands of people have been killed or seriously injured. The road to this national tragedy runs parallel to that of Namibia and Mozambique.

On January 4, 1996, when all parties thought that peace would prevail in Angola, fifty people were killed during a dawn attack by rebels from the UNITA movement. The fact that this attack took place while government leaders and UNITA forces returned from negotiations to end the crisis that began twenty-one years earlier shows the tragic nature of the problem in Angola.

The drama of national conflict and the agony of social change have been played out in more painful ways in South Africa than in any other country in all of southern Africa. Since the official introduction of the notorious policy of apartheid in 1948, South Africa has been steadily edging perilously close to the brink of a major national disaster. On January 25, 1944, Daniel Malan (1874–1959), an ordained minister in the Dutch Reformed Church and an active member in Nationalist Party politics, expressed his political philosophy relative to the future of South Africa as intended "to ensure the safety of the white race by maintaining the principle of apartheid."[25] Malan was expressing the prevailing thinking among the die-hard Afrikaners that the Africans must never expect to have social equality with whites. Unaware of the extent of the national conflict that would emerge as a result of this policy, Malan and the Nationalist Party, which he now led, exploited this prevailing thinking to win the elections of 1948.

It is a tragic reality that from 1948 to 1990 the Afrikaners refused to acknowledge the fact that the Bantustan Homelands, more than any other component of the policy of apartheid, were not only one of the greatest tragedies in the history of South Africa, but were also the major conflict in southern Africa as a whole. The enactment of the Group Areas Act in 1950, the Native Passes Act, 1952, and the Bantu Education Act in 1953 ushered in the beginning of the unprecedented suffering to which apartheid has subjected the Africans. It is for this reason that in 1976 the Soweto uprising captured the news headlines around the world. During a visit to South Africa in December 1994, we had an opportunity to see the evidence of the damage that apartheid inflicted on the country while it was in place.

Before and after the Soweto tragedy, the Africans of South Africa were constantly reminded that every moment of their life, from sunrise to sunset, from birth to death, they were, indeed, a conquered and enslaved people—politically, socially, and economically—and that forgetting this basic fact constituted a criminal offense. The meeting held between Nelson Mandela and former president Pieter Botha in July 1989, and the one between Mandela and F. W. de Klerk in December 1989, came as a painful reminder of the supremacy of apartheid. Both leaders reminded Mandela that apartheid is a part of history that could not be changed overnight. The tragic truth of apartheid is that the Afrikaners were guided by the views that Paul Kruger (1825–1904), president of the ill-fated Transvaal Republic from 1883 to 1900, expressed in a statement of policy that stated, "The black man must be taught that he belongs to an inferior class of people who must learn to obey."[26]

The truth of the matter is that Afrikaners did not waver from this principle until 1990 when the pressure from the international community combined with the increased guerrilla warfare to make conditions unbearable. Suddenly, de Klerk announced on February 2, 1990, that Mandela would be released unconditionally and that the ban on ANC and other political parties would be lifted. Many people responded with measured skepticism and disbelief because de Klerk himself subscribed to the principle that apartheid must remain the policy of South Africa until conditions forced him to accept the inevitability of change. The fact that de Klerk recognized the imperative of change in the structure of apartheid suggests a critical need to initiate a transformation of South Africa. But the task of initiating such a change rested on the shoulders of Nelson Mandela, whom the policy of apartheid had put away for twenty-seven years because he was opposed to it.

The important thing for Afrikaners to remember, in a situation in which choices are few, is that the transformation of the South African political system could best be accomplished in the context of educational reform. This is the line of thinking that Brian Carlson, headmaster of St. Andrew's Preparatory School in Grahamstown, South Africa, took into consideration when he wrote in 1988, "Education is a powerful instrument of social change. Reform in it has an important role to play in building a new society."[27]

Up to this point, the government of South Africa defied the voice of the international community calling for fundamental social change. It would have spared the country the agony of this inevitable change if its leaders had listened to one of its own people. The advertisement that was placed in the *Chronicle of Higher Education* of May 16, 1990, by the University of Cape Town inviting researchers from the international community to go there and help establish a new process of change was in line with Carlson's call. In this context, the call for a new thrust for national development in South Africa has now acquired an international dimension.

While efforts to dismantle apartheid were being made on an international level, events on the home front were quite different. In December 1995, a total of 230 people had been killed in Natal, bringing the total to fourteen thousand people since the ethnic fighting broke out in 1985. Twenty-eight people were killed during the Christmas season alone.[28] Among the worst incidents of violence since the beginning of the Christmas season was the massacre of fourteen people by a militia group of about six hundred men near the coastal resort of Port Shepestone.

In response to this tragedy, Frank Mdlalose, the provincial premier, called on the police to create what he called a long-term environment for people in Natal. Creating an environment for peace is tantamount to creating conditions for the social transformation of the country. It remained to be seen if the people of South Africa, who have been subjected to the violence of apartheid, could now respond to a different call to place the country back on the road to a new thrust for national development.

THE ECONOMIC CRISIS

Economic conditions continue to compound the social problems of Third World countries. The action taken by the U.S. House of Representatives on August 12, 1988, to ban nearly all trade with South Africa in protest against apartheid heightened a growing international determination to let the Nationalist government know that it faced an increasing isolation from the world community as long as it maintained apartheid. When James Baker, U.S. secretary of state, visited South Africa on March 22, 1990, after attending an independence celebration for Namibia the previous day, he reminded de Klerk of that fact and that South Africa must commit itself to move toward an irreversible course to end apartheid as a condition of peaceful transformation.

The abandonment of the so-called Sullivan principles as a means to improve the economic plight of Africans meant that other alternatives must be explored to achieve an end to the apartheid system. What the world readily recognized as a painful fact of apartheid is that it really did not matter how well educated Africans were, they were still subjected to the socioeconomic and political humiliation due to the color of their skin. This was a central tenet of the policy of apartheid.

Efforts to improve the economy in South Africa are a reflection of the rapidly deteriorating economic and social crisis in all of southern Africa. For example, the fact that in Mozambique in 1988 the urgent need for famine relief that put 640,000 people in refugee camps shows how bad the economic situation had become. In 1989, when the number of refugees had risen to 780,000, the UN Food Program sounded an alarm of desperation and called for an educational reform that would help the people of Mozambique to understand and utilize new agricultural technology, to study weather conditions, and to make a collective effort to resolve this problem.[29]

In a similar fashion, the civil war in Angola had created a shortage of food production to the extent that the country needed more than 258,000 metric tons of food shipments in 1988.[30] The announcement made in July 1989 by the government of Mozambique that it was abandoning its Marxist economic principles could have well been made in Angola, where a lack of trained personnel and a stagnation in economic development combined to place heavy demands on socioeconomic change in conjunction with reform in education. The warring parties in Angola had yet to realize that this much needed development could take place only when the country was at peace. With an unemployment rate of 40 percent in 1989, both Mozambique and Angola are slowly but steadily edging closer to a seriously tragic economic fate.

In Zambia, the government of Kenneth Kaunda was forced to close its borders in August 1989 to introduce a new system of currency in an effort to revive the sagging economy. If the Zambian government had recognized the need for educational reform soon after attaining independence in October 1964, this crisis could have been averted. In May, 1987, Kaunda broke relations with the International Monetary Fund (IMF) because he thought that his government would initiate viable economic self-sufficiency programs not only to give Zambia the greater degree of economic independence it needed for national development but also to serve as a model for other countries in southern Africa.

But Kaunda was unaware that the decline in the monetary value of copper would force him and his government to devalue the *kwacha* to a point where it was no longer able to compete with other monetary systems on the world market. This forced the production of copper to decline from 700,000 tons in 1979 to 417,00 in 1989.[31] There is no question that this economic crisis was caused primarily by an inability that is so common among African nations to relate education to other important national programs.

Zambia's economic problems must be seen in the context of its rapidly declining political system as well. This is apparent in the letter that Henry Kalenga, a member of the banned ANC, wrote in March 1990 from his political prison in Kitwe to Amnesty International to say,

I write as one of the victims of Zambia's injustice and oppression, especially the draconian laws on detention without trial that the government has introduced as part of its standard operation. At a time when human rights are being internationalized, it is disheartening to note that Zambia violates human rights with impunity.[32]

It is ironic that in 1996 Kaunda was seeking nomination as a candidate for president to oppose Frederick Chiluba, who had defeated him four years earlier.

Elsewhere in southern Africa events were unfolding that hindered national development. In March 1990, Mobuto Sese Seko of Zaire argued, "Zaire has no need for *perestroika* because its one-party state system is the most elaborate form of democracy in Africa,"[33] he neglected to say that the rapid decline in the economy was a direct result of the fallacy of a one-party system as a democracy.

Although Zimbabwe was recognized in 1988 by the Hunger Project as leading Africa in food production as a basis of economic development,[34] its economy was considered fragile. The rapid decline of the dollar threatened national infrastructures that are essential to national development.[35] The lack of trained personnel to initiate innovative strategies poses problems that make it necessary for Zimbabwe to brace itself for possible serious economic difficulties. Unless the government does something to halt the rapid decline of the dollar, which in itself causes rapidly rising inflation, it will continue to experience rising unemployment. The twin problems of rapidly rising inflation and rising population have combined to create a set of social, economic, and political problems that Zimbabwe may find hard to solve unless it makes a new effort to reform its educational system to make it relevant to the needs of the times.

SUMMARY AND CONCLUSION

What has been discussed in this chapter leads to two conclusions. The first is that problems of national development in all of southern Africa became so complex that they required something of a much better standard and a far more viable national resource than conventional wisdom would suggest. In all practical realities, education has often been regarded as a means to resolve these problems. However, the situation in all of southern Africa leads to the conclusion that the current educational process is far too inadequate to help solve these problems. What is therefore needed is a fundamental change or reform in education to meet the needs of an increasingly complex situation.

The fact of the matter is that in human experience, education provides that needed catalyst to understand national problems from their proper context. This is the only environment in which solutions can be found. Therefore, for southern Africa, educational reform is the most viable basis of finding solutions to the political, economic, and social problems that exist. Initiating educational reform forms an imperative condition of seeking solutions to the problems of the region as a whole. It would help nations see the situations they face from their proper perspective. No matter how much effort is made in seeking solutions to problems of national development, that effort is bound to fail if it is not related in practical ways to making an effort to reform the educational process. The various aspects of that reform are the subject of this study.

The second conclusion is that like politics, social and economic development help shape a national character. Therefore, efforts made toward national development are possible only if individual citizens are able to advance themselves economically and socially. In southern Africa, more than in any other region of Africa, the more citizens are educated, the more they contribute to their own social and economic development and the development of their nation. This suggests the conclusion that because of the delicate nature of the economy, all the countries of southern Africa need educational reform not only to sustain them, but also to strengthen them to reshape the emergence of new national characters.

An important consideration for the countries of southern Africa to keep in mind is what J. C. Eisher recognized by saying, "It is important to ascertain that the limited resources at the disposal of the persons or institutions who make educational input are utilized in the most effective way possible in pursuing national objectives."[36] To achieve this objective, education must be reformed. This suggests the conclusion that it would be very difficult to introduce a new political and economic system without introducing a new system of education that promotes the social advancement and national development.

With a clamor for fundamental social advancement in Eastern Europe in 1989, the call for fundamental change in political and socioeconomic spheres of national life in Africa went out much louder than it had been in the past. In 1996, that call had reached every corner of this vital region of Africa. The existence of the system of one-party governments in any country of southern Africa has no place now or in the future. It is in this kind of environment that educational reform must become an endeavor for social advancement and for national development.

NOTES

1. The geographical definition of southern Africa is that part of Africa south of the equator. The countries in this region include Angola, Botswana, Lesotho, Mozambique, Namibia, South Africa, Swaziland, Tanzania, Zaire, Zambia, and Zimbabwe. These countries are the focus of this study.

2. For details see, for example, Dickson A. Mungazi, *Gathering under the Mango Tree: Values in Traditional Culture in Africa* (New York: Peter Lang Publishing, 1996), p. 150.

3. The film *The Gods Must Be Crazy*, which features the Khoi, was produced in Botswana. The movie is a classic example of how the white race has tried to perpetuate some myths about the Africans. One is led to the conclusion that the reason the Khoi were the subject of this form of Western humor and comedy is that they have declined to accept Western culture. That the film depicts the Khoi as regarding the whites as gods suggests the strength of this myth.

4. Dickson A. Mungazi, *To Honor the Sacred Trust of Civilization: History, Politics, and Education in Southern Africa* (Cambridge, Mass.: Schenkman Publishers, 1983), p. 4.

5. *New York Times*, July 15, 1990.

6. Philip H. Coombs, *World Crisis in Education: The View from the Eighties* (New York: Oxford University Press, 1985), p. 84.

7. Ibid., p. 81.

8. In his study, *The Struggle for Social Change in Southern Africa: Visions of Liberty* (New York: Taylor and Francis, 1989), Dickson A. Mungazi argues that the policy of apartheid was initiated at the inception of the Dutch East India Company rule in 1652.

9. Robert Mugabe, "Zimbabwe: For the Record, Number 2," An address to the OAU, Freetown, Sierra Leone, July 2, 1980. The Zimbabwe Ministry of Information.

10. Harold Dow, CBS-TV *Evening News*, May 4, 1990.

11. ABC-TV, *20/20*, March 2, 1990.

12. On February 15, 1990 Dickson A. Mungazi wrote a letter to President de Klerk advising him that his overtures of peace to ANC in South Africa would be futile if he did not stop supporting UNITA and Renamo activities.

13. *Washington Post*, August 1, 1989.

14. Indeed, in July 1990, Kenya was rocked by violent demonstrations against the Moi government. That the demonstrators demanded an end to one-party rule, which Moi instituted in 1982, suggests a critical need for innovation in Kenya itself.

15. OAU, *A Communiqué on Mozambique*. Nairobi, Kenya, August 8, 1989.

16. For the names of these officials and the extent of their involvement in the scandal, see *Herald*, April 13, 1989, p. 7.

17. Ibid., p. 45.

18. Faye Chung became minister of education on August 4, 1989, when Dzingai Mutumbuka was forced to resign from the government following his conviction on charges of gross corruption.

19. Zimbabwe, *Herald*, August 11, 1989, p.9.

20. Ibid.

21. *Time*, July 9, 1990, p. 38.

22. *Herald* (Harare, Zimbabwe), January 5, 1996, p. 3.

23. John Dugard, *The Southwest Africa/Namibia Dispute* (Berkeley: University of California Press, 1973), p. 89.

24. *New York Times*, December 21, 1989.

25. Brian Bunting, "The Origins of Apartheid," in Alex La Guma (ed.), *Apartheid: A Collection of Writings in South African Racism by South Africans* (New York: International Publishers, 1971), p. 24.

26. Ibid., p. 35.

27. Brian Carlson, "American Education: A South African Perspective in the Process of Desegregation," *Kappa Delta Phi*, Summer, 1988, p. 99.

28. Zimbabwe, *Herald*, January 3, 1996, p. 1.

29. *Christian Science Monitor*, July 26, 1988, p.4.

30. Ibid.

31. *Economist*, September 30, 1989, p. 11.

32. George Ayittey, "In Africa Independence Is a Far Cry from Freedom," *Wall Street Journal*, March 28, 1990, p. 15.

33. Ibid.

34. *New York Times*, September 16, 1988, sec. 2.

35. In December 1985, the rate of exchange was 1 US\$ = Z\$8.9, but in January 1996 it was 1 US\$ = Z\$9.2.

36. J. C. Eicher, *Educational Costing and Financing in Developing Countries: Focus on Sub-Sahara Africa*. (Washington, D.C.: World Bank, 1984), p. 3.

2

The Imperative of Educational Reform in a Historical Context

> The purpose of education is to train children, not only with reference to their success in the present state of society, but also to a better possible state in accordance with an ideal conception of humanity.
>
> Immanuel Kant, 1781

> Education must light the path of social change. The social and economic problems confronting us are growing in complexity. Our ultimate security is based upon the individual's character. This responsibility rests squarely upon those who direct education.
>
> Theodore Roosevelt, 1902

THE PURPOSE OF EDUCATION

The Swiss psychologist and educator Jean Piaget discusses the purpose of education, saying, "The principal goal of education is to create men and women who are capable of doing new things, not simply reflecting what other generations have done, men and women who are creative, inventive, and who are discoveries."[1] From this view of the purpose of education, Piaget stresses the thinking among educators that the universality of the purpose of education is to prepare students to live and function efficiently in a changed social environment that allows them to be discoverers.

One can see the importance of change that has taken place in the twentieth century, not for its own sake but to meet human needs; one must understand and accept change as an important factor or prior condition of human development. And human development is the first condition of national transformation. Any nation or society that does not seem to accept the concept of change denies itself an opportunity for its own advancement. Advancement itself can only occur when the elements of its transformation are in place. But the question is, How do these elements come into place? In their struggle for development, the nations of southern Africa should be mindful that throughout human history the transformation of society has greater meaning when the purpose of education is clearly defined.

This is the perspective that Immanuel Kant (1724–1804) takes into account in arguing, "The purpose of education is to train children, not only with reference to their success in the present state of society, but also to a better possible state in accordance with an ideal conception of humanity."[2] A conception of humanity requires an articulation of conditions that, when properly observed, would elevate mankind to a higher level than what is perceived. In a similar manner, Theodore Roosevelt (1857–1919), president of the United States from 1901 to 1909, presented an imperative of the perspective of educational reform in a universal sense, saying,

Education must light the path for social change. The social and economic problems confronting us are growing in complexity. The more complex and difficult these problems become, the more essential it is to provide a broad and complete education to all students. Our ultimate security is based upon the individual's character, information and attitude. This responsibility rests squarely upon those who direct education.[3]

One reaches two conclusions from what Piaget, Kant, and Roosevelt said about the universal imperative of educational reform. The first conclusion is that from the most advanced societies to the least developed, from ancient times to modern times, in good times and bad, human society has endeavored to initiate change, not for its own sake, but to improve the conditions that promote the quality of human life. Therefore, any society that refuses to acknowledge the importance of change for the benefit of society, such as South Africa did from 1910 to 1990, denies itself an opportunity to make an effort to initiate the process of transformation to ensure its own development.

Refusal or unwillingness to accept and implement the concept of change as an important condition of human and social development inhibits the ability of all people. To critically examine a society and appraise the essential components that constitute its existence, the people must implement change. Unwillingness or the inability of the people to call for change creates an environment where the thrust for national development loses its meaning, and the citizens are subjected to the agony of underdevelopment and stagnation. The world witnessed and watched this agony in South Africa from 1948 to 1994, a period during which apartheid ruled supreme. The concept of change requires the

acknowledgment of the inadequacy of the existing system and a clear understanding of the nature of the change to be initiated. Because this exercise
requires high-level skills, many countries of Africa would rather stay in the mud
of underdevelopment than initiate new programs of change.

The second conclusion is that any social change that fails to relate effectively
to educational reform also loses the purpose for which it is initiated. It must
be recognized that educational reform is different from other forms of social
change in some very important aspects. For example, educational reform must
be initiated from the perspective of seeking the improvement of the educational
system. This is how it can improve the quality of life of the people. It enables
students to set individual goals and objectives consistent with national operative political, social, and economic principles.

Educational reform also promotes the development of a nation by developing
the potential of the individual. It must seek to promote and manifest individual
endeavors as it helps initiate the formation of a new national character so
essential to national purpose and endeavor. It must help in defining that purpose
to allow people to set objectives in a way that embraces collective and common
action that leads to demonstrated and tangible results that benefit the country
as a whole. The combination of these forms of educational reform brings out
the best in every student as he functions in an enriched environment that makes
it possible for him to see new possibilities for himself and for his country.

THE IMPERATIVE OF EDUCATIONAL REFORM
IN SOUTHERN AFRICA TODAY

Whether or not educational reform is universal in its meaning, one would
have to say that it is far more important in its application to conditions that
exist in southern Africa than any other region of the continent and the world,
because the problems that exist there demand immediate action in seeking
solutions. This is why, with reference to the situation in the Third World in
general, Paulo Freire, a Brazilian thinker and author, suggests that educational
reform involves much more than is implied in the search for a new meaning
in an effort to eliminate the contradiction that exists between the powerful and
the dispossessed and handicaps national purpose.[4] Therefore, educational
reform must, in effect, be initiated under the influence of a national climate
that is intended to create an environment of collective understanding of its
importance so that those national goals can be defined in terms of human need
and individual goals. These are the elements that make educational reform
imperative in all of southern Africa.

Failure to realize the importance of these elements and to make a decision to accept them as imperative for national endeavors means that the region would continue to languish in the mire of stagnation and underdevelopment. To understand the importance of educational reform in southern Africa today, all concerned need to understand the purpose of education in traditional society as it existed before the colonial period. A brief discussion of educational systems in traditional culture in Africa contributing to an effort for the development of all people in southern Africa follows.

THE ROLE OF EDUCATION IN TRADITIONAL SOCIETY IN AFRICA

In traditional societies in southern Africa, the educational process began as soon as the child was considered able to understand the importance of functioning in his environment, both physical and social. Instruction was conducted in the belief that society would have experienced a transformation by the time the learner was ready to take his place in it. This means that the concept relevance of the educational process formed the essential components of the process of providing education to the learner. The educational process was adopted to changing conditions to make it more applicable and effective in meeting the needs of the learner and those of his society.

Western perception was that the educational process in traditional society in Africa was irrelevant because it lacked a structured and formal curricular content. To the contrary, education in traditional society in Africa was designed and understood by the Africans themselves to be more effective and meaningful than Western education because it was meant to be for Africans in their own cultural context. To view education in traditional society in Africa from a Western perspective is to miss its importance to African society. As soon as the child could walk, his education began to take a definite form. First, he learned the basic components of his culture and society and how to function in them. Those people in positions to influence his educational effort and development, such as members of his immediate family and the entire community,[5] often taught him by both example and precept. As Michael Gelfand concludes, the learner's society taught him "that some things are right and that others are wrong,"[6] and that he was expected to make a clear distinction between the two.

The emphasis that traditional society in Africa placed on instruction suggests that coming early in the life of the learner as it did, the instruction of moral values held an especially important place in the educational process. The underlying consideration in stressing the importance of moral values was that as an adult person, the learner needed to embrace basic moral principles to have meaningful relationships with other people, either in business activity or in personal association. Africans considered any person whose conduct or social behavior manifested a lack of moral and social values to have missed some essential aspects of his or her education.[7] It therefore became very difficult for such a person to have meaningful relationships with other people unless he or she demonstrated a desire to learn the importance of moral values.

The traditional African approach was in the knowledge that as an adult, the learner was expected to demonstrate understanding of the value of the human person as an indispensable component of the character of society itself because the character of society resulted from the thought process and behavior patterns of the individual members. This behavior demonstrated their character. In this context, the character of individuals was closely related to the character of society. That understanding was often measured in terms of a concerted effort to uphold and embrace a universal definition of human dignity and worth as a central modus operandi. This means that the instruction of social values was inseparable from the instruction given in the importance of democratic values.

One can see that the Western concept of separation between church and state was not a norm applicable to social behavior in traditional society in Africa because the king and subjects alike were considered equal before the law. Their conduct or behavior was determined by how they demonstrated commitment to sustain moral and social values as fundamental tenets of the success of their educational endeavors.[8] In this setting, Africans considered the educational system in their traditional society more effective than education in Western social settings in the way it was expected to sustain the universal principle: *Society must be governed by law, not by man.*

As the child grew and gained new experiences that he needed to lead a successful life, his education began to take on more advanced principles and ideas. The inclusive nature of the educational process also involved critical components of diversity and individuality, not only in the educational process itself, but also in methods of instruction. Its cautiously protected development was expected to conform to the developmental process of the learner. It was also intended to help him to relate to human environmental factors that included the physical, emotional, spiritual and mental characteristics of his society, all considered essential components of human existence and growth.

The structure of the educational system in traditional society in Africa suggests that it had relevance and application to human life far beyond itself because it was designed to train individuals to become capable of exercising social responsibility and to discharge duty in a much larger social order. Common educational experiences were considered important to uphold social institutional values. The only reason the colonial governments regarded this educational process a product of a primitive culture is that they wanted to justify their colonial objectives.

Another serious misconception that formed the basis of attitudes and policies designed by the colonial government for the education of Africans was their view that African life and society were marked distinctly by the absence of democratic principles. The colonial governments also argued that African society consisted of fragmented units of unstructured communities headed by autocratic chiefs. But a study of institutional operations in traditional society in southern Africa would yield substantial and clear evidence to show that the contrary was, in fact, the case. To understand how education was designed to sustain democratic values, one needs to understand the structure of society itself and how its members endeavored to sustain democratic principles. At the head of the African society was the king.[9] V. W. Turner suggests that the African king "symbolized the unity of the whole society structured to sustain its collective values."[10] This suggests a demonstrated commitment to democratic principles.

Although the king was a hereditary leader and was not elected, people knew who was next in the line of succession. The king had a clear responsibility to operate under a set of principles and values that were distinctly different from those of Western societies. He was not at liberty to issue executive orders, as is the case in Western societies. Rather, he was required to consult members of the council before he could make decisions or take action on any matter. In this context, the king represented justice, equality before the law, fairness, and freedom of all people in all aspects of life. Lawrence Vambe concludes that in carrying out his duties, the king "ruled by consent of his people and therefore enjoyed popular loyalty born of genuine patriotism."[11]

There is yet another feature that suggests the conclusion that the Africans in traditional society applied democratic principles in their social and political behavior. Society itself was divided into three levels. These were the ward, district, and village. Over each ward was a ward head, and over each village was a village head. Their duties and functions included coordinating activities designed to promote and protect the interests of all the people to sustain the integrity of society. A team of councilors assisted both the ward head and the village head in discharging their responsibilities. There was no room for even a powerful individual to resort to dictatorial behavior to have his own way prevail, because the major restraints were the bonds that existed between the leaders and the people. These came into being as a result of observing valued cultural traditions and the knowledge that leaders had an obligation to respect the wishes of the people they represented. Council meetings were always open to the public.

There is no doubt that the king, the ward head, and the village head, and their respective councils, deliberated on issues and made decisions that were based on the collective belief that they were in the best interests of the people. William Raynor suggests that this practice evinces the observance of democratic principles in a universal sense.[12] Africans understood the importance of observing democratic principles in a much broader dimension than the members of the colonial governments were able to understand. This was the reason why the educational process itself acquired elements that were critical to the sustenance of the vitality and integrity of their society.

Therefore, the educational process in traditional society in Africa was quite complete and relevant to the needs of the students. Some members of the colonial governments themselves recognized this completeness and relevance to society as a whole. For example, speaking in March 1965 to the Rotary Club International in Harare, Zimbabwe, F. G. Loveridge, who was a senior education officer in colonial Zimbabwe with responsibility for the conduct of African education, observed that the importance of education in traditional society in Africa was cultural in comparison with Western education. Loveridge said,

In his traditional society the African was given all the education which he needed to function in his culture. Today, he has fallen away because Western education does not prepare him to function in Western culture. At the same time it does not prepare him to function in his own culture. Therefore, the African who goes to school in a Western cultural setting is placed in a socioeconomic limbo.[13]

Yet another misconception that Westerners had about education in traditional African society was their view that it lacked a defined curricular content. But an examination of what was learned would furnish clear evidence to prove that what was learned was comprehensive because it included components that were essential to seeking improvement in the conditions that controlled human life. Because the educational process entailed utilitarian purpose, it required the learners to demonstrate competencies in whatever they learned to do. Michael Gelfand (1911–1985), a British medical practitioner who lived most of his life in Zimbabwe and studied African culture, describes the comprehensive nature of education in traditional society in Africa as he saw it there, saying,

The son watches his father make a circular hole in the ground and places in it some charcoal. Air is forced through a tunnel into the hole. The charcoal is lit with lighted sticks and embers to a high temperature. When the iron in the fire turns red, the father uses a source-shaped implement to grip the top. His son holds it firmly while he hits it with a hammer to fashion the molten iron into a desired object.[14]

One can see that among other things, this form of education instilled in the learner a purpose that was essential to the sustenance of diverse components of society and individuality. In turn, this made such diversity a critical element of human existence needed everywhere. Therefore, to conclude that the learning process helped transform the individual from being merely a person into being a finished product because the educational process was comprehensive is to acknowledge its completeness. For the colonial governments in Africa to conclude that education in traditional society in Africa had no definite curricular content indicates yet another piece of evidence that they had no clear understanding of the African culture itself.

One must be aware that a discussion of education in traditional African society would be incomplete if it did not address the question of how components of what was learned were related to the totality of life in the community itself. In concluding that education in traditional African society meant nothing more than a practice of superstitious beliefs, Westerners, including the nineteenth-century missionaries to southern Africa, missed a critically important aspect of their claimed knowledge of Africans and their culture. B. A. Powers concludes that the fact that education in traditional African culture, like that of any culture, was designed to place emphasis on cultural values that were considered essential to the well-being of society and its members must be understood in the context of a universal purpose of education.[15]

Because Africans had a tremendous respect for human life, learning to show respect for elders and children, to say prayers before a journey, to feed children or give them a bath, to celebrate the harvest, to clean the house, to fetch water from the village well, or to dig the ground all entailed the observance of religious principles and social values that had to be learned fully and acquired carefully. In a similar fashion, learning to embrace human qualities, such as integrity, honesty, truthfulness, and faithfulness, was considered an essential component of the educational process. This knowledge must never be taken for granted. For this reason, the educational system was being constantly reformed to make it relevant to the needs of the students and the transformation of society to ensure its development.

In 1974, an elderly African in Zimbabwe described the completeness of education in traditional society in Africa, saying,

Before the coming of Europeans to our country, no aspect of our life, no boy or girl was ever neglected by our educational system because it was constantly being innovated to make it relevant to the needs of all students. Every person had an opportunity for education. Today, we are told that only so many can go to school. Why so many only and not all? Neither the missionaries nor the colonial government succeeded in convincing us of the wisdom of accepting both Western education and Christianity.

Do you fail to see the intent of the colonial government in the education of our children today?[16]

Michael Gelfand agrees with this view of the completeness of education in traditional African society and adds that the educational system covered all aspects of life, including law, religion, medicine, trade and commerce, agriculture, social ethics, language and music.[17] They all formed essential components of the learning process so critical for success in life. The absence of formal education, as it is understood in the West, did not in any way diminish the quality of education. Gelfand explains why, saying,

There were no professional schools or teachers in the traditional society in Africa. But the child learned from various members of the family and community as he grew. He learned from his grandparents, parents, and members of the community. Yet, his entire education was as complete as it is in Western culture, whether it was agricultural pursuit or taking part in games.[18]

In 1971, Gelfand might have failed to envision the need for human understanding on a global level when he acknowledged the sufficiency of traditional education.

What has been presented relative to the educational process in traditional African society leads to two basic conclusions. The first conclusion is that Africans found their education complete, therefore there was no reason for Africans to abandon their system simply because the white man told them to do so, saying it was designed to sustain a primitive culture. The second conclusion is that the colonial governments used the argument that both the education and the African culture in which it was cast were primitive. They were therefore unable to see the need to utilize the positive attributes inherent in African society to initiate a new relationship with Africans based on mutual trust. This lack of appreciation is why the colonial governments introduced educational systems of their own to train Africans to serve their own purposes. The purpose of the introduction of Western education to southern Africa is presented to show how it created problems that demanded educational reform in the region as a condition of its transformation.

THE PURPOSE OF COLONIAL EDUCATION IN SOUTHERN AFRICA

When the Portuguese established colonies in Angola and Mozambique in 1575, they faced a situation they had not anticipated. They encountered the strength of the African culture, the viability of the educational system within it, and its relevance to the life-style of Africans. It was the combination of the social viability, political and economic structure, and the educational system that presented the Portuguese with the problems of how to control Africans to subject them to colonial rule. During the next forty years, Africans resisted not only the colonization of their land but also the form of education the Portuguese were pressuring them to accept as part of their new life.[19]

When Brazil declared itself independent from Portugal in 1822, the Portuguese redirected their efforts, creating an environment that forced Africans to need some form of education as defined by the Portuguese. Under the policy called *Estado Novo*, the Portuguese had an opportunity to define the purpose of their education for Africans, which included an ability to speak the Portuguese language. In this manner, the process of acculturation had begun and the life-style Africans had known for centuries was altered permanently.

From the very beginning, the purpose of Portuguese education in Angola and Mozambique was to maintain distinctions between the level of development for Africans and for Portuguese nationals.[20] This was done because the Portuguese colonial government feared that education for Africans, in the context of Portuguese colonial culture, would have the same effect that it had on the people of Brazil. It would increase the level of their consciousness outside the control of the colonial government and could eventually lead to rebellion.

Through the efforts of one determined and brilliant African, Antonio de Miranda, who had taught himself how to read and write the Portuguese language, Africans in Angola began to believe that the Portuguese colonial officials were afraid that the African form of education would enable Africans to see the injustice of the colonial system itself. Therefore, the consciousness that the Portuguese colonial officials feared education would help raise among Africans became a new reality through trying to deny it to them.

By the time the Berlin Conference concluded its deliberations on the colonization of Africa in February 1885, its participants had outlined strategies for training Africans. The Victorian goal for Africans was to train them as laborers to gain profit in the wake of the magnanimous expectations envisaged by the Great Industrial Revolution. The newly established colonial governments began to formulate new theories and philosophies of education for Africans consistent with the purposes they wished to accomplish. In this way, the spokesmen of the colonial establishments sharpened the cause and the strategies that the colonial governments had designed to ensure that Africans were trained to fulfill stated purposes. There are other examples of the political, economic, and social purposes that the colonial governments established for African education throughout southern Africa.

German Policy

In the German colony of Namibia, the responsibility for formulating a colonial policy, known as *Deutsche Kolonialbund*, fell on the shoulders of General von Trotha. His appointment as commander-in-chief of the colonial armed forces was not made lightly; it was the result of a carefully calculated and seriously considered policy. He had a distinguished military record greatly admired by Erwin Rommel (1891–1944), who was nicknamed the Desert Fox. A brilliant German general who commanded German forces during the Second World War, Rommel's military strategy almost paralyzed Allied operations in northern Africa. His tragic death in 1944 spelled the demise of Adolf Hitler and his Third Reich. He was responsible for every aspect of policy, including education.

General von Trotha was mystic and flamboyant and was a classic example of colonial contradiction. He wanted Africans trained as laborers but did not want them trained to gain political and economic skills. First, he ordered Africans to move from their land to make room for German settlers. Then, after the African rebellion was crushed in 1907, he demanded that Africans be trained as laborers.[21] General von Trotha pursued this colonial educational purpose for Africans with the same intensity as the level of brutality he had used to crush the rebellion. This shows the extent to which the German colonial officials were committed to the policy to train Africans as laborers.

In 1894, the German colonial government allowed the missionaries to open schools for Africans. It stipulated a condition that the major curricular component be practical training and basic literacy to ensure an adequate supply of labor.[22] It also reserved the right to inspect those schools to ensure compliance with its requirements. The missionaries wanted to emphasize the teaching of religion, suggesting that the education of Africans was placed in a conflicting position. This created conflict between two colonial institutions, the government and the church. This was the situation that placed Africans at an educational disadvantage, as their education was so manipulated that it could not accrue real social benefits to them but to the German nationals themselves. The colonial officials, at the urging of von Trotha, concluded that this practical training as laborers was the only form of education from which Africans could benefit. They were considered inferior to the white man, suggesting that the strength of the Victorian misconception characterized the attitudes of the colonial governments toward them.

The implementation of this policy and the fact that Africans had been subjected to colonial domination combined to create a damaging doubt among African about the value of their culture and their worth as human beings. The German policy is why four Africans were considered to be equal in social status to one white person. The notion that Germans were superior to Africans was carried to dangerous limits by Adolf Hitler. Until German forces were defeated in Namibia by Allied forces in 1915, German colonial officials pursued this policy with impunity.

British Policy

In the British colonial government, the purpose of education for Africans followed similar lines as in the German colonies. As soon as he arrived in South Africa in 1870 in search of fortune, Cecil John Rhodes (1853–1902) began to formulate his own philosophy and policy toward Africans. Although the British had been in control of South Africa since the Boer migration of 1835, the formulation of a policy toward Africans became the exclusive domain of Rhodes and his associates. He used the massive wealth he acquired after arriving in South Africa to pave his way to the top rung of the political ladder. Rhodes, as prime minister of the Cape Province in 1896, felt ready to enunciate his own philosophy of both the place and education of the Africans, saying,

I say that the Natives are like children. They are just emerging from barbarism. If I may venture a comparison, I should compare the Natives with regard to European civilization to the tribes of the Druids. I think that we have been extremely liberal in granting barbarism forty or fifty years of training what we ourselves obtained only after many hundreds of civilization.[23]

In constantly reminding Africans that they and their culture were barbarian, Rhodes and the British colonial establishment subjected them to what Canaan Banana concludes was a confused state of *cultural dualism*, which forced them to doubt their own values without being accepted into those of the white man.[24] This is precisely what F. G. Loveridge meant when he said in March 1965 that the Africans who were educated in a Western cultural context were placed in a political and socioeconomic limbo. If this was not a deliberate educational purpose for Africans, it certainly was the effect it had on them.

Rhodes's political behavior and policy toward Africans manifested a classic example of colonial contradiction. Speaking on June 23, 1887, in the Cape Parliament on the second reading of the Native Registration Bill, Rhodes received a standing ovation when he argued,

I will lay down my own policy on the Native question. Either you receive them on equal footing as citizens, or you call them a subject race. I have made up my mind that there must be a class legislation, and that we have got to treat the Natives where they are, in a state of barbarism. We are to be lords over them. We will continue to treat them as a subject race as long as they remain in a state of barbarism. What is civilized man? It is a person with sufficient education to enable him to write his name. The Natives should be a source of assistance to the white man as laborers. This must be the main purpose of his education.[25]

It is therefore not surprising that during and after his life, Rhodes remained the crown prince of British colonial policy toward the development of Africans. He had become the unquestioned mentor to future colonial officials who followed his footprints. They became loyal ideological disciples seeking to sustain the presumed wisdom of a man they revered and regarded as infallible in the process of human thought and action. They also elevated the ideals he represented to a new height of the white man's power over Africans.

Rhodes's influence on educational policy for Africans in the British colonies in southern Africa was profound. For example, Paul Kruger (1825–1904), the president of the Transvaal Province in South Africa, was an archenemy of Rhodes. However, they had one philosophical belief in common about the place of Africans in colonial society. Kruger, a poorly educated man but an uncompromising believer in the colonial myth of white superiority, repeatedly urged that Africans be trained so that they would fulfill tasks appropriate to their presumed intellectual and social inferiority. This is why he stated his own philosophy of education for Africans, saying, "The black man must be taught to understand that he belongs to an inferior class and that his function in society is to serve as a laborer."[26]

The policy of apartheid was officially introduced following the elections of 1948. In this election, the Nationalist Party was returned to power. Under the nationalist government, the need to sustain white superiority through education became so strong that it exerted a major influence in the enactment of the Bantu Education Act of 1953. In that same year, Hendrik Verwoerd (1902–1966), then minister of Bantu affairs, who was responsible for African education, explained the purpose of education provided for them by legislation, saying, "Native education must be controlled in such a way that it should be in accord with the policy of the state. If the Native is being taught to expect that he will live his adult life under a policy of equal rights, he is making a big mistake. The Native who attends school must know that he must be the laborer in the country."[27] Two decades before the Soweto uprising in June 1976, it had been recognized that the education of Africans was "being perverted to create bondage out of a racial setting and to restrict the productivity of the Africans to local and subservient tasks."[28] One can conclude that in defying a call for educational reform, national leaders of southern Africa are bound to lead their countries to a major national catastrophe.

The effect of this policy on African education was quite consistent with the effect in the other countries of southern Africa during the colonial period. For example, in Zimbabwe the colonial officials designed an educational policy that was quite consistent with Rhodes's philosophy. Earl Grey (1851–1917), who served as administrator of colonial Zimbabwe from April 12, 1896, to December 4, 1898, argued in 1898 when he introduced an education bill that the purpose of education for Africans was to train them as laborers. Grey added, "I am convinced that the very first step towards civilizing the Natives lies in a course of industrial training and manual labor which must precede the teaching of religious dogma."[29]

To conclude that the colonial government in Zimbabwe formulated an educational policy for Africans to serve its own political, social, and economic purposes is to acknowledge that it could not have been designed along any other line of thinking. The negative attitude of the colonial government toward Africans forced them to conclude that traditional education was uncivilized because it was different. Once this attitude became a basic operative principle of their action, colonial officials were not likely to see the positive attributes of the African culture. This is the reason why the chief native commissioner argued in 1905, "It is cheap labor which we need in this country, and it has yet to be proved that the Native who can read and write turns out to be a good laborer. As far as we can determine, the Native who can read and write will not work on farms and in mines."[30]

To give effect to this line of thinking, the colonial government enacted Ordinance Number 133 in 1907 to provide for manual labor as a viable form of education for Africans. There is no question that the strategy that the colonial government in Zimbabwe designed to reduce the education of Africans to a level where it helped serve the labor needs of the colonial society was synonymous with its desire to have education prepare Africans to serve its own political, social, and economic purposes.

The enactment of Ordinance Number 133 is the reason a senior colonial government official wrote a letter to the editor of the *Rhodesia Herald* in June 1912, to state what he believed must be the purpose of African education as he saw it, saying, "I do not consider it right that we should educate the Native in any way that will unfit him for service. The Native is and should always be the hewer of wood and the drawer of water for his white master."[31] This is also why Ethel Tawse Jollie (1874–1950), one of a very few women to be elected to the colonial legislature, was quite candid in arguing that Africans must be educated differently to prepare them to function as laborers, saying during a debate in the legislature in 1927, "We do not intend to hand over this country to the Natives, or to admit them to the same political and social position as we

ourselves enjoy. Let us therefore make no pretense of educating them in the
same way we educate whites."[32] In supporting Jollie's argument, Hugh Williams went a step further to argue, "If we close every school and stop all this
talk of fostering education and development of Natives, we would much sooner
become an asset to the British Empire."[33]

One can see that from the time Rhodes formulated his philosophy of
education to the end of the colonial rule of Zimbabwe in 1979, the education
of Africans was controlled to sustain this segregational bias. This bias is evinced
by the statement that Andrew Skeen, a member and spokesman of the Rhodesia
Front (RF) Party that ruled Zimbabwe from 1962 to 1979, made in the
legislature in 1969 when he said, "We in the Rhodesia Front Government are
determined to control the rate of African political advancement till time and
education make it a safe possibility. Besides we wish to retain the power to
retard the advancement of the Africans through education to make sure that
the government remains in responsible [white] hands."[34]

In 1983, Ian Smith, the last RF colonial prime minister, defended the
educational policy of his government, saying during an interview, "We knew
that there was a gap between white education and African education. This was
not due to anything that we did, this was part of our history. Before the Second
World War, the Africans did not believe in education because they thought
that it was something that belonged to the white man."[35] What Smith was
saying, in effect, is that although his government knew that there was a need
to reform education to serve the needs of all students, it was not possible to do
so because it would be going against the precedence of history. Cecil John
Rhodes could not have been happier to hear one of his protégés express his
own views so well. What can we learn from the historical perspective of Rhodes
as well as the views and perspectives of Jean Piaget, Immanuel Kant, and
Theodore Roosevelt?

THE RESULTS OF COLONIAL EDUCATIONAL
POLICY

The educational system in southern African needs reform because the
original purpose of formal education was defined from a narrow perspective
to suit the interests of the colonial society. The purposes of education imposed
by colonial governments underscore two basic imperatives. The first is that all
societies, regardless of their level of development, must accept the principle of
change or reform to ensure their own transformation. The second imperative
is that any transformation that fails to utilize education as the principal

instrument of change loses the social, political, and economic purposes for which education is designed.

Because education in traditional society in Africa was complete and comprehensive, Africans could not abandon it in favor of accepting Western education without losing some important components of their culture. This is why Canaan Banana, a Zimbabwean author, concludes, "In traditional society in Africa, education was an integral part of the entire social, economic and cultural system. It was related to the individual, the human group and the environment. Each part was essential to the coherent operation and sustenance of the whole system."[36]

This line of thinking is also the reason why Aldon Southall argues in his essay, *The Illusion of Tribe*, that when a people has lost the essential components of its culture in an attempt to accept those of another, it not only loses its own sense of self, but also fails to grasp the essentials of the culture it is trying to accept as a new modus vivendi. In this manner, it hangs perilously on the cliff of confusion.[37] This is the plight that Africans of the nineteenth century faced as they considered the limited number of options that were before them. This is the plight that Africans will face in the twenty-first century if educational reform is not initiated.

SUMMARY AND CONCLUSIONS

The discussion in this chapter leads to three conclusions. The first conclusion is that the relevance of education in traditional African society made it possible for all students to have access to it. This was because the purpose of education was well defined, with functionalism as its major guiding principle—functionalism for self-sufficiency rather than functionalism for colonial labor. In this context, African society regarded education as a means to an end, not an end in itself. This explains why the educational process was a lifelong endeavor, fully integrating it into major institutional structures and making it applicable and relevant to the needs of society from one generation to the next. With reference to education in traditional society in Africa, Babs Fafunwa discusses this integration and goes on to add, "The warrior, the hunter, the medicine man, the priest, the farmer, the nobleman, the man of character who combined and embraced features of knowledge in its comprehensive form with specific skills on a variety of whom society benefited was a properly educated person."[38]

One is led to the conclusion that the purpose of education in traditional African society and its relevance to the human condition are what the colonial governments saw as the backbone of the African culture itself. To break the resistance of Africans to the intrusion of their society, colonial governments designed a strategy to discredit it as a justification for colonization. This is why the colonial officials constantly argued that African culture was primitive and that Africans were immersed in barbarism. In this kind of setting, educational reform, or the small amount of it that took place in colonial settings, was intended to improve the skills of Africans as laborers, an objective that was not compatible with universal purposes of education. This set the stage for a major conflict to emerge between Africans and the colonial governments when the time was right.

The second conclusion is that one would have thought that having succeeded in discrediting education in traditional African society, the colonial governments would have provided a better system of education that would have had the effect of promoting the development of Africans in new political, social, and economic settings. But what actually came out of the educational system of the colonial governments was a practice that was not only based on race but was also calculated to place Africans at a political, social, and economic disadvantage. This is what Hilda Bernstein sees as one of the most crippling features of education during the colonial period. In 1971, Bernstein concluded that the education of the Africans was being perverted to create bondage out of a racial setting. Bernstein went on to suggest that in ignoring the universality of the purpose of education, the colonial governments set in motion a spiraling process that ultimately led to confrontation with the Africans.[39] This was the ultimate effect of the colonial educational policy in Africa.

The third conclusion is that throughout its history, the educational system in colonial southern Africa demonstrated serious shortcomings in traditional society in Africa. The attitudes of the colonial officials, such as Cecil John Rhodes, Paul Kruger, Earl Grey, Ethel Tawse Jollie, Hugh Williams, and Ian Smith, demonstrate a purpose of education for Africans that was incompatible with basic social, political, and economic needs. The need for cheap labor and the desire to limit political, social, and economic development of Africans placed them on a level of bare existence and suffering. This made it difficult for them to function in a larger social context.

This situation is what Methodist Bishop James Crane Hartzell (1842–1928)[40] saw when he wrote in 1918, "Africa has suffered many evils. Slave trade and exploitation by the white man have, through many years, preyed upon the life of the people and have left them uncertain about the future. To their dismay, the Natives of Africa have realized that the white man has offered them his form of education only to enable them to function as laborers."[41] Albert Schweitzer (1825–1965), a German missionary to nineteenth-century Africa, agreed when he wrote, "Who can describe the misery, the injustice, and the cruelties that the Africans have suffered at the hands of Europeans? If a record could be compiled, it would make a book containing pages which the reader would have to turn unread because their contents would be too horrible."[42]

One can see that from its inception colonial education needed reform because it was inadequate. It was inadequate because it was unable to meet the needs of all people as defined by themselves in the context of a new social, economic, and political system in which it was cast. When, from time to time, the colonial governments introduced what they considered reform, they did so not in accordance with universal principles of educational reform, but to train Africans to serve better as laborers. Such an educational system was destined to create a climate of conflict, repression, and human misunderstanding.

NOTES

1. William van Til, *Education: A Beginning* (Boston: Houghton Mifflin Company, 1974), p. 417.

2. Ibid., p. 418.

3. Ibid., p. 419.

4. Paulo Freire, *Pedagogy of the Oppressed*, trans. Myra Bergman Ramos (New York: Continuum, 1983), p. 132.

5. Indeed, in Africa the responsibility of educating a child rests on the shoulders of all the members of the community. This is why Africans get credit for the saying "It takes the whole village to raise a child."

6. Michael Gelfand, *Growing Up in Shona Society* (Gweru: Mambo Press, 1985), p. 11.

7. Dickson A. Mungazi, *The Struggle for Social Change in Southern Africa: Visions of Liberty* (New York: Taylor and Francis, 1989), p. 53.

8. Ibid., p. 54.

9. The European governments that instituted colonies in Africa refused to accept the concept of kings and decided to refer to them as chiefs to make a case to substantiate their claim that African society was primitive. For Europeans to recognize African leaders as kings would be to place those leaders at the same level as kings in Europe. If they did this, then they would not be able to justify their colonial intentions.

10. V. W. Turner, *Schism and Continuity in an African Society* (Manchester: Manchester University Press, 1957), p. 318.

11. Lawrence Vambe, *An Ill-Fated People: Zimbabwe Before and After Rhodes* (Pittsburgh: Pittsburgh University Press, 1957), p. 317.

12. William Raynor, *The Tribe and Its Successors: An Account of African Traditional Life After European Settlement in Southern Rhodesia* (New York: Frederick Praeger, 1962), p. 49.

13. F. G. Loveridge, Senior Education Officer in Colonial Zimbabwe, "Disturbing Reality of Western Education in Southern Africa," an address to the Rotary Club International, Harare, Zimbabwe, March 13, 1965. Quoted by permission of the Old Mutare Methodist Archives.

14. Michael Gelfand, *Diet and Tradition in African Culture* (London: E. S. Livingstone, 1971), p. 45.

15. B. A. Powers, *Religion and Education in Tswana Chiefdom* (London: Oxford University Press, 1961), p. 29.

16. An elderly African, during an interview in Mutare, Zimbabwe, May 15, 1974, in Dickson A. Mungazi, "The Change of Black Attitudes Towards Education in Rhodesia, 1900–1975" (dissertation, the University of Nebraska, Lincoln, 1977), p. 80.

17. Michael Gelfand, *Growing Up in Shona Society*, p. 217.

18. Ibid., p. 220.

19. Lawrence Henderson, *Angola: Five Centuries of Conflict* (Ithaca, NY: Cornell University Press, 1979), p. 15.

20. Ibid., p. 18.

21. Marion O'Callaghan, *Namibia: The Effects of Apartheid on Culture and Education* (Paris: UNESCO, 1977), p. 19.

22. Ibid., p. 96.

23. Stanlake Samkange, *What Rhodes Really Said About Africa* (Harare: Harare Publishing House, 1982), p. 14.

24. Canaan Banana, *Theology of Promise: The Dynamics of Self-Reliance* (Harare: The College Press, 1982), p. 53.

25. Ibid., p. 26.

26. La Guma, *Apartheid*, p. 13.

27. Hilda Bernstein, "Schools for Servitude," in La Guma, *Apartheid*, p. 43.

28. Ibid., p. 44.

29. British South Africa Company Records, Earl Grey, 1896–1898: Folio AV/1/11/:GR/1/1/11:547–548. By permission of the Zimbabwe National Archives.

30. Southern Rhodesia, "The Annual Report of the Chief Native Commissioner for Moshonaland, 1905." By permission of the Zimbabwe National Archives.

31. *Rhodesia Herald*, June 28, 1812.

32. Southern Rhodesia, *Legislative Debates*, 1927.

33. Ibid.

34. Rhodesia, *Parliamentary Debates*, 1969.

35. Ian Smith, RF prime minister of colonial Zimbabwe from 1964 to 1979, during an interview in Harare, Zimbabwe, July 20, 1983.

36. Banana, *Theology of Promise: The Dynamics of Self-Reliance,* p. 73.

37. Aldon Southall, *The Illusion of Tribe* (The Netherlands: R. J. Brill, 1970).

38. Babs Fafunwa, *History of Education in Nigeria* (London: George Allen and Unwin, 1974), p. 16.

39. Hilda Bernstein, "Schools for Servitude," in La Guma, *Apartheid*, p. 43.

40. Bishop of the Methodist Episcopal Church in Africa from 1896 to 1916. Hartzell Secondary School at Old Mutare Methodist Center outside Mutare in Zimbabwe is named after him.

41. James C. Hartzell, "The Future of Africa," *African Advance*, Vol. 12, No. 1, July 1918, p. 5.

42. "Missionaries in Africa," *Christian Century*, Vol. 2, No. 1, October 8, 1975, p. 5.

3

The Purpose of Educational Reform in Southern Africa

We must never think of a man as a form of automation who must receive and carry out orders irrespective of whether he understands them or has assimilated them.

Samora Machel, 1972

Africa needs change to ensure its development. Reform in education must be the starting point towards meaningful social change.

Julius Nyerere, 1974

PROBLEMS CREATED BY COLONIAL POLICY

The purpose of formulating and implementing colonial policies such as *Estado Novo*, *evalue*, *Deutsche Kolonialbund*, and indirect rule was to protect the political, social, and economic interests of the colonial governments in southern Africa. These policies were not intended to promote the development of Africans. The formulation and implementation of these colonial policies were quite compatible with the behavior of colonial establishments everywhere, and there was nothing unusual in the application. In the countries of southern Africa, however, the effect was quite different. The restrictive nature of education under colonial control meant that Africans were isolated from their own people when they made a concerted effort to secure an education.[1] Only a small number of Africans were able to get an education. Those who obtained an education were isolated from their uneducated brothers and sisters. The psychological effects of that isolation were devastating. Africans educated under these policies failed to identify themselves with either the white community or the African community.

The achievement of political independence in Africa demanded immediate resolution of these problems if the Africans were to have a better future. One major way of doing so was to initiate considerations of a new purpose of educational reform. This is the challenge that nations of southern Africa face today. In December 1995 Boutros Boutros-Ghali, secretary-general to the United Nations (UN), declared the year 1996 as the international year of eradicating poverty. Boutros-Ghali indicated that the only way to end poverty was to reform education throughout the world to prepare all people for an effective role in society by earning a decent income. Boutros-Ghali said that the lack of educational opportunities was the cause of poverty, and poverty was the cause of the increasing wave of crime throughout the world. Boutros-Ghali said that over 1.3 billion people in the world were struggling to survive on less than one dollar per day. He argued that five years earlier the number was three hundred million. Another billion people in 1995 lacked the ability to meet their basic needs. Boutros-Ghali concluded, "Eradication of poverty is an ethical, social, political, and economic imperative of humankind."[2]

To succeed in this effort, the nations of southern Africa need to resolve problems that were left behind by the colonial governments. It must be understood that in their desire to exploit African resources, both human and material, the colonial governments created problems that they simply did not know how to resolve, problems that are prevalent today. The task now rests on the shoulders of Africans for resolution. The formulation and implementation of colonial policy instituted a set of problems that had far-reaching consequences on the development of Africans and their continent. As time went on, these problems became more complex, making them harder to resolve. It is equally important for the nations of southern Africa to recognize the seriousness of the problems that they are facing before attempting to solve them through educational reform. They must also realize that total commitment to national purpose is a critical factor of their efforts. Educational reform alone does not guarantee the success of efforts directed toward national development.

One of the most difficult problems that the colonial systems created in southern Africa is the distribution of land. The enactment of the Land Act in South Africa in 1913, for example, allocated 13 percent of the land to Africans and the remaining 87 percent to whites. John Daniszewski stated that, after attaining majority rule in 1994,

Blacks began to wonder if they had won democracy only to be condemned to be paupers in their own country. Less than 15 percent of the population, whites, now own more than 30 percent of the farmland. The struggle over land is central to South Africa's troubled racist past. The Dutch settlers, known as Boers, trekked into the interior in the nineteenth century buying land and founding vast farms. Then in 1913 the Union of South Africa decreed that blacks would not own or rent land. The only way blacks would escape being forced into native reserves was to go to work for white landowners as sharecroppers.[3]

As soon as the Nationalist Party was returned to power in the elections of 1948 the government led by Daniel Malan ended the system of sharecroppers and forcibly moved Africans into the native Bantustan reserves. Now the government of Nelson Mandela faces the problem of redistribution of land in a system that is fair to both whites and blacks. This presents a monumental challenge.

PROBLEMS OF EDUCATIONAL REFORM IN SOUTHERN AFRICA

To meet the challenges of the twenty-first century, a discussion of some fundamental purposes of educational reform in contemporary southern Africa is important. Before this is done, a discussion of some of the educational problems left behind by the colonial governments will underscore the need for educational reform. Because the educational policies of the colonial governments were directed toward fulfilling purposes that were incompatible with the development of Africans, the educational process itself left a legacy of problems that African nations have not been able to resolve.

In a special report on problems of education in Africa in general issued in October 1981, the *Chicago Tribune* outlined the following problems as the legacy left behind in Africa as a result of the action of the colonial governments in pursuing their purposes. Of every eight teachers in the primary school, six had completed only ninth grade. For every 360 children in the primary school, two hundred dropped out before they reached fourth grade, wiping out any literacy they may have acquired. This means that of Africa's 430 million people in 1981, only 11 percent could read and write.[4]

The economic legacy of the policies pursued by the colonial governments in Africa can also be seen in the financial outlay for education. The average expenditure for education in 1981 was $149.00 per student per year compared with the average for the world of $612.00. With a population growth rate of 3.9 percent annually in 1989, this means that in twenty years, the per pupil expenditure would decline sharply, putting national developmental efforts in

Africa perilously on the brink of disaster. The lack of financial resources also means that only 56.4 percent of all primary age children actually attend school, but only 20 percent continue their education to the end of primary school.

The *Chicago Tribune* also reported that an average of nearly 50 percent of all teachers in the primary schools failed to meet the qualification criteria established by their governments. In addition, the teacher-to-student ratio of 1:45 was among the worst in the world. Because the colonial governments often emphasized practical training for African girls to have them serve as domestic servants, a practice emerged among African parents of preferring to send their sons to school, not daughters, in the hope that they would secure better employment opportunities in industry. As a result, in 1981 girls constituted only 41 percent of the students in primary school, 37 percent in secondary school, and 31 percent in higher education.[5]

When the countries of southern Africa achieved political independence, they came face to face with the hard realities of these problems. No country has been immune. When Zimbabwe achieved independence in April 1980, it was forced to recruit teachers heavily from other countries. At that time, it had an enrollment of 790,000 students, but within one year that enrollment had jumped to 1.82 million students, and Zimbabwe could not produce teachers fast enough to meet the need.[6] In addition to finding a workable solution to this problem, Zimbabwe had to borrow $1.8 billion from the International Monetary Fund (IMF) to develop the educational facilities left behind by the colonial government of South Africa.[7]

It was soon evident that the three hundred million dollars that the government of Zimbabwe had allocated toward education during the first year of independence was insufficient to meet the need. All the countries of southern Africa went through this experience and have shown how they were trying to offset the adverse effect of the colonial legacy. When Namibia achieved independence in March 1990, it encountered these same problems—the result of seven decades of benign neglect by the government of South Africa, which administered it from 1920 to 1990.

Three areas that must become the focus of reform for the transformation of southern Africa are social, political, and economic. A discussion of each and how its influence is felt on the need for educational reform follows. This discussion does not address the process of educational reform. Rather, it presents only the relationships of educational reform to those aspects of national development that are its products.

In his annual budget statement presented to the parliament of Zimbabwe in July 1990, Bernard Chidzero, the minister of finance and economic planning, recognized that the introduction of free primary education had resulted in the increase of students from 1.6 in 1980 to 2.3 million in 1989. At the secondary level, the figures for the same period were 74,966 to 695,612. Chidzero concluded that these figure raised the budget from 14.8 percent in 1980 to 23.1 percent in 1990.[8] Chidzero also urged the government to reexamine the policy of free education, saying,

There are two reasons why the government should review the system of financing education. The first reason is that although education represents a long-term investment in the development of human resources, its provision needs to be balanced with investment in immediately productive areas if the economy is to sustain the costs implied. The trend so far has been to social sectors as education grows at the expense of the productive sectors. The second reason is that there appear to be anomalies in the present system of financing education. While education is supposed to be free, parents of various social groups are called upon to contribute to the building fund in money or in kind. It is not always the richest who pay the heaviest levies.[9]

Unfortunately, Chidzero's views were the basis of the decision made by the government of Zimbabwe to end free primary education in 1991, causing larger political, social, and economic problems. Once free primary education was introduced it should have been maintained at all costs.

In his annual budget statement for fiscal year 1995–96, A. M. Chambati, Chidzero's successor, did not even address the problems that the ending of free primary education had created in the form of a lack of financial resources by parents, an increasing rate of illiteracy, rising unemployment, and a lack of morale and hope for the future. Instead, Chambati directed his budget proposals toward higher education, saying.

Under the ministry of higher education, a provision of $90 million has been made to cover on-going works for the faculty of commerce, the hall of residence as well as the completion of the administration block at the National University of Science and Technology. Additional to this, provisions have been made to the University of Zimbabwe for the health science complex. Under the Ministries of Education and of Sports Recreation and Culture, a provision of $42 million has been made for completion of facilities, renovation of Venus and computerization of the All Africa Games.[10]

The fact that both Chidzero and Chambati failed to address the need for a balanced approach to all levels of education indicates a dire need to reestablish new purposes of educational reform. In an article to the *Sunday Mail* of January 7, 1996, Paradzai Chihwape, a teacher in a rural school in Zimbabwe, addressed this need, saying,

The government must build secondary schools in near farms so that primary school graduates will find it easier to have access to secondary school education. Children in farms are also being starved of reading materials and this has a negative impact on their academic achievements. Efforts should be made to secure funds and books so as to establish libraries in these areas. Members of parliament whose constituencies cover farms should strive to get some donations for the development of schools in the areas they represent. This is a challenge to the government and the human rights groups to rise to the occasion and bring salvation to the farm children who are in agony of abuse through neglect and a lack of educational reform. Farm children should be incorporated into all educational programs.[11]

 It is clear from Chihwape's views that both Chidzero and Chambati did not appear to have a sharp purpose of educational reform. Leaders of the nations of southern Africa must recognize that it is not possible to initiate successful educational reform without taking all levels of education into consideration. These levels include all dimensions of education, such as Chihwape addressed in this article.

THE STRUGGLE FOR LIBERATION THROUGH LITERACY

Experience in developed countries shows that the success of education lies in what are known as the basics: reading, writing, and arithmetic. There is no reason to think that developing nations do not wish to develop the basics for their own people. These universal elements of education have been recognized worldwide as fundamental tenets of national development. If anything, they are far more critical to Third World nations today than to developed nations because Third World nations are struggling for transformation. Concern for reform in southern Africa must, by the nature of its form, extend far beyond school enrollment. It must be woven into the political, economic, and social fiber of the national character.

In a much larger context, all the countries of southern Africa are encountering serious problems in their national developmental efforts because in 1990, illiteracy was also rising at a disturbing rate.[12]

Literacy is also important to national endeavors in that it must come first in any national educational programs. Literacy is the touchstone that opens the door of opportunity to all other areas of human enterprise. Without literacy, there is no escape for the individual and the nation from the oppression of the tentacles of an old and vicious octopus, ignorance. Literacy is the ultimate form of human liberation. President Mugabe recognized this fact when he launched a national literacy campaign in July 1983. He also acknowledged the critical nature of literacy as a means to self-fulfillment by both the individual and the nation. Paulo Freire suggests that self-consciousness itself invokes in the individual an ability to think critically and "the ability to communicate ideas consistent with the essence of being human."[13] In this context, educational reform acquires a compelling influence to place the individual on the level of human effort that every person in society is entitled to, to ensure his development as a condition of national development. This is the global right of a global citizen.

Unlike political liberation, the struggle for national liberation through literacy makes possible the liberation of the human mind as an absolute necessity for the creation of a social, economic, and political environment. The educational process itself must serve its intended purpose. This is the setting that makes self-determination an indispensable human quality that is needed to distinguish man from other living species. Self-determination enables one to set goals, to establish priorities, and to design strategies to fulfill them. In 1983, Ndabaningi Sithole, veteran nationalist leader, thinker, and political activist, recognized the importance of literacy as a form of human liberation and equated it with the universal definition of education and what it does for the individual. Sithole observed,

Education provides the individual who has certain feelings and thoughts with a mechanism of articulation and self-expression. Before one acquires basic literacy it is impossible for one to articulate sufficiently what one wants to communicate. Literacy translates into education which gives one a wide scope and a depth to one's thinking. It provides one a comprehensive grasp of who one really is, and the problems that one faces. Adjustment to a new social environment is virtually impossible without literacy. Reform of the educational system must seek to accomplish literacy as a basic component of its purpose to ensure the absolute liberation of the individual as a condition of national liberation.[14]

There are two basic elements that must be understood as forming the important core that is the heart of the struggle for liberation through literacy. Literacy is the key to self-determination as an outcome of educational reform in southern Africa. The first element is that an enlightened and genuinely liberated nation can emerge only from enlightened and liberated individuals. Many nations of Africa have yet to come to grips with this reality. Without enlightened citizens, a nation will always be oppressed by a combination of forces such as social ills, racial or ethnic bigotry, tribal conflict, and political dissension. In short, illiterate individuals cannot build an enlightened nation.

In 1996 Paradzai Chihwape addressed the imperative of government involvement in seeking to end illiteracy. Chihwape said,

After the attainment of independence the government declared war against illiteracy and made primary education compulsory for all school-going age people. In an endeavor to realize its objective, education at the primary level was made free. It is unfortunate that illiteracy is on the increase in farms as many children are not going to school or are dropping out of school at an early age. One of the major causes of this situation is that many parents in the rural community do not know the importance of sending their children to school. They do not encourage them to strive and proceed in their studies. As I see it, government and non-government organizations should embark on a serious campaign for educational reform in all its aspects including farm schools. They can move from farm to farm carrying out a survey to establish the true statistics of those going to school and those who are not.[15]

On January 8, 1996, in an unprecedented move to dramatize the need for educational reform in all segments of education in Zimbabwe, William Sithole, the director of the Council for the Blind, proposed that the government open more schools for the blind to allow more students to acquire the basic education they need to function in society. Sithole said that only sixty-six schools in Zimbabwe were equipped to educate blind students in line with the integrated educational policy. Sithole added, "We expect blind students to go to the same schools as other students, but only 66 schools have the resources and the specialist teachers needed to get the students integrated into the conventional school system. These schools are far from enough."[16] Sithole added that blind children had to attend special schools created for the blind, but that these schools were too far for the students to travel. He concluded that it was important for the government to realize that providing adequate educational facilities for the handicapped students was in the best interest of the country. But to accomplish this objective, it was necessary to initiate reform in the educational system itself.

Throughout Africa, it has been recognized that illiteracy is a harmful legacy of the colonial period that all countries of southern Africa have not yet been able to eliminate. This inability suggests that educational reform is an imperative condition for seeking solutions. The fact that the colonial governments were interested in literacy among the Africans only as a means of improving their labor capacity suggests the reason why the nations of southern African must make a greater effort to provide basic literacy to their people. The following figures illustrate this confusion:

Literacy in Southern Africa: 1983 and 1990 Compared

Country	1983		1990	
	Percentage of 5–19 pop. in school	Literacy percentage	Percentage of 5–19 pop. in school	Literacy percentage
Angola	28	12	30	30
Botswana	56	30	35	61
Mozambique	20	20	14	25
Namibia	—	15	13	40
South Africa	55	98 white	99 white	
		55 black	50 black	71
Tanzania	60	60	85	89
Zaire	40	40	55	62
Zambia	50	50	54	75
Zimbabwe	37	30	50	78

Source: World Almanac and Book of Facts, 1983 and 1990.

The second element is that all the governments of southern Africa must recognize that basic literacy is a right that belongs to all citizens and must therefore endeavor to direct their energies and national resources to the full development of the human potential that is so critical to national development. This endeavor must be undertaken in the full knowledge that, ultimately, it is the nation that will benefit from the development of the people. To emphasize this line of thinking, Mugabe rhetorically asked, "How can a farmer improve his farming if he cannot read instructions on the use of fertilizers?"[17]

In making his point, Mugabe rhetorically asked the question, "How can the people themselves run their own factories and shops if they cannot count their money and write their budgets?"[18] What Mugabe was implying is that citizens who are self-sufficient, providing a home and food for their families and running their own affairs, will provide the essential elements of a developing society that is happy and stable. Experience in other countries shows that governments are secure only when their people are secure. Unlike the colonial governments, the independent governments of southern Africa become the major beneficiaries of the life insurance policy that the people, through literacy, can be guaranteed. This requires a favorable response to government policy designed to ensure the advancement of all.

In launching this literacy campaign to achieve human liberation, Mugabe was aware that the inability of the citizens to develop their mental capacity perpetuates oppression of the nation itself because ignorance of the ideas expressed by others and inability to communicate create a condition of exploitation. This was a situation created by the colonial educational policy, which the governments of southern Africa must now seek to eliminate. This is why Mugabe concluded, "It was therefore not by accident that the white settler regimes of our colonial past denied the majority of the African people the opportunity of going to school."[19] It is for this reason that Mugabe acknowledged the fact that the campaign for literacy was not aimed merely at some illiterate people, but at all adults outside the formal educational process. He tried to convince his fellow Zimbabweans that achieving 100 percent literacy was a condition for national liberation.

The nations of southern Africa must recognize that basic literacy is a major objective of educational reform, and that it benefits the nation because it benefits all individuals. The reality of this situation translates into an imperative: a realization that universal basic education is paramount for a new reality in all of southern Africa. There should be no reason why children are not educated. Achieving this fundamental objective must become a major national commitment and challenge understood by those who are charged with the responsibility of planning and implementing educational programs to ensure reform as a condition of national transformation.

CULTURAL PLURALISM AS A NATIONAL ENRICHMENT

If there is a part of the world that must recognize, appreciate, and cultivate the importance of cultural diversity as a national enrichment, it is Africa. Some leaders of African nations fail to realize that the existence of many ethnic groups creates a national variety that can only act as a spice of national life. Many of them, instead, regard cultural diversity as a threat to their own definition of national unity and their own political power. It is true that members of a cultural or ethnic minority group create an inner circle whose ideas may be considered incompatible with national policies. It is also true that the preponderance of ethnic groups in southern Africa creates a situation in which members of an ethnic group consider themselves loyal to it before they consider themselves members of the country in which they live. This often creates a conflict situation between the group and the government.

For better understanding, one must discuss this serious problem of national development in southern Africa in the context of the policies adopted by the colonial governments. In practicing the policy of *divide and rule*, the colonial governments devised a strategy that they used to conclude that some ethnic groups were better than others. For example, in South Africa, the government portrayed the Zulus as better than the Xhosas. In colonial Zimbabwe, the government told the Shonas that they were better than the Ndebeles. In Zambia, the Bembas were considered better than the Lozi. It was this cultural and colonial setting that allowed the colonial governments to provide education to different ethnic groups in different ways.

This colonial practice of the policy of divide and rule was so pervasive in southern Africa that some ethnic groups were set against others. Violent clashes between different ethnic groups, such as those that took place in the mining compounds in South Africa beginning in 1936, played into the hands of the colonial officials as they exploited cultural and ethnic differences to conclude that Africans were uncivilized. The competition and the climate of conflict that the South African government often created between different ethnic groups did not help Africans in resolving the problems created by the colonial governments. In South Africa, the government's secret involvement in promoting violence between different ethnic groups has created a situation that is close to a major national disaster.

Indeed, it is not by coincidence that since the release of Nelson Mandela from prison on February 11, 1990, Inkatha, a Zulu political and cultural group led by Chief Mangosuthu Buthelezi, intensified its fight against the supporters of the United Democratic Front (UDF), which supported African National Congress (ANC), which Mandela, who is Xhosa, leads. That Buthelezi and the South African government hold periodic consultations indicates the extent of government involvement in the renewed fighting, which, by the end of March, 1990, had cost twenty-five hundred lives.[20] On April 1, 1990, Buthelezi blamed ANC for the violence, instead of the continuation of apartheid, and the fact that he and Adrian Vlok, the South African minister of law and order, held secret talks on the situation suggests the tragic outcome of the South African government's strategy to apply the old principle of divide and rule to new settings. The fact that the fighting was mainly between rivalry members of the same Zulu group did not mean anything to Buthelezi and the government of South Africa. One must therefore conclude that although, by 1990, the government of South Africa did not openly accuse ANC of the violence, it had not abandoned its secret involvement in promoting violence between different ethnic groups and the application of the colonial principle of divide and rule.

What came out of the application of the colonial educational policy is what Canaan Banana of Zimbabwe calls a culture of poverty.[21] This means that the colonial governments repeatedly belittled and discredited African culture to the extent that the African self-image was reduced to the level where it had confused meaning in their life. This was done to serve the purposes of the colonial governments themselves. Translated into the kind of relationships that emerged between Africans and the colonial government as a result of this strategy and between the educational process and the concept of cultural diversity, the colonial purpose of putting ethnic differences into the educational system created social, economic, and psychological conditions that inhibited the ability of Africans to function in a larger social order.

One can see that the resulting situation was, in reality, a colonial cultural imposition. It was clear that the problems of education in the colonial setting were, in themselves, a mirror of cultural domination and alienation so effectively put in place for the sole purpose of controlling Africans and reducing the influence of their culture in their endeavors toward development so that they were educated to fulfill the larger purpose of the colonial culture. It was therefore the intent of the colonial governments to utilize its system of education as the principal instrument of ensuring colonial cultural supremacy. Dzingai Mutumbuka argued that, "The colonial condition of cultural domination and alienation as a consequence of colonial domination was also a consequence of economic, political, and educational domination."[22]

What Mutumbuka said must not be regarded as flogging a dead horse, but as a critical appraisal of all relevant aspects of the past to chart a new course to the future. Therefore, when Mutumbuka calls on all the nations of southern Africa to redirect their efforts toward educational innovation to restore their cultural heritage and pride,[23] he is, in effect, suggesting the emergence of an entirely new dimension of cultural diversity as a purpose of educational innovation.

One must search for a wider perspective from which to understand the concept of cultural diversity as a purpose of educational reform in southern Africa. When Paulo Freire concludes that efforts of the oppressed to restore their belittled culture constitute an essential step toward self-rediscovery,[24] he is suggesting that the educational process must be divorced from the culture of the oppressor. For nations of southern Africa, this suggests establishing a new purpose of cultural enrichment as an outcome of a new educational process in a new social, economic, and political order. Samora Machel discusses the importance of this line of thinking when he says that cultural rediscovery creates a new social ideology, formulated in the context of new conditions and promoted by a new system of education to strengthen it.[25]

The recognition of the importance of cultural rediscovery suggests that for southern Africa as a region, redefining cultural values as a purpose of educational innovation has an importance that cannot be taken for granted. It entails the provision of values to students at the primary school level that are of a rudimentary nature but are critical to the wider application of life-style in a multiethnic society. It is here that education plays an important role in teaching students early in life the spirit of cultural tolerance and acceptance, not of division and conflict, as was the case during the colonial period. Once students experience an elimination of cultural prejudice, they will see all human beings, not as members of distinct ethnic groups with stereotypes so characteristic of the colonial period, but as members of an embracing human family. Once this objective has been accomplished, tribal or ethnic conflicts that paralyze national efforts toward advancement will also become manageable.

Beyond solving the problems of human conflict, cultural acceptance and diversity extends to all people a sense of confidence in themselves and their national leaders as they are made to believe that the notion of the superior-inferior complex has no place in the new social system. When education emphasizes the national character of a plural cultural enrichment, no ethnic group is threatened, and no ethnic group feels dominated. In this new societal environment, equal opportunity is practiced to the fullest. The tragedy of cultural domination that exploded into a bitter civil war in Nigeria in 1967 must be avoided at all costs.

There is another important reason for having educational innovation seek the improvement of cultural diversity as a national enrichment in southern Africa. One of the major worries of national leaders all over Africa has always been their inability to establish what they have regarded as a *national cultural identity:* an identity in which all citizens seek to identify themselves with a single national symbol. From Kwame Nkrumah of Ghana in 1957 to Sam Nujoma of Namibia in 1990, this objective has remained elusive for three basic reasons. The first reason is that Africans consider themselves first members of their ethnic group before they consider themselves citizens of their country.

The second reason is that national leaders often come from one of the dominant ethnic groups and often exclude members of other groups from the government. Examples include the Hausas, the Yorubas, and the Ibos in Nigeria; the Nyanjas and the Chewas in Malawi; the Senas and Ndawus in Mozambique; and the Shona and the Nbebeles in Zimbabwe. It was not until there was persistent conflict between the two groups in Zimbabwe that President Robert Mugabe's predominantly Shona government decided to include the Ndebele representatives under the leadership of Joshua Nkomo, and solution to a critical problem was finally found.

The third reason is that the inability of the African leaders to carve out a new national cultural identity has also resulted in their inability to resolve conflict situations that often emerge in the question of who comes first, the individual or society. Because national leaders often argue that society must come first, there has been a strategy to demand absolute loyalty of every citizen. This means that the concept of individuality must be subordinated to the concept of national unity, in which individual interests come second to what is considered national interests. The problem has been that what national leaders have regarded as national interests has been nothing more than seeking to sustain their own political interests.

This scenario created a situation in which some ethnic groups that had been excluded from participation in government withdrew from national programs to place their loyalty with their ethnic groups. This voluntary self-alienation furthered an environment of conflict because excluded ethnic groups felt that they were being exploited for political reasons. African national leaders felt uncomfortable with the criticism, especially from the West, that they were intolerant of cultural differences.[26] For Western nations to level this kind of criticism, however, was to neglect their own role in creating the situation in the first place.

One does not have to search far for evidence that cultural diversity as a purpose of educational innovation must be considered an essential element of national development. Although young Africans seem to be placed at the crossroads of traditional cultural values and the emerging values, the problem can be resolved by designing an educational system that convinces the students of the wisdom of restoring the important components of the African culture itself. They would soon learn that a people without a set of cultural values has nothing of importance to build a future on. The ultimate result of a cultural void would be what Canaan Banana sees as a consequence of a misguided education, producing what he sees as "scores of black *Europeans* who debase their own culture."[27]

In 1970, Samora Machel took this line of thinking to add, "Colonial education accentuated ethnic and cultural divisions. The purpose of educational reform in post-colonial southern Africa must be to accentuate cultural diversity as a national enrichment."[28] Seven years later, in 1977, the education commission of Botswana saw cultural diversity in the context of both social change and educational innovation, adding, "Social change which is meant to improve the quality of human life is the main purpose of educational innovation."[29] What these examples show is that instead of regarding cultural plurality as a negative feature of national life, the nations of southern Africa should regard it as national enrichment. But to do that, the national priority must be transformed through the educational process to meet the needs of all people. This demands an honest, open-minded willingness to meet the challenge of educational reform.

THE NEED FOR TECHNOLOGICAL DEVELOPMENT

When, in 1970, Samora Machel expressed the need for technological development in southern Africa as an outcome of change in the educational system to meet the needs of a changing technological society, he was recognizing the imperative of educational reform and was rejecting the educational status quo because it would mean, in effect, sustaining the educational system of the colonial governments. Machel went on to add,

The principal task of change in the educational system is to promote the advancement of science and technology, to facilitate the development of industry, to improve agriculture, medical services, and transport and communication. These are the elements that help us revitalize our society. These are the elements that make educational reform a necessary condition for national development.[30]

The world has changed much in terms of technology, and the nations of southern Africa must come into line with trends of the future if national transformation is to take place. The need for technological development is perhaps more profoundly felt in southern Africa than in any other part of the continent because the region faces more serious problems of development than any other region. For many years, Africa has been exploited by Western nations because it did not have developed industry and technology. In fact, the colonial governments prohibited the development of industry to protect the system of monopoly that helped sustain the colonial systems themselves. After independence, the absence of industries diminished the economic independence of African nations to the extent that African leaders accused Western nations of engaging in the practice of neocolonialism. Without economic independence, the political independence for which Africans fought hard for so many years became meaningless. An educational system that fails to help the nations of southern Africa initiate industrial development fails to achieve the purpose for which it exists.

With a rapid population increase, the need for educational reform to ensure agricultural technology becomes a critical factor of national development. When one sees pictures of masses in Ethiopia and Mozambique starving because they have not developed new agricultural methods to produce enough food to feed their rising population, one is reminded of the need to ensure an adequate supply of food to create a climate of political stability. The massive starvation in both Angola and Mozambique in 1990, although there was a scourge of civil wars, stresses the importance of educational innovation to increase agricultural production. In the same way, the need for technological development in medicine, transport, and communication through educational innovation must be recognized as an imperative of national development in all of southern Africa.

THE NEED FOR ECONOMIC DEVELOPMENT

The importance of economic development in developing countries must be discussed in the context of its relation to the purpose of educational reform. There is a symbiotic relationship between the economy and the sociatics (i.e., education, health and welfare) of the individual through employment. The reality that the colonial governments used the education of Africans to strengthen their own social, economic, and political positions suggests the reason countries of southern Africa must state their own purposes of educational reform to guide their developmental efforts. The fact of the matter is that stating new purposes can be done at the time educational reform is initiated. Developed nations have wrestled with the question of what to develop first, the economy or education. Education is a national priority and an individual right as promised by the UN Bill of Rights of 1948. For Third World nations this is a question of what comes first, the chicken or the egg, because conditions compel them to recognize that without the one, the other cannot take place. Without political support and economical input, educational reform will be slow, and the sociatics will remain Third World.

During the colonial period, the Africans who received some form of Western education regarded it as a way of escaping the scourge of deprivation and poverty. They came to realize that success in life, whatever definition it implied, came only by achieving success in education as defined by the colonial governments themselves. For Africans to function as teachers, preachers, messengers, or domestic servants was, in essence, an escape from poverty, because they were considered to have achieved success in education. This meant that economic success and educational success could not be separated, and it highlighted the importance of the government. The obsession of the colonial governments with practical training and manual labor as the only viable form of education for Africans translated into a policy of economic deprivation of the African population.

This is the context that George Stark, director of native education in colonial Zimbabwe from 1934 to 1954, used to argue in 1940, "A Native who has completed a course of study in practical training is not as efficient as a European[31] artisan."[32] In 1996, Mugabe, who based his entire political career on fighting against this negative attitude, recognized the negative effect it was having on the ability of Africans to make a viable contribution to the economic development of Zimbabwe. Mugabe observed, "Your economy becomes that of others and we do not want to become that sort of a country. We do not need economic colonization which we have suffered from already."[33] But while Mugabe was speaking, the economy was in a state of stagnation as the Zimbabwean dollar declined in purchasing power.

In an interview conducted by Tommy Sithole, the editor-in-chief of the *Herald* and published on January 1, 1996, Mugabe outlined three major goals that he said his government hoped to achieve during the next four years. These are rapid industrialization, better operational institutional infrastructures, and better participation by the people in various activities related to national development. Mugabe stated his economic philosophy, saying,

Zimbabwe has to grow to a stage where industry is the main employer while a well-developed agricultural sector sustains the people. By processing minerals and farm produce before export, the growing wealth would be distributed widely among the people. Boosting exports of primary products would not necessarily benefit large numbers of people, hence the need for industrialization to accompany the development of mining and agriculture.[34]

But without outlining the strategies to ensure success of the program, Mugabe left room for doubt as to whether and how the agenda would be fulfilled. Leaving room for doubt about equitable distribution of resources is the very core of what is wrong with the national social, economic, and political programs in all the nations of southern Africa.

In southern Africa today, the economic purpose of educational reform must entail considerations that are critical to development of a viable economic system. The introduction of a less restrictive, and, thus, a more productive economy, would demand skilled manpower. This will create difficulties in calculating the effect of a better educational preparation. It is also an endeavor African nations must undertake in the context of educational reform to have parallel development of the economy and education itself. It is not in the best interest of the African nations to rank-order the two. Each is critical to the development of the other. Experience in developed countries seems to suggest that educational innovation is best achieved in the context of increasing economic production. This is only one side of the triangle possible with better trained personnel needed to run it.

Another fundamental economic consideration related to educational reform must, by necessity, be diversifying the economy itself so that it can be sustained should its mainstay be disrupted, such as the production of copper in Zambia and Zaire, agriculture in Mozambique, chromium ore in Zimbabwe, and natural gas in Angola. Because agriculture is critical to sustaining the economy in general, African nations must guard its development carefully because it determines both the pace and direction of national development.[35] In this respect, the Southern Africa Development Coordination Corporation (SADCC) can play a crucial role in the development of a regional economy so that there is regional cooperation in seeking solutions to a critical problem.

This approach would ensure that prices are stable, inflation is controlled, competition from more developed nations has a promotional effect, and that currency devaluation is more effectively controlled. The present system of international trade in which Third World nations owe billions of dollars in interest on loans reduces the ability of African nations to set new economic goals and to establish national developmental programs. The combination of educational reform and regional economic planning would enable the nations of southern Africa to accept the challenges of national development in a more meaningful way. Once this is done the process of reform can have a greater significance than it would in any other strategy.

Among the essential components of the economic purpose of educational reform is building an economic system that creates new employment opportunities for all. George Psacharopoulos concludes that the higher the rate of unemployment a country experiences, the less its rate of economic development.[36] To reduce the chances of that happening, the nations of southern Africa must broaden the base of their economic development so that as many people as possible are employed. Unemployment undercuts a national effort to initiate effective planning for the future. It also reduces the best national resources, the people, to the level of mere existence, destroys national morale, and weakens a national resolve to build the infrastructure that is essential to national development. This is what George Psacharopoulos, an official of the World Bank, means when he argues, "When unemployment occurs between graduation from school and the first attempt to secure employment, it is often misinterpreted as inefficiency of the school system itself to produce graduates needed to sustain the needs of the national economy."[37] This misinterpretation of the role of the school in strengthening the national economy arises from an effort to rank-order the two. We reject this approach to the relation that must exist among economic development, political backing, and educational reform.

It can be seen that under the political error of rank-ordering economic development and educational reform, both education and the economy are hurt. Central to this reality is that Third World nations must observe the concept of free enterprise. The rush to nationalize the economy hurts the purpose for which educational reform must be initiated. The fact of the matter is that a country is far more secure when its citizens are economically secure. This should become one of the major objectives of governments everywhere. Corruption among government officials must be regarded as a cancer that destroys the vital parts of national life and must never be allowed, tolerated, or practiced. The oppressed who are returned to power must never take on the airs of their oppressors. They must not oppress their own once they obtain political power, economic success, or become educationally advanced.

An important consideration of the economic purpose of educational reform in all developing nations that must be taken into account for relating education reform to efforts toward national economic development is that all citizens must be allowed to have the dignity of earning a decent income to allow them a reasonably good standard of living. This allows them to own their own homes and enables them to provide their families a decent standard of living. This is a prerequisite of the self-pride, or self-actualization, so critical to national development and stability; this is the right of all global citizens. Any government that is based on stratified social, economic, or political structures is bound to lose something important in its endeavor to anchor the country on a soundly developed foundation. This is how a fragile economy threatens the very basis of the government's own survival. Decent income, decent conditions of living, and freedom of choice combine to produce the ideal conditions of a happy society. This sense of economic security, in turn, constitutes elements that are required to make educational reform relevant to individual needs and national efforts to ensure social, economic, and political development of the citizens and of the country.

In January 1996, Funny Mushava, a reporter for the Zimbabwean *Business Herald*, reported what she observed to be a conversation between a motorist and a street boy as follows:

"Sir, can I guard your car?" a street kid asks a motorist. "Sure, no problem," comes the reply. An hour later the motorist returns and pays the street kid twenty cents. "Only this? But, sir, I can't even buy a bun," pleads the street kid before the motorist has a sudden change of heart and tops the twenty cents with fifty cents. Such is the value of the Zimbabwean dollar. With double digit rates of inflation in the past six years, the dollar is buying less and less.[38]

Mushava goes on to describe how the declining value of the dollar has hurt the economic development of Zimbabwe and suggests that the solution to this problem is to reform the educational system so that the resulting educational process is directed at enabling the people to ensure entrepreneurship that seeks to strengthen the economy, add to the self-esteem of the citizens, and strengthen the national character.

Another important consideration of the economic purpose of educational reform is the importance of sustaining good public health. The health of the citizens is a critical factor of national development. The increase in the slums or, as they are called in Africa, *shanty towns*; the increasing number of the unemployed and the homeless; and the increase in differences in the standard of living between people in the rural areas and those in the urban areas are erosive problems. Government must form a major national endeavor to resolve these problems if economic development and educational reform are to combine to give the nation a distinctive purposeful direction. It is in the best interest of the governments themselves to ensure that national resources are directed toward improving sociatics, the health, and the education of the people.

In Africa, there are malnutrition, malaria, measles, and other diseases that are common in places where sanitation, water supply, and preservation of food are inadequate. Diseases rob the nations of Africa of the best national resources they need for development, the people, the culture. The following are among the things that governments must do to ensure good sociatics for the health of the people—providing health education, teaching the people proper nutrition, creating recreational facilities, teaching the people how to preserve food, providing child care, and establishing educational clinics where information on food and health issues are readily available to all people. The establishment of these facilities creates a national climate in which educational reform takes on powerful and more meaningful dimensions. This climate also helps generate a national feeling among citizens that their governments are interested in cooperating with them in their effort to secure the kind of education that is pertinent to their needs as a prerequisite of meeting national needs.

It is a well-known fact that the nations of Africa have been riddled with corruption at various levels of government. Corruption among government officials must be regarded as a cancer that destroys the vital tissue of national life. Corruption and inhumanity must be eliminated once and for all. All over Africa, the people are tired of corruption. The problem is how to get rid of it.[39] In different countries and at different times, Africans have addressed the problem of corruption and the need to end it. In an editorial in January 1996, the *Sunday Mail* of Zimbabwe discussed how the cancer of corruption has been destroying national life, saying, "There is still a need to completely stamp out corruption in the government departments and introduce a new commitment to national duty. A visit to any of these departments will reveal that most government officials do not seriously apply themselves to duty. Whether this is because they are poorly paid or the management system is not conducive to efficient operations needs to be looked into."[40]

In an editorial of December 14, 1995, the *Financial Gazette* of Zimbabwe decried what it called a wave of corruption in the process of extending scholarships to students. The editorial stated,

The scholarship fund, intended to boost national human resources development, has fallen victim of greedy politicians and civil servants who have raided it to subsidize the external education of their kith and kin. In what has become the norm, public funds have been monopolized by those charged with making them accessible to the taxpaying public.

Zimbabwe is a poor developing country whose future is wholly dependent on the prudent use of its human and financial resources. The responsibility to ensure that this happens to the optimum benefit of the nation is vested in our public officials whose conduct is naturally expected to be beyond reproach. This has often not been the case.[41]

What this suggests is that without seeking to eliminate corruption in government, every other effort directed at seeking improvement in national life will fail. It is not possible to initiate educational reform within the environment of corruption. This suggests that seeking to end corruption is an important purpose of educational reform. Signs of corruption include sudden financial expansion of those who are in political office, abundance, and waste of taxpayers' money.

THE THRUST FOR NATIONAL POLITICAL INTEGRATION AND UNITY

The fact that the colonial governments did not practice democracy in Africa because they argued that Africans were not sufficiently educated to understand its complex process must dictate a fundamental change in both the political process and the educational system. Central to this reality is the question, If the colonial governments believed that the lack of educational opportunity inhibited the political abilities of Africans, then why did they not do something to change the situation? Realizing that this line of thinking was not in the scheme of things of the colonial governments is precisely why African nations must initiate an educational reform to realize the importance of political integration, economic support, and national unity as critical factors of national development.

Earlier in this chapter, we concluded that economic development and literacy must benefit the individual before they can benefit society itself. In the same way, educational reform intended to realize some political objectives must first be directed at improving the position of the individual in society as a supreme political being. But the process of becoming a supreme political being demands an education that is comprehensive enough to enable students to grasp the essential components of a political society. The symbiosis is ongoing.

British writer on problems of education in Africa, A. R. Thompson, argues that to serve the needs of the people in a way it was intended to do, education must not be removed from focusing on the political interests of the individual first and then of society as a whole.[42] Thompson goes on to argue that national governments "must recognize that the growing scale and complexity of educational planning must be met largely from the public purse and must therefore be subject to political accountability."[43] Thompson is actually suggesting that educational reform must be directed toward political integration and national unity. One must therefore ask the question: What do political integration and national unity mean?

Thompson argues that it has been recognized that in southern Africa, education and politics have remained as far apart as they were during the colonial period because of an inherent unwillingness to acknowledge their interdependence. The proper thing for the developing nations of southern Africa to do is to formulate national policies that seek to bring education and politics together in a productive manner. Change in the educational system is essential to that fundamental objective. It would enable all people to view the political process from a perspective of healthy activity intended to ensure national development. This kind of setting creates a new social environment that enables citizens to develop a collective political identity, which suggests that although they hold different political views and belong to different political parties, as they must to sustain democratic principles, they would still subscribe to a common national endeavor to sustain a national posture and political goals compatible with commonly held national values. In essence, these are the elements that constitute a definition of political integration and national unity.

The important thing for the nations of southern Africa to remember is that once these elements are in place, they would provide all citizens an opportunity to appreciate the fact that political diversity and freedom of expression are sacred principles that must be preserved at all times, and that this cannot be done through maintaining the status quo in education. This is why Thompson suggests that the pursuit of national goals in terms of political integration and national unity can best be achieved through reform of the system of education. Thompson goes on to conclude, "Schools are the principal instrument through which individuals take up positions of leadership within their society."[44]

One must therefore conclude that the nations of southern Africa have a solemn duty, not only to preserve democracy but also to ensure that it is never threatened. The system of one-party rule or presidents for life that some African nations have adopted is a sure recipe for national disaster.[45] It is important for government leaders to recognize that no one, from the president to the average citizen, is above the law. Educational reform intended to offer basic courses in civics or political studies would underscore the importance of all people respecting the law. But when law is dictated from a president who holds office for life, it serves as an instrument of oppression, and citizens have a right to demand a fundamental change in the government itself.

The recognition that law must result from a democratic process is the reason why it is important to initiate educational reform along similar lines to ensure the compatibility of these institutions. This is how basic human and political values are sustained. The inclusion of psychology, sociology, civics, and political studies into the educational system would remind all the people that the calling of a president for life or the one-party rule by any name does not really conceal its true dictatorial character.

In normal practice, educational systems tend to seek the sustenance of social, economic, and political systems because they are designed to operate as instruments of distributing rewards to individuals. But, because developing nations cannot afford to maintain outdated systems, an endeavor for educational reform must inculcate in all students the principle of equal opportunity as a basic component of political integration and national unity. This enables them to rise up to the top rung of the political ladder and make a viable contribution to the development of their country.

A disturbing practice has been emerging in southern Africa in recent years. Those leaders who were in the forefront of the struggle for political independence have assumed that only they have the right to form exclusive political clubs, which become intolerant of change or a more inclusive political structure once they are in the seat of government. They therefore regard their experience in the independence movement as a badge of honor. Some of the political soldiers for independence consider anyone who has not been directly involved in the struggle less patriotic and so less qualified to run for political office. In this way, some African governments oppress their own people far more severely than the colonial governments they replaced.

The reality of the fact is that flexibility in educational reform will mean a corresponding flexibility in the political process. It is important for the nations of southern Africa to recognize that a more inclusive political system based on diverse political ideology is the cornerstone of a truly democratic state. The system of political patronage and conditions of offering political benefits only to party members is prominent in southern Africa. Admission to the party on the assumption that the governing party enjoys the exclusive support of all the people is an illusion that robs the nations of Southern Africa of a vital element of their developmental efforts. The conclusion that educational reform parallels political inclusiveness and diversity must become an operative principle, or an article of faith, in all national endeavors.

It can be seen that if educational reform is designed to ensure political integration and national unity, then those who design it must first define the kind of society that a political system must seek to create. In the same way, the educational system that emerges as a result of reform must endeavor to define the kind of political skills students need to acquire to play a role in effecting political integration and national unity. In no way must the schools teach students the notion that the definition of political values and formulating plans for change to envisage a future different from the past is the exclusive power or right of the government. Rather, students must be taught to recognize the importance of collective action and responsibility. This is one viable definition of political integration and national unity. Unlike the political thought process of the colonial period, political integration and national unity in contemporary southern Africa must make it possible for all to understand the essential nature of sustaining distinct multi-party political structure.

It is also important to recognize that political integration and national unity as objects of educational reform do not demand a blind acceptance of the existing political system or loyalty to the ruling party. Rather, they encourage the concept of political diversity to allow all citizens to examine all possible political options before they cast their ballots in elections, both local and national. The democratic process is so important that it must not be left to chance, but should form a major component of the educational system itself. It is for this reason that educational reform must take into account the principle of multi-party participatory democracy.

Participation in the political process as a product of the educational process ensures the stability of society because it extends to the individual a sense of belonging and a sense of esteem. The elections held in Namibia in November 1989 stand out as an example of the applicability of this critical concept. The nations of southern Africa must also realize that participation in the economic and political processes cannot be isolated from participation in the educational process. The principle of participatory democracy must operate in the sociatic or educational process, the economic process, and the political process to ensure political integration and national unity. While education may not enable the nation to find solutions to all its problems, it helps create a safe and nurturing environment in which solutions can be found.

It is quite clear that if education is expected to equip citizens with economic and political skills so that they can function effectively in their society, it cannot do so in its existing form. The political structure must support a system that is broad enough to enable students to make a thrust to determine precisely the nature and the extent of their involvement in political decisions that are made for the benefit of all. They can best be informed decision makers from an educationally enlightened point of view. Educational innovation, therefore, must seek to broaden the range of human talent and potential to inculcate in all students, not a passive or conforming frame of mind or social norms, but the adoption of creative and imaginative attitudes that are essential to making a continuous effort to improve the conditions under which people live. Julius Nyerere of Tanzania took this line of thinking when he said in 1974, "Africa needs change to ensure its development. Innovation in education must be the starting point towards meaningful social change, not just for the sake of change, but in order to improve the quality of human life."[46]

Samora Machel (1935–1986), arguing that because both political leadership and national responsibility must, by their very nature, be collective, it is the responsibility of those in government to ensure that all citizens receive an education that enables them to participate in both. Machel then goes on to add,

We must never think of man as a form of automation who must receive and carry out orders irrespective of whether he understands them or has assimilated them. Leaders must fight against the harmful tendency of seeking solutions to political problems through administrative decisions arbitrarily imposed on the people. This tendency leads to a bureaucratic dictatorship and creates sharp contradictions with the rank and file. To avoid this tendency, the national educational system must embrace the concept of change to allow a greater degree of participation in the political process.[47]

There is no doubt that Machel was suggesting that participation in the political process must be regarded as one of the best ways of increasing political integration and national unity and that educational innovation could help facilitate the process. This is why he called for a new form of education, saying,

In our children's future we as a struggling people have three decisive tasks. The first is to educate the new generation and to instill a new way of thinking which will make true champions of the revolution. The second is to teach students so that they master science and become agents of the transformation of society. The third is to educate all people to accept women as equal partners in the struggle for national advancement.[48]

Conventional wisdom suggests that these three goals constitute an important dimension of the political purpose of educational innovation.

SUMMARY AND CONCLUSION

The discussion in this chapter leads to two basic conclusions regarding the purpose of educational reform in southern Africa. The first is that because the purpose of education of the colonial governments was directed toward sustaining the interests of the colonial society, it had no real value to the development of Africans. Because the purpose of the colonial governments was incompatible with the real needs of Africans, the educational process that it produced also had no real value. Therefore, because the educational process in the colonial settings was intended to strengthen the colonial status quo, it lacked a distinct quality to envisage the importance of change to improve the quality of life of all the people. An innovative approach to major national issues, including education, was not a hallmark of the colonial systems.

The second conclusion is that recognizing the reality that purpose shapes the character of education, the independent nations of southern Africa face an enormous task of relating the educational process to a new purpose. This is the real challenge that nations of this critical region face, because to formulate a purpose without a technical strategy to make it compatible with the educational process becomes an exercise in futility. A definite strategy to make that purpose compatible with the educational process requires considerable ability to formulate national objectives that enable the nations to serve the needs of the people.

The only way in which this can be done is by initiating a collective action that includes observance of democratic principles. A low literacy rate and the paternal attitudes of some leaders combine to present formidable problems to that challenge. But it is one that must be undertaken in the knowledge that purpose cannot be separated from the thrust for educational reform, and that the purpose of educational reform is to ensure national development, but that national development is not possible without the development of the individual.

NOTES

1. Canaan Banana, *Theology of Promise: The Dynamics of Self-Reliance* (Harare: The College Press, 1982), p. 53.

2. "UN Declares 1996 Year of Eradicating Poverty," *Daily Nation* (Kenya), December 19, 1995, p. 9.

3. John Daniszewski, "The Land Is the Issue: White Owners Evicting Black Sharecroppers in South Africa," *Arizona Daily Star*, November 26, 1995, p. 15.

4. *Chicago Tribune*, October 1, 1981, sec. 1, p. 2.

5. Ibid.

6. Government of Zimbabwe, *Parliamentary Debates*, August 3, 1983.

7. Dickson A. Mungazi, "Educational Innovation in Zimbabwe: Possibilities and Problems," *Journal of Negro Education*, Vol. 54, No. 4 (1985), pp.196–212.

8. Bernard Chidzero, Budget statement presented to the Parliament of Zimbabwe, July 26, 1990, p. 9.

9. Ibid.

10. A. M. Chambati, Budget statement presented to the Parliament of Zimbabwe, July 27, 1995, p. 21.

11. Paradzai Chihwape, "Children in Farms Must Be Involved in Youth Programs," *Sunday Mail*, January 7, 1996, p. 7.

12. *World Almanac and Book of Facts*, New York: Pharos Books, pp. 729–731. 1990.

13. Paulo Freire, *Pedagogy of the Oppressed*. Translated by Myra Bergman Ramos (New York: Continuum, 1983), p. 62.

14. Ndabaningi Sithole, during an interview in Harare, Zimbabwe, July 22, 1983.

15. Paradzai Chihwape, "Children in Farms Must Be Involved in Youth Programs," *Sunday Mail*, January 7, 1996, p. 6.

16. "Call to Increase Schools for the Blind," *Herald*, January 8, 1996, p. 4.

17. Robert G. Mugabe, "Literacy for all in Five Years," a statement of policy: Harare, July 18, 1983. The objective of trying to reach 100 percent literacy was stated by the San Francisco Conference in 1945 as a condition of increasing knowledge among the people to ensure their liberation to eliminate the possibility of war in the future. As of 1996 no country has reached that goal. This does not mean that the goal cannot be reached, but that it is hard to reach.

18. Ibid.

19. Ibid.

20. *New York Times*, April 1, 1990, p. 4.

21. Banana, *Theology of Promise: The Dynamics of Self-Reliance*, p. 34.

22. Dzingai Mutumbuka, "Zimbabwe's Educational Challenge," paper read at the World University Services Conference, London, December 1979.

23. Ibid.

24. Freire, *Pedagogy of the Oppressed*, p. 33.

25. Samora Machel, "The Liberation of Women as a Fundamental Necessity for Revolution," an opening address to the First Conference of Mozambique Women, Maputo, Mozambique, March 4, 1973.

26. A. R. Thompson, *Education and Development in Africa* (New York: St. Martin's Press, 1981), p. 77.

27. Banana, *Theology of Promise: The Dynamics of Self-Reliance*, p. 53.

28. Samora Machel, "Educate Men to Win the War, Create a New Society, and Develop a Country," a speech given at the Second Conference on Education and Culture, Maputo, Mozambique, September 1970.

29. Botswana, *Report of the National Commission on Education*, April 1977, p. 23.

30. Machel, "Educate Men to Win the War, Create a New Society, and Develop a Country."

31. As it was used in colonial Africa, the term *European* meant anyone of European origin.

32. George Stark, Director of Native Education in colonial Zimbabwe, 1934–1954, in Southern Rhodesia, *The Annual Report of the Director of Native Education*, 1940, p. 15. For detailed discussion of Stark's philosophy of education for Africans, see Dickson A. Mungazi, "To Bind Ties Between the School and Tribal Life:

Educational Policy for Africans Under George Stark in Zimbabwe," *Journal of Negro Education*, Vol. 58, No. 4, Fall 1989, p. 468.

33. Zimbabwe, *Sunday Mail*, January 7, 1996, p. 6.

34. Tommy Sithole, "Mugabe's Vision for Next Term," *Herald* (Zimbabwe), January 1, 1996, p. 1.

35. George Psacharopoulos, *Higher Education in Developing Countries. A Cost Benefit Analysis* (Washington, D.C.: World Bank, 1980), p. 19.

36. Ibid., p. 46.

37. Ibid., p. 48.

38. Funny Mushawa, "Cost of Living Beyond Reach of Many," *Business Herald* (Zimbabwe), January 4, 1996, p. 7.

39. In the concluding chapter of *The Mind of Black Africa* (Praeger, 1996), Dickson A. Mungazi suggests some methods for eliminating corruption among government officials in Africa.

40. Zimbabwe, *Sunday Mail*, An Editorial, January 7, 1996, p. 6.

41. *Financial Gazette* (Zimbabwe), December 14, 1995, p. 4.

42. Thompson, *Education and Development in Africa*, p. 47.

43. Ibid., p. 48.

44. Ibid., p. 49.

45. Chapter 1 discusses how Kamuzu Hastings Banda of Malawi and Kenneth Kaunda of Zambia became victims of the system of one-party government.

46. Julius Nyerere, during a speech to the Dag Hammerskjold Conference in Dar es Salaam, May 20, 1974.

47. Samora Machel, "Leadership Is Collective, Responsibility Is Collective," a speech given to the Joint Meeting of Frelimo Instructors, February 2, 1972. Courtesy of Mozambique Ministry of Information.

48. Ibid.

4

Prerequisites of Educational Reform

A study of history enables us to understand that the main battle we encounter in our struggle for development is against illiteracy. The knowledge of this reality forms an important prerequisite of our efforts to reform the educational system to ensure the transformation of our country.

Samora Machel, 1970

UNDERSTANDING PREREQUISITES OF EDUCATIONAL REFORM

In an address to the nation delivered on December 31, 1980, President Robert Mugabe of Zimbabwe outlined some prerequisites that he said his administration would utilize in seeking improvement of education. Mugabe said, "The envisaged educational program will be designed to absorb every child completing his primary education into secondary school. Because of the shortage of secondary school teachers, a recruitment drive for this category of teachers is being carried out by the Ministry of Education overseas and elsewhere in Africa."[1] In 1992, facing increasing costs and a rapidly rising population, Mugabe's government was confronted by a difficult question: How far could Zimbabwe provide universal primary education through higher education and maintain a steady flow of graduates into the secondary and higher-education-level school system? At that point, primary education was consuming 80 percent of the education budget, leaving only 20 percent for secondary education and higher education. This spelled the end of free primary education. The critical issue here is that higher education is also provided free.

There are two critical conditions Mugabe might have stated as essential to making efforts to bring about reform in education, not only in Zimbabwe but also in all the countries of southern Africa. The first condition is the recognition of the right of every student to primary schooling. The second condition is the availability of resources. This includes human, physical, and fiscal resources and a pool of adequately trained teachers. Mugabe must have been aware that educational reform does not necessarily occur when these two conditions are met, because there are other important prerequisites that must be fulfilled as well before a country can initiate reform.

In this chapter, six prerequisites that we believe must be fulfilled to have educational reform consistent with national goals and objectives are presented. These are the influence of history, theoretical assumptions, educational objectives, projection of population increase, economic development, and the need to eliminate inadequacies in the existing system of government and education. A discussion of these prerequisites must not lead to the conclusion that they are the only ones essential to educational reform, but should be regarded as a suggestion that they are among the most important. In this presentation, we hope that the nations of southern Africa will see the imperative nature of articulating prerequisites that may guide them in their endeavor to initiate educational reform as an important condition of initiating the transformation of their nations. Failure to initiate this undertaking will lead to national disaster.

THE INFLUENCE OF HISTORY

Among the prerequisites that the nations of southern Africa must observe as essential to educational reform is the influence of history. It has been implied that aspirations toward universal primary education have a national and regional appeal to Africans because they see primary education as basic to all forms of individual and national development. In 1983 Ian Smith, the last colonial leader of Zimbabwe (serving from 1964 to 1979), said during an interview, "We knew that there was a gap between African education and white education. This was not due to anything that we did, this was part of our history."[2] It is quite clear that Smith was trying to place the blame on history for the inadequacy of his own government's educational policy. That is why Smith defended that policy, arguing that it was a direct product of history.

During the time he led a government that was under severe attack, Smith was unable to overcome the negative influence of history in designing his policy. For Smith and other government leaders to be able to overcome the negative influence of history would require a new vision on which to base an articulation of a national endeavor outside the control of political expediency.

The kind of political vision that empowered the colonized was not a hallmark of the colonial systems. The method was rather to perpetuate the inadequacy of the existing system instead of initiating change. Ultimately, Smith himself became the victim of his own efforts to maintain the influence of history.

By the outbreak of the war of independence in April 1966,[3] Smith's government was spending $206.00 per white student, compared to $18.00 per African student.[4] This great inequality in spending for education suggests the strength of historical influence that Smith accepted and utilized as a prerequisite of his government's policy. It can be seen that the educational policy of Smith's government was one tragic outcome of the educational policies designed by the colonial governments in southern Africa. Those policies were designed not to meet the developmental needs of Africans or of change in the conditions of the existing systems of education, but to provide a continuum that was in effect compatible with the needs of the white people but not compatible with the blacks'. In this kind of setting, the educational policy of the Smith government became a major contributing cause of the war of independence.[5]

What Smith said about the influence of history on the educational policy of his government was not an isolated example, but an established practice among colonial officials. For example, after establishing an administrative system at the Cape in 1652, the Dutch East India Company ordered Jan van Riebeeck to open schools for both white children and children of slaves imported from the Indian subcontinent. By 1658, Riebeeck had formulated a policy that provided for segregation, not only in the educational process but also in the curriculum itself.[6] The purpose of formulating a policy for each racial group was to provide an opportunity for white students to exercise dominant power over Africans. For the next three hundred years, the whites of South Africa lived a life of luxury, believing that they were superior to Africans in every way. The seeds of conflict were sown in this kind of early environment, and they have germinated down through three and four generations.

The purpose of education for children of slaves was to turn them into more efficient cheap laborers. The policy of apartheid had its origins in these developments. Once cast in historical settings, this policy became supreme in every way. When slavery ended in South Africa in the early nineteenth century, the improvement in the apartheid system assumed its functions. From that time the Africans were reminded that their future would be controlled by that policy. By 1992, however, the Africans themselves, like Africans elsewhere under colonial control, recognized the imperative need to alter the course of history to initiate a new approach. When Nelson Mandela assumed the reins of government in April 1994 he came face to face with the hard realities of the influence of history.

That the education of children of slaves was designed to make them more efficient laborers indicates its oppressive character. This is why many of them ran away, forcing many schools for Africans to close.[7] The fact that children of slaves received an education that turned them into cheap labor indicates that they were oppressed. This situation created an awareness, a knowledge of the necessity to reject a system of education that was oppressive. By the nineteenth century, however, the educational conditions imposed by the Dutch East India Company had destroyed the cultural values of Africans and their socioeconomic system. These conditions forced Africans to seek low-paying employment opportunities to escape from the economic deprivation and extreme social poverty to which they were subjected. The realization that they were victims of the influence of history motivated Africans to seek change in the conditions that controlled their lives.

These developments required that a new start be made to provide the kind of education that would enable all students to function effectively in a new social system that recognized all people as equal. Unfortunately, the official end of slavery in 1858 did not bring an end to segregated education in South Africa. There was no significant improvement in the kind of education Africans received because the influence of history inhibited the ability of the government to perceive new prerequisites that would require educational reform. This is why from time to time African students protested and boycotted schools. Educational character was essentially the same as it had been during slavery; it stressed manual labor as a viable form of education for Africans, just like it had during slavery. Because Africans wanted something substantially more, conflict became inevitable. This is how the seeds of a major struggle were sown between Africans and the apartheid system. In 1994, a few months before a black majority government was installed in South Africa, Ziyad Motala discussed the influence of history on all aspects of life in South Africa, saying,

In South Africa the black majority have historically been excluded from the central political process. Successive governments have been formed exclusively at the whim of the minority white electorate. The legality doctrine does not address itself to notions of fundamental liberty such as freedom of speech, property, or movement, tenets that are today considered essential in liberal society.[8]

The escalation of protests by African students from 1948 to 1976 reflected the need to end the negative influence of history and the apartheid system itself.

In South Africa, the Bantu Education Act of 1953 entrenched the oppressive elements that had been in place since 1658. This created a new situation that permitted neither a new reappraisal nor a new approach to the educational process. Indeed, the Bantu Education Act of 1953 was, in itself, a product of the influence of history, which means that the law would be amended or reformed only in the context of the influence of history. This is why Hendrik Verwoerd (1901–1966), then minister of Bantu Affairs Administration, argued in 1957, "I will reform the Bantu Education Act so that Natives will be taught from childhood that equality with whites is not for them."[9] Yes, Verwoerd reformed the educational system under the prerequisites of seeking to sustain the policy of apartheid, but he paid a personal price when he was assassinated by a disillusioned white man in 1966, setting the stage for the acceleration of conflict in the country.

Verwoerd's idea of reforming education to sustain apartheid is the same line of thinking that Riebeeck had used in 1658 to introduce segregation in education. Verwoerd's argument is precisely the same line of thinking that his successor, John Vorster, who served as president of South Africa from 1966 to 1978, used to amend the Bantu Education Act in 1975 to entrench the educational practices of the past. Pieter W. Botha, who served from 1978 to 1987 as Vorster's successor, had no idea that by his desire to sustain the influence of history he had placed the country on an explosive course. This amendment led to the uprising in Soweto in 1976 and violent demonstrations in Cape Town in 1990. There is no question that one of F. W. de Klerk's major tasks from 1987 to 1994 was to find a formula for educational reform to create a new system that would avert further disaster in South Africa.

To accomplish this objective, de Klerk had to overcome the influence of history. In 1990, when he finally succeeded in breaking the chain of the influence of history, the solutions that had eluded the government of South Africa for three centuries were in sight. De Klerk's decision to release Nelson Mandela and to initiate dialogue with the African National Congress paved the way for the transformation of South Africa in April 1994. At that time, Mandela, the man the apartheid system had sent to prison for twenty-seven years, became the new president of South Africa. Mandela now faces the challenge of articulating a new set of prerequisites for educational reform to elevate the process of the transformation of South Africa to a higher scale.

The colonization of Namibia by Germany in 1885 led to fears that if Africans were educated in the same way as whites they would demand equal rights in society. The end of the German colonial rule in Africa in 1915 transferred the responsibility for administration and education to South Africa. The meeting that was held between government officials of South Africa and church leaders of Namibia in 1926 resulted in a partnership between the two institutions such that the church would operate the schools and the governments would provide financial support and formulate policy and requirements.

The introduction of the provisions of the Bantu Education Act in Namibia in 1955 altered the character of education in that the development of Africans was now in accordance with the requirements of apartheid. It is not surprising that by the time Namibia achieved political independence on March 21, 1990, it needed a crash course in educational programming to bring about much needed improvement, not only in education but also in the character of society itself. In its efforts to bring about educational reform in Namibia the administration of Sam Nujoma came face to face with problems created by the influence of history; the legacy of the past was beyond its ability to resolve.

In the Portuguese colonies of Angola and Mozambique, Antonio Salazar's decision in 1932 to reactivate and implement the policy of *Estado Novo* created a new historical condition that would have a serious impact for the future. By 1961, the policy of *Estado Novo* had bonded Portugal to its past and left a legacy for the future that made it hard for Africans at the time of independence. In 1975, both Angola and Mozambique had no clear sense of a new direction to take in their struggle for development. As a result, these countries have endured the scourge of underdevelopment more than any other countries in southern Africa. Political conflict, sociatic disintegration, and economic decay have all preyed on the life of the people in painful ways. This was the reason why the OAU dispatched the Moi-Mugabe mission to Mozambique in 1989 in an effort to bring conflict to an end so that Mozambiquians would have an opportunity to start afresh in rebuilding a country destroyed by the policies of the past.

In 1977, Samora Machel concluded that for three hundred years Portugal had maintained a system of education designed to preserve the colonial status quo. He recognized that independent Mozambique must make a new thrust to reform its educational system so that social transformation could take place to ensure national development. He went on to argue that any strategy adopted by a country in southern Africa to ensure educational reform must first seek to eliminate the influence of history,[10] or to learn from it. The attempt by Portugal to use the policy of *Estado Novo* to integrate some Africans into Portuguese culture, rather than to create a new society in an African cultural setting, furnishes clear evidence that Portugal utilized the influence of history in designing its policy for the future. How would educational reform occur if it was initiated under the influence of this negative historical context unless it repeated that history?

There is no question that the Portuguese colonial government failed to alter the influence of history as a factor of educational reform. It was not possible for Portuguese colonial officials to operate under the universal meaning of reform for the future. This is why, by 1950, Portuguese colonial policy became a major topic of discussion among members of the international community.

In that year UNESCO estimated that less than forty thousand Africans in Angola alone had attained the status of assimilados, yet less than 3 percent of the entire population had acquired basic literacy.[11] Samora Machel recognized the harmful effect of this influence of history when he argued in 1970, during the height of the struggle for independence, that,

A study of history enables us to understand that the main battle we encounter in our struggle for development is against illiteracy. Without the active participation of the masses in the battle against illiteracy it will not be possible to wipe it out because we are victims of the influence of history. The knowledge of this reality forms an important prerequisite of our efforts to reform the educational system to ensure social transformation of our country.[12]

What Machel was suggesting is that the influence of history often has two possible effects. The first effect is that it retards the course of reform so that it fails to promote its basic objective. The acknowledgment that society is never constant was not a hallmark of vision and foresight of colonial governments. Instead, it was a reality that they seemed to struggle against to sustain the social status quo. The second possible effect of the influence of history can be seen in the context of the colonial conditions history left behind. Many African national leaders today find the task of reform so big that they fail to measure up and meet the challenge. The only thing that these leaders do is to try to persuade their people to believe that things are going well.

In this manner, national leaders strengthen the status quo more than did the colonial governments. Therefore, any change initiated in the prerequisites of educational reform to accommodate the aspirations of Africans was also not possible, because the influence of history had become stronger than it was during the colonial period. This situation does not permit the leaders of the countries of contemporary southern Africa to see things other than in terms of the past. As time goes on, however, it slowly becomes evident to these governments that it is not possible to sustain the status quo, and it becomes apparent that reform must take place that includes provisions for a democratic form of self-determination, which requires visionary thinkers, articulate speakers and writers, and a literate populace. This realization often comes with a cost to the leaders themselves. This is why Kenneth Kaunda of Zambia and Kamuzu Hastings Banda of Malawi fell from office in 1994. For nearly thirty years, they had tried to maintain the conditions put in place by the colonial governments.

One of the most important results that came from the influence of history is that the countries of contemporary southern Africa have been forced to accept the concept of change to ensure national development. Since national character is a product of history, it is the duty of every citizen to make a contribution to the concept of reform based on the positive attributes of history so that it has a positive influence on his thought process and action. This will help shape the kind of future of society that is compatible with the aspirations of its members. This is also why the nations of southern Africa must recognize the influence of history as an important prerequisite of educational reform. It is not possible to initiate reform without taking this influence into account.

FORMULATING THEORY OF EDUCATIONAL REFORM

One of the major prerequisites of educational reform is the formulation of theory. The nations of southern Africa must recognize the fact that any national endeavor that lacks theory has no meaning or purpose. Theory helps to determine educational goals and objectives. It assists in defining the purpose of education itself. Without theory, there is no good education. In the same way, without theory, there cannot be educational reform. In 1967, President Julius Nyerere of Tanzania said, "The purpose of education is liberation through the development of the person as a member of society. Therefore, the education that serves the needs of the individual has to be reformed to enable him to serve the needs of society."[13] Nyerere was, in effect, recognizing the importance of a new theoretical perspective as a prerequisite of Tanzania's effort to design a new educational system to suit the demands of the times. For Nyerere to urge his country's people to think in terms of the liberation of the individual in a larger social context was to urge them to formulate a new theoretical component that had not been taken into consideration before. Educational reform is the necessary component to set a new stage for the political, economical, and societal transformation of Tanzania.

The reformation of education to serve the needs of the individual must be recognized as a condition of meeting the needs of society. This perspective demands fundamental change and cultural inclusion in the way Africans view themselves with high esteem and in the future of their society. The role of education in shaping new social structures must also be recognized. This thinking demands that education be reformed to enable it to accomplish the objectives that are needed for self-determination and vision. The importance of the individual in society must be recognized as a critical condition that must exist to erase the negative influence that colonial conditions imposed on the ability of Africans to envisage themselves and their future. In 1983, a thirteen-year-old girl in eastern Zimbabwe explained to us this new way of viewing educational reform.

Having observed the enthusiasm and the determination with which she applied herself to the process of her schooling, we could not resist the temptation to ask what we had always regarded as a question unbecoming well-informed persons: asking school children of that age what they plan to do after their education was completed. After all, if college students are often not sure of what they plan to do, how does one expect school children to know that much in advance? However, the girl, with a sense of self-assurance and confidence in her future, never hesitated as she responded,

You really want to know what I will do after my education is completed? I have absolutely no doubt about that. After completing my primary school here I will go to St. Augustine's Secondary School.[14] Then, with a first-class pass, I will go to the University of Zimbabwe to study to be a doctor. I will then get married and have two children, one boy and one girl. You see, without the educational development of the individual, there is no development of society. But for education to accomplish that goal it must be reformed under conditions that make it possible to transform society. Any other course of action is bound to fail.[15]

Without a young girl's expanded knowledge she is not equipped to envision a future other than her experience.

One sees that while political independence is an essential manifestation of collective liberation required to give people a new national identity, it is the educational development of the individual that evinces the ultimate liberation of society itself. The essential nature of the relationship that must exist between the individual and society is that the development of the individual and of the society is a product of a new form of education. It is equally true that while collective action comes only from individual commitment to a national endeavor, it is the vision and action of the individual that originates it. Therefore, the educational development of the individual is essential to the development of society itself. But a fundamental tenet of this relationship must be reinforced by the imperative of reform of the educational system. If educational reform does not occur, or if it takes place under inadequate conditions, social transformation has no meaning, and society experiences the scourge of underdevelopment, depression, and decay.

Placing emphasis on the educational development of the individual as a prerequisite of the development of society in the emerging nations of southern Africa underscores two critical factors of theoretical considerations of educational reform. The first factor is that without reforming the educational process, the individual is handicapped in discharging his responsibility, first to himself, then to his society. The second factor is the thought that the individual comes before society. This is a reversal of traditional African philosophy of the proper relationships between the individual and society. They must be willing to expand their thinking to include some forms of human rights of the individual, and since Africans have accepted various forms of social change to make progress, they must be willing to accept changes in their thinking. They will realize that by pursuing this line of thinking the interests of society will be sustained by sustaining those of the individual first. This gives an individual ability to think in expanded realms.

It is true that traditional society in Africa, by the imperative of its cultural practices, was a collective one. That is, traditional society in Africa placed the interests of society above those of the individual. Any individual who tried to place his own interests above those of society was considered to be miseducated.[16] Indeed, the emerging nations of southern Africa are struggling to set their own developmental priorities by trying to resolve the conflict that exists in this setting. In 1982, Robert Mugabe discussed the efforts that his government was making to reconcile these two conflicting perspectives. Mugabe said,

We feel that there is a link between the Marxist-Leninist thinking and our traditional collective ideas, and we are linking these together. On the basis of this we are evolving a philosophy which we hope will be acceptable to our people that there is individuality in a collective society. But we want to emphasize the collective aspect of our society and still allow room for individuality as a principal factor of the new society we are trying to build.[17]

Indeed, this conflict between the interests of the individual and those of society is one of the major challenges that the emerging nations of southern Africa are facing in their endeavor for national development. To initiate reform in their educational systems, the nations of southern Africa must now recognize that change in the relationship between the individual and society is essential. They must also realize that unlike traditional society, their perception of the role of the individual in shaping the character of society is largely determined by the kind and level of education that the individual receives, which can be done only on an individual basis. This is not to suggest that Africans must reject their own cultural traditions and values, but rather that they need to recognize the importance of change in the character of society as a condition of national development. One must therefore conclude that the perception of the place of the individual, in relation to his society, constitutes an important component of a new theory as a prerequisite of educational reform.

Another critical component of theory as an important prerequisite of educational reform is the concept of equality in educational opportunity and in society as a whole. In 1979, President Kenneth Kaunda of Zambia equated equality in both the educational process and in society with what he called *humanism.*[18] The philosophy of humanism, as a basic principle of equality in society, takes the position that *man* and society—in their universal definition— are quite capable of attaining perfection through educational reform. Kaunda went further to argue,

For us as a nation to embrace humanism as a social ideology and as a condition of educational change is a futile exercise unless it is done with a full appreciation and knowledge that equality of educational opportunity combines with the practice of democracy to allow power in the hands of the humblest citizens of our country. Equality of educational opportunity cannot become a reality unless it becomes a prerequisite of educational reform.[19]

What made Kaunda's statement hollow is that he never saw the serious contradiction in which he made it. He had introduced a one-party system of government in 1972, and now, in 1979, he was calling for educational reform and equality in the educational process itself. The people of Zambia would not accept Kaunda's message because it was cast in this contradiction.

The reality of acknowledging the need for educational reform to bring about equality of educational opportunity would help the nations of southern Africans to set educational goals and programs that are consistent with the purpose of education as defined by the individual. One can see that the nations of southern Africa must now recognize that both educational reform and equality in both education and society have become a principal factor of social transformation as an important condition of national development. Perhaps this is why Kaunda concluded, "There will be no genuine or lasting peace until man has developed society to such an extent that it is based on the theory that all people are entitled to equal educational opportunity as a condition of national development."[20] It would appear that Kaunda was suggesting that a new thrust must be initiated in efforts to reform the educational process so that it would help in sustaining the principle of equality to create a new society. One can see that the concept of equality is an important condition of educational reform. There is no question that Kaunda was trying to base a new approach to education on what he considered to be the accomplishment of Zambia since it attained independence in October 1964 under his leadership. Had he not introduced a one-party system of government, he might well have succeeded in his efforts.

From 1964 to 1971, the Zambian Ministry of Education tried to carry out an ambitious reform program in education, as the Ministry of Information put it, "a complete transformation of the educational scene to make the transformation of our society possible."[21] Indeed, enrollment in primary school increased from 378,400 in 1964 to 810,739 in 1973.[22] At the same time, the number of students starting primary school in 1974 had increased considerably. This increase could not have occurred if the educational process had not changed enough to accommodate it. This means that, when properly defined and applied, the combination of the philosophy of humanism and the theory of educational reform can have meaning to the nations of southern Africa in important dimensions of social transformation. It can become a guiding principle in creating new relationships between the individual and society.

This combination can help initiate purposeful reform in many national institutions based on the belief that each person has value to society because he sees value in himself. It can help transmit a new conviction that men and women must liberate themselves before they can liberate their society. It can assist in creating a new educational system that brings out the best in each student by giving him confidence in his potential. It can aid in guiding individual growth and development in a way that offers mutual benefit to the person and society.[23] It can enable all people in articulating a new concept of national endeavor and unity of purpose beyond the peripheral goals of self-interest.

The nations of southern Africa must realize that a fundamental tenet of theory as a critical prerequisite of educational reform is that it must be utilized to protect the concept of the freedom of the human mind. Julius Nyerere agrees with Paulo Freire when he concludes that this liberating theme must reverse the process of domination of the mind of the universal human being as it was practiced by the colonial systems. Nyerere goes on to add,

The ideas imparted by education or released in the human mind through educational reform, should be liberating ideas. The skills acquired by an individual through education should be liberating skills. Nothing else can properly be called liberation of the human mind if the individual is not free to exercise freedom of thought process. We cannot call it reformed education if it fails to uphold this basic tenet of human endeavor.[24]

Ngagiwa Thiongo, a Kenyan educational thinker, suggests that freedom of the human mind is an indispensable condition of being human and that education must take account of it if it is to be meaningful to national development. Thiongo argues that education can accomplish this objective only if it is reformed. Thiongo concludes,

Education for the liberation of the human mind must also aim at producing a fully developed individual who understands the forces at work in society, an individual who uses Reason to understand reasons of his role in society. This cannot happen by maintaining status quo in education, but by initiating reform. Therefore, freedom of the human mind must stand out as a principal condition of educational reform.[25]

One must therefore conclude that the liberation of the human mind is a critical prerequisite of educational reform that the nations of southern Africa must take into account.

A central question that must be asked in considering the components of theory as prerequisite of educational reform is: What is education intended to accomplish? The answer determines some important principles that guide its development. Without keeping the answer to this question in mind, educational reform loses its meaning. As a result, the emerging educational process becomes an exercise in futility. Keeping this question in mind also helps put all relevant aspects of the process of reform in proper perspective. But the formation of theory is in itself undertaken in the context of creating an environment in which it is cast. It cannot be done haphazardly. The challenge before the nations of southern Africa is to formulate theoretical assumptions to direct the course of educational reform.

SETTING EDUCATIONAL GOALS AND OBJECTIVES

Conventional wisdom suggests that setting goals and objectives constitutes a critical prerequisite of educational reform. Without establishing goals and objectives, the entire educational process loses its meaning. In 1974, Kenneth Kaunda seemed to understand this basic truth when he argued that Zambia needed a set of goals and objectives to guide its endeavor to initiate educational reform. Kaunda added that free and universal primary education was an important condition of the educational reform that the ministry of education was proposing. Kaunda went on to outline a set of goals and objectives that he said must influence the development of educational reform, saying,

The introduction of free and universal primary education must form a basic condition which must direct our efforts to reform the educational system. We must look at the expanded educational facilities in every district. We need more teachers, colleges, technical colleges, more secondary schools, more primary schools, and more trade institutions. We must expand university facilities rapidly in terms of student enrollment, the curriculum, and the acquisition of skills so that the nation benefits from the contribution of an educated population. The thrust for educational reform cannot take a back seat to any other national program because it is vital to social transformation and national development.[26]

The conditions that Kaunda specified as essentials of educational reform constituted a seriously challenging national endeavor. Did Zambia have national resources in sufficient amounts to realize these goals and objectives so as to realize educational reform envisaged in their fulfillment? The fact that the literacy rate in Zambia had increased from 50 percent in 1983 to 54 percent in 1990 suggests how difficult it was to realize these important goals and objectives. In 1995, this challenge still remained to be met. In his enthusiasm to initiate reform, Kaunda was setting a national agenda beyond his ability to fulfill it. The reason is that the people Zambia, having been disillusioned by grant promises from the government, lacked the interest and the enthusiasm to accept the challenge.

There is no doubt that the nations of southern Africa have tried to work sincerely toward accomplishing universal and free primary education as a condition of social transformation and national development. It is evinced by their efforts to accomplish it. This is precisely what Robert Mugabe had in mind when, on July 18, 1983, he launched a national campaign to raise the literacy rate from 30 percent to 100 percent in 1988.[27] But that Zimbabwe's literacy rate increased from 30 percent in 1983 to 50 percent in 1990 suggests that this objective has remained elusive. In a similar manner, President Samora Machel of Mozambique promised in 1970 that by 1980 the country must achieve a universal primary education to achieve a 100 percent literacy rate. But the literacy rate in Mozambique actually declined from 20 percent in 1983 to 14 percent in 1990,[28] also suggesting that Mozambique was having great difficulties in trying to reach this objective.

A common thread that ran through all the countries of southern Africa in 1993, except South Africa, is that efforts to introduce free and universal primary education were made in the belief that reaching a 100 percent literacy rate would produce a more functional population able to contribute to efforts directed at social transformation and national development. A troubling question must therefore be asked. Why has the objective of universal literacy not been reached? There are three possible answers. The first answer is that nations of southern Africa do not have sufficient resources to meet this goal. The second answer is that educational reform itself may not have been designed to fulfill objectives consistent with other forms of national development. The third answer is that the implementation plans might have been flawed. The objective of universal and free primary education cannot be fulfilled in this kind of environment. However, the knowledge that setting goals and objectives is an important prerequisite of educational reform has helped the nations of southern Africa in seeking solutions to this monumental problem.

The struggle for literacy as a principal educational objective in southern Africa must also be seen in the context of other national goals and objectives. The concept of national unity and identity has eluded many nations of Africa simply because the leaders themselves fail to understand the basic tenets of democracy and have failed to convince their people that the governments are there to serve them. The people see government operations as a means of enriching the bureaucrats themselves and their party. While the leaders are increasingly aware of this serious problem, they have done little to change the situation to create an environment of trust and public support through popular participation. This is the message that Kenneth Kaunda made a futile attempt to convey to his people when he said in 1979, "The government belongs to no one person, not even to the most active members of it. The government belongs to all the people. Therefore, every Zambian is a shareholder in this institution. No one owns the government and no one can take it away from you."[29]

Kaunda must have ignored an important consideration, and that is the action of turning the country into a one-party state is hardly an environment in which the government can have the full trust and support of all the people. As long as the governments of southern Africa impose a one-party system, they should not expect their people to have full confidence in them. Therefore, the introduction of a multi-party democracy is an important prerequisite of educational reform. The introduction of a one-party system of government suggests the conclusion that the government really belongs only to those who run it and that the services it offers are exclusively to their prerogatives. This is hardly the kind of one-party political policy or sociatic climate that a nation needs to initiate progressive educational reform to make social transformation possible.

Indeed, we do not share the reasons that some national leaders of southern Africa have repeatedly advanced to argue in favor of a one-party system of government. Among these reasons are that a one-party system brings about national unity; that multi-party democracy is a Western imposition; that a one party-system is consistent with African cultural and social practices; that a multi-party system is too costly; that a multi-party system distracts from making efforts to solve the problems of national development as politicians oppose the government for opposition's sake; and that a multi-party system creates an environment of conflict as the simple and unsophisticated citizens get confused and begin to focus on the negative features of the government, rather than on its policies, accomplishments, and issues.

We dispute and reject all these reasons. On the contrary, a multi-party system of government ensures that all relevant points of view are taken into consideration in formulating national policy and implementing it. There is room for input from an enlightened citizenry that perhaps evolves a new visionary from that citizenry. No matter how much the leaders argue, the existence of a one-party system of government is nothing less than a form of dictatorship. The sad part of this situation is that the leaders fail to prove opportunity to do less than to see things this way. Instead, they begin to blame other conditions for their own failure or inadequacy. It must be realized that educational reform is meaningless under political conditions that are less than absolute in affording the people freedom of choice in their political activities.

It is equally sad that leaders of one-party governments mislead their people by claiming that they are democracies. The reality of the situation is that they do not know that a multi-party system of government is in their own interest as citizens of a global community. In this kind of national environment, establishing goals and objectives as a prerequisite of educational reform becomes a peripheral exercise void of any real meaning. This is why in all his powerful statements Kaunda could not convince his people of his sincerity in saying that the government belonged to all people. Instead they threw him out of office in 1990.

MAKING PROJECTIONS OF POPULATION INCREASE

If there is a major national problem that African nations are unable to solve and so handicaps their ability to solve other national problems, it is the rapidly rising population rate. Worse still, the inability of African nations to make accurate projections of population increase paralyzes their efforts to provide adequate services to their people. The rapidly rising population, the illiteracy rate, birth control, AIDS education, declining economies, unfavorable trade balances, and other sociatics combine to create a frustrating situation for African nations.

The average population growth rate of southern Africa increased from 2.3 percent per year in 1960 to 3.1 percent per year in 1984.[30] This has placed heavy demands on national resources. In 1984, children under the age of fifteen years accounted for 45 percent of the population compared with 37 percent in Asia and 40 percent in Latin America.[31] The problem of keeping accurate projections of population increases the problems of keeping accurate records. This problem, in turn, translates into a serious problem in making effective health and education plans. That "Education is critical to slowing down population growth rate"[32] suggests the need for an important change in a fundamental aspect of African culture, the desire among Africans, especially those in the rural areas, to have a large number of children.

Somewhere within the scheme of things among African nations, a basic change must take place in shifting the emphasis from dependence on children in old age to political and economic self-sufficiency. This requires a major social transformation and a radical restructuring of the economic system so that during their years of production, people build a sound financial base to live comfortably on in their retirement. This would reduce dependence on children for support and so reduce the need for large numbers of children. While this requires a considerable financial outlay by the government at the initial stage, the results in the long term can be beneficial. But to do this, two essential ingredients are necessary. The first ingredient is for the government to build a solid economic base that makes it possible to initiate such a program.

The second ingredient is to create confidence in the people so that they do not fear that they will lose the money they have taken years to save. The advantage of this approach is that it enables the government to make plans for the future based on an accurate projection of population increase. This is important because educational reform must take into account the projected number of students in the future. This, in turn, would determine facilities to be built, the number of teachers to be trained and employed, the operational budget, and the teacher-student ratio.

In 1977, the Report of the National Commission on Education in Botswana recognized the imperative of seeking solutions to this problem when it concluded,

The rapid population growth rate of 3.00% per year puts considerable strain on both the economy and the educational system. It results in large numbers of students in school without sufficient financial resources. An unbalanced population structure creates its own peculiar problems in terms of reforming the educational system itself.[33]

It is, indeed, ironic that Botswana, with an area of 582,000 square kilometers and a population of 712,000 in 1977, was considered sparsely populated. But when population had increased to 1.2 million with a literacy rate of 35 percent in 1990, the situation had been transformed in magnitude. The mass migration from rural areas to urban areas increased the urban population by 12 percent per year. Botswana seemed to panic as it considered the problem it was facing, not only for the present but also for the future.

This situation has created immense economic, social, and educational problems so that, in spite of political efforts to plan educational development of the country, it was not possible to have an accurate projection of population increase to adapt educational reform to this critical consideration. Even the Education Commission itself concluded that its projection of an increase in urban population of 45 percent by 1990[34] was nothing more than a guess. However, the commission concluded that without an accurate projection of population increase it would be hard for Botswana to make adequate educational plans for the future because "social infrastructures, including new schools, are more expensive to provide."[35]

The World Bank has suggested that it is very important for developing nations to keep an accurate census and projection of population figures to make accurate budget allocations to various national items. If this is not done those countries will always endure the adverse effects of underdevelopment because it is always difficult to make plans for national development without a full grasp of the essential facts of population figures.[36] Therefore, projection of population increase is an important prerequisite of educational reform.

RECOGNIZING THE NEED TO ENSURE ECONOMIC GROWTH

National and regional economic development must be seen as another important prerequisite of educational reform. This is a reality that all national leaders in southern Africa must take into consideration. It is the driving force they will need as they attempt to place their nations on the road to development. With the tremendous national resources that nations of southern Africa possess, one would like to think that the task of developing them is much lighter than in other regions. But the truth of the matter is that this is not the case for a number of reasons. In his budget proposals presented to the Zimbabwean parliament in 1990, Bernard T. Chidzero, the minister of finance and economic planning, addressed the importance of educational reform to make economic development possible. Chidzero said,

The government must be aware that unless there are structural changes in education designed to address the problems the economy is facing, the rate of economic growth will continue to fall below that needed to maintain reasonable standards of living and to provide employment for the majority of the population.[37]

Among the reasons for failure to develop national resources are the following: in South Africa, the international boycott from 1990 to 1993 reduced the production of minerals considerably. During the Smith government in colonial Zimbabwe, sanctions imposed by the UN had a devastating effect on the economy. In Angola and Mozambique, the civil wars have hurt the economy badly. In Namibia, the conflict between the UN and South Africa over its future eroded away the confidence of investors to the extent that a national economic system was not developed until the attainment of independence in March 1990. In Zambia and Zaire, competition on the world market has hurt the production of copper. This is why Chidzero suggested five things that the government of Zimbabwe could do to initiate improvement. The first thing was to ensure balance of payment and trade. The second thing was to have a price and income policy. The third thing was to have labor regulations. The fourth thing was to develop conditions that would attract investment. The fifth thing was to put in place a financial and monetary policy.[38]

In general, the economic development of southern Africa has been experiencing considerable difficulties due to a combination of factors. The gross national product grew at an average rate of 3.6 percent per year from 1970 to 3.8 percent in 1980. This was a healthy sign. But with a population increase rate of 3.2 percent per year, per capita income dropped from 4.00 percent in 1970 to 3.4 percent in 1980.[39] Because the mainstay of the economy in southern Africa is agriculture, the combination of extended drought, population increase, and the policies of the multi-corporations have combined to hurt agricultural productivity. Massive starvation in Mozambique and Angola, caused by continuing civil wars, played into the hands of South Africa until 1994 as much as it put economic strain on Zimbabwe due to its decision to take care of refugees from Mozambique and South Africa. Industrial production had declined considerably, to the extent that basic essentials were hard to secure. "Poor investment choices, failure to develop export opportunity, falling domestic income, inadequate foreign exchange for materials and spare parts"[40] and the destabilizing activity of South Africa have all created a situation in which the economy of southern Africa has become vulnerable.[41]

Following the achievement of independence, many countries of southern Africa made an impressive attempt to build their economies. This made it possible to invest in education and build supporting infrastructures. But as national leaders remained in office longer than they should, the confidence and excitement of the people about the future transformed into a general state of depression, an inability to move, and a loss of morale. When corruption and unwillingness of government officials forced the economy into a spinning decline, depression among the people translated into apathy in the political process. The social and economic transformation of southern Africa, once envisaged as the foundation of educational reform, was not only steadily being halted but was being eroded. This created a situation in which government leaders found it easier to place blame elsewhere than at their own doorsteps.

In April, 1980, the black-ruled countries of southern Africa formed an organization known as the Southern Africa Development Coordination Conference (SADCC), and it was anticipated that at last they had found a solution to the economic problems of regional development. With its main objective of reducing economic dependence on South Africa, the SADCC felt that black-ruled countries in the region would no longer be vulnerable to South Africa's destabilizing tactics. But because the SADCC's success depended on the ability of its members to mobilize national resources and cooperate in developing them in the first place, the technology needed to make it possible was not readily available. Therefore, the economic salvation that the SADCC was expected to be to the countries of southern Africa actually turned out to be a mirage as a combination of factors derailed the expected economic growth needed to invest in education.

Note that we neither dispute the basic objectives of the development of southern Africa nor question the national economic policies. The point we are making is that political and economic problems must be resolved at the same time as, and as an important prerequisite to, educational reform. We are also arguing that economic development is so important to educational develop-ment that it has to be achieved and maintained at a healthy level to make that reform possible. When this is done, educational reform can take place at all the desired levels to make it viable for all people. This is one of the challenges that the nations of southern Africa face. Neither the formation of the SADCC nor the objectives established by the Lagos Plan of Economic Action in 1980 has yielded the desired results. It is not possible to envisage educational reform under conditions that have serious implication for doubt about the economy. Educational reform and the economy are supplemental and symbiotic.

The question now arises: What must nations of southern Africa do to ensure economic development so that they can invest in educational development? Among other things, they need to control the price of goods. They must provide an assessment of global needs and also identify the natural resources that are needed on that global market. They must play a role in shaping international trade. They must diversify their economies. They must provide opportunities for free enterprise and resist the temptation to nationalize major industries. They must provide educational and production incentives to both the workers and the management. They must provide tax breaks to business and wage earners so that they can invest in expansion and self-determination. They must reduce both national spending and taxes. They must design uniform domestic production and trade policies. They must resist the temp-tation to overtax the people so that they can spend less and save more. They must encourage competition, which is good for the economy.

An important dimension of economic development, which national leaders of southern Africa do not seem to understand as an important prerequisite of educational reform, is the need to maintain political stability. Without political stability with constitutions, it is very hard to develop short-term and long-term plans for economic development. The conditions of political stability are as important to educational reform as economic growth and development. An important factor that many nations of Africa seem to ignore is that political stability must result from popular participation in the political process. Na-tional policy and national programs must be determined by popular action and need not to be dictated by the government. The notion that one-party rule or one-man government provides political stability is a farce that many national leaders have yet to recognize.

In 1964, United Methodist Bishop Ralph Dodge, who served in Zimbabwe from 1956 to 1964, argued on this point, saying,

The strength of a political system and stability depends upon the full and free participation of its citizens. The citizens of every country should have access to all essential information regarding the policies of their government. National security must not be imposed to justify illegal activities directed against any person. When law and order are imposed under these conditions, the confidence of the people is eroded away. With it the economy suffers and educational development is hurt.[42]

This is a reality that the nations of southern Africa must recognize in seeking improvement of the economy as an important prerequisite of educational reform. It is true that without a strong economic system many national programs cannot be undertaken.

RECOGNIZING THE INADEQUACY OF THE EXISTING SYSTEM OF EDUCATION

Another important prerequisite of educational reform that the nations of southern Africa must take into account is the recognition of the inadequacy of the existing system of education. Costs, low literacy rates, wide differences between rural and urban schools, shrinking budget allocations, imbalances in teacher-student ratios, rigid examination systems, irrelevant curricula, shortages of trained personnel, poor working conditions for teachers, and excessive government regulations are among the problems that the nations of southern Africa must recognize. These realities and issues need immediate change to create a climate for educational reform.

While some nations of southern Africa, such as Zimbabwe and Botswana, have made commendable efforts to provide universal primary education, failure to make fundamental changes in important areas of education has hurt their developmental strategies. In many respects, the continuation of these problems leads one to the conclusion that some nations have hurt the educational system more than the colonial governments they replaced. It is true that some nations of southern Africa, such as Zambia, Botswana, and Zimbabwe, have inadvertently maintained inadequacies existing in the educational process as a result the policies designed by the colonial governments by arguing that they are trying to maintain educational standards. We contend that the old model is being used because the administration and teachers have not been exposed to "new" sorts of ways. For example, maintaining the distinction between the "O" level and the "A"[43] level leads not only to fewer numbers of students going on to college, but is also wasteful in terms of finances and students who are frustrated because they cannot continue their education beyond high school.

The examinations conducted at the end of the year at various levels of the educational process place serious strains that are detrimental to the educational advancement of the students. In a similar manner, continuing to require certain courses for one sex only, such as home economics for girls and shop for boys, is an educational practice that can no longer be justified under contemporary conditions. Therefore, the recognition that the existing system of education carries some serious inadequacies constitutes another important prerequisite of educational reform.

Another situation that tends to perpetuate inadequacies in the existing educational systems in countries of southern Africa and that must be eliminated as a prerequisite of educational reform is the fact that the system of education in most countries of the region is based on models that have been imported from developed countries and have not been adopted to suit local conditions. For example, emphasis on Western history has the effect of alienating students from their own cultural history. At the same time, the emphasis placed on passing government-controlled examinations as a measure of educational achievement is done at the detriment of the actual learning itself. The belief that passing public examinations as proof of educational achievement is a myth that is still alive in all countries of southern Africa. The thinking that when one fails to pass public examinations one has failed in education has a damaging and retarding psychological effect on students and cultures.

The main task of the school in contemporary southern Africa is to teach the students that learning is far more important than passing public examinations. Placing emphasis on passing these examinations forces students to memorize facts. In this situation, their ability to engage in critical thinking is severely impaired. Public examinations also have a negative effect on teaching itself. They deny teachers the flexibility and freedom they must have to expose their students to the wide range of learning activities that is needed to produce well-rounded, educated citizens.

Public examinations also tend to develop in students a dependence complex as they begin to rely on the lectures given by their teachers with little or no opportunity to examine critically the wider implications of what they are learning.[44] The practice of a national curriculum undercuts the very essence of the philosophy of education as an outcome of the concept of academic freedom and forces all the schools in the country to approach the teaching and the learning processes in a mechanical manner. For educational reform to be meaningful, it has to remove these serious inadequacies. The nations of southern Africa must also realize that there is no single strategy that can be used to accomplish this objective, but that economic and political conditions can combine to create a national climate in which the need to remove inadequacies can be understood in its proper perspective as a blending of the cultures within the political boundaries, with an opportunity to extract knowledge about the education and economics of the past.

SUMMARY AND CONCLUSION

The discussion in this chapter leads to three basic conclusions. The first conclusion is that while economic, social, and political conditions have a profound impact on the development of education, nations of southern Africa must avoid the temptation to rank-order them because in its own way, each has a considerable impact on educational reform and development. In their formative stage, and most nations of Africa are in their formative stage, many nations of the Third World find it hard to determine policies for national development because they do not establish a clear agenda for corrective action. It is for this reason that we warn against putting educational development and economic development in a rank order. In a similar manner, political stability and economic development depend on each other, but both are dependent on a foundation of education. The best that developing nations can do is try their best to improve all these conditions so that they combine to influence the development of education so critical to endeavors for national development.

The second conclusion is that there is no question that an essential outcome of the thinking about ways of improving education in southern Africa has been the emergence of the concept of how conditions outside the educational process affect education itself. Among these conditions are the sociatic, economic, and political factors. (Sociatic is defined as the health and education of jobs.) While the nations of southern Africa strive toward their own definitions of national unity and progress, they seem to neglect the fact, as UNESCO put it in 1976, that "Education in Africa is a maze of innovative activity. Innovation may be defined as a deliberate effort to improve a particular component of the educational system."[45]

This suggests the conclusion that African nations must recognize that change is not necessarily an innovation or reform unless it is designed to ensure improvement. When, on April 5, 1990, de Klerk announced that segregated state schools for whites would be able to admit black students if 90 percent of the white parents in any school so voted, there was a feeling that he was not quite sincere in claiming that his government wanted to have dialogue with the ANC to resolve the problems South Africa was facing. Nelson Mandela responded, "This is inadequate because the parents' voting requirement would paralyze the whole initiative."[46] To experience genuine reform the prerequisites discussed in this chapter, as well as others that have not been presented here, must be observed and applied.

The third conclusion is that the nature and extent of the applicability of the prerequisites of educational reform have implications on management or strategies for seeking improvement. While human factors and political considerations have inhibited educational reform in the past, they can become national assets when the spirit of urgency prevails at all levels of authority from the people to the government. Mutuality of understanding and respect will enable the nations of southern Africa to approach the task of educational reform from a perspective of a national endeavor to improve the system so as to serve the developmental needs of all the people in order to serve the developmental needs of the nation. Any other course of action is likely to yield limited results.

NOTES

1. Zimbabwe, "President's End of the Year Message to the Nation: Policy Statement Number 2," December 31, 1980. By courtesy of the Zimbabwe Ministry of Information.

2. Ian Smith, during an interview with Dickson Mungazi in Harare, Zimbabwe, July 22, 1983.

3. Smith himself told Dickson Mungazi that the war started in 1962, but recorded evidence seems to point to April 1966.

4. Dickson A. Mungazi, "Educational Innovation in Zimbabwe: Possibilities and Problems," in *Journal of Negro Education*, Vol. 54, No. 4 (1985), p. 198.

5. For details to support this conclusion, see Dickson A. Mungazi, *The Fall of the Mantle: The Educational Policy of the Rhodesia Front Government and Conflict in Zimbabwe* (New York: Peter Lang Publishers, 1993).

6. Kathy Bond-Stewart, *Education in Southern Africa* (Gweru: Mambo Press, 1986), p. 15.

7. Ibid., p. 16.

8. Ziyad Motala, *Constitutional Opinions for a Democratic South Africa: A Comparative Perspective* (Washington, D.C.: Howard University Press, 1994), p. 11.

9. Bond-Stewart, *Education in Southern Africa*, p. 16.

10. Machel Samuels, "The New Look in Angolan Education," *Africa Report*, November 1967, p. 63.

11. Ibid.

12. Samora Machel, "Educate Man to Win the War, Create a New Society, and Develop Our Country," September 1970.

13. Tanzania, *Education for Self-Reliance* (Dar es Salaam: Government Printer, 1967).

14. St. Augustine's Secondary School was the first secondary school for Africans in Zimbabwe. It was opened in 1939 by the Anglican Church.

15. A thirteen-year-old girl during an interview in eastern Zimbabwe, July 15, 1983.

16. Dickson Mungazi, *The Struggle for Social Change in Southern Africa: Visions of Liberty* (New York: Taylor and Francis, 1989), p. 51.

17. *Not in a Thousand Years: From Rhodesia to Zimbabwe*, a documentary film, PBS, 1982.

18. Kenneth Kaunda, "Zambia: Blueprint for and Economic Development," an address to an economic conference, Mulunguishi Hall, Lusaka, October 8, 1979.

19. Ibid.

20. Ibid.

21. Zambia, Zambia Information Service, *Zambia in Brief* (Lusaka: Government Printer, 1975), p. 15.

22. Ibid.

23. Zambia, *Educational Reform*, Lusaka, Zambia, 1977, p. 5.

24. C. William Smith, *Nyerere of Tanzania* (Harare: Zimbabwe Publishing House, 1981), p. 15.

25. Bond-Stewart, *Education in Southern Africa*, p. 5.

26. Kenneth Kaunda, "Zambia: Blueprint for Economic Development," 1979.

27. Robert Mugabe, "Literacy for All in Five Years," radio and television speech in Harare, Zimbabwe, July 18, 1988.

28. *World Almanac and Book of Facts*, 1990.

29. Kenneth Kaunda, "Zambia: Blueprint for Economic Development," 1979.

30. World Bank, *Toward Sustained Development in Sub-Sahara Africa* (Washington, D.C.: Author, 1984), p. 26.

31. Ibid., p. 27.

32. Ibid., p. 28.

33. Botswana, *Report of the National Commission on Education* (Gaberone: Government Printer, 1977), p. 10.

34. Ibid.

35. Ibid.

36. World Bank, *Toward Sustained Development in Sub-Sahara Africa*, p. 28.

37. Bernard T. Chidzero, "Budget Statement" presented to the Parliament of Zimbabwe, July 26, 1990, p. 24.

38. Ibid., p. 25.

39. World Bank, *Toward Sustained Development in Sub-Sahara Africa*, p. 2.

40. Ibid.

41. Dickson A. Mungazi saw evidence of the rapidly declining economy while he was on a study trip to Southern Africa in 1989.

42. Dickson A. Mungazi, *The Honored Crusade: Ralph Dodge's Theology of Liberation and Initiative for Social Change in Zimbabwe* (Gweru: Mambo Press, 1991), p. 57.

43. The "O" level and the "A" level are systems used in the British system of education to indicate a difference in educational attainment. The "A" level is for those students who seek to qualify for entrance into college.

44. Botswana, *Report of the National Commission on Education*, p. 19.

45. UNESCO, *Educational Studies and Documents, Number 25: Education in Africa in Light of the Lagos Conference* (Paris: Author, 1976), p. 16.

46. Anthony Lewis, "The Harsh Reality Is that Apartheid Is Still in Place," *New York Times*, April 6, 1990, sec. 2, p. 15.

5

Theory of Educational Reform in Contemporary Southern Africa

Claims of educational reform during the colonial rule was a strategy to sustain the fossilized structure of the African culture.

Samora Machel, 1981

It is important for Third World Nations, especially those of southern Africa, to recognize that the individual cannot find educational fulfillment without freedom to choose his own course of study.

Conference of Catholic Bishops, Zimbabwe, 1987

THE IMPORTANCE OF THEORY OF EDUCATIONAL REFORM

On August 14, 1941, President Franklin Roosevelt (1882–1945) and Prime Minister Winston Churchill (1874–1965) issued the *Atlantic Charter*, stating: "We respect the right of all people to choose the form of government under which they will live and wish to see sovereign rights and self-determination restored to those who have been denied them."[1] In this statement, the two leaders were actually recognizing the fact that the Second World War, devastating as it was, had created a climate of unprecedented need for fundamental social change. The two leaders were also convinced that the conditions that had created an environment of the war in 1939 must be altered to avoid another conflict in the future. They, therefore, concluded that one of the major conditions for future security of all people in all nations was to change the manner in which governments were structured.

If the *Atlantic Charter* was issued under the pressure of the conditions that came out of the war, Roosevelt and Churchill subsequently disagreed about to whom the message contained in this document was directed. On the one hand, Roosevelt thought that the charter was directed toward changing the systems of government all over the world to bring out the representative character. This concept is essential to national development through individual and popular participation, which in all aspects of government operations and functions could benefit from the social transformation through educational reform. This is why, in 1943, while he was on his way to the Casablanca Conference, President Roosevelt stopped in the French colony of Gambia to lay the groundwork for better understanding and implementation of the self-determined national charter. Roosevelt was so profoundly disturbed when he observed the conditions of life of Africans that he expressed his deep disappointment with France's colonial policy. Roosevelt felt that he had a duty to call for a fundamental change of that policy. As an American leader, Roosevelt was aware that his own country had a serious racial problem that he felt could be resolved through international cooperation. At the San Francisco Conference held in 1945, Roosevelt's ideas formed the basis of an international effort to restructure the world order at the conclusion of the war. President Harry S. Truman (1884–1972), Roosevelt's successor, championed that course of action.

On the other hand, Churchill did not think that the concept of self-determination and the process of instituting governments on Western principles included responding affirmatively to the needs of Africans in the British empire. He therefore argued in defiance that " I have not become the King's[2] First Minister in order to preside over the liquidation of the British Empire. We mean to hold our own."[3] The difference of opinion between Roosevelt and Churchill about the meaning of social transformation said something very important about what its purpose was. As the leader of a nation that had a vast colonial empire, Churchill saw social transformation from its narrow perspective of colonialization rather than globalization.

Roosevelt saw it from a broader and more inclusive perspective. But the real message of the *Atlantic Charter* was its call for more representative forms of government. This was, indeed, a call for reform in its more inclusive terms as a prerequisite of national development imperative on the development of the individual. It is quite evident that in issuing the *Atlantic Charter*, Roosevelt and Churchill were laying the foundation for new theoretical considerations that would have to have a profound impact on the entire world community if conflict was to be avoided in the future.

A question must now be raised: How did the message contained in the *Atlantic Charter* influence the evolution of the concept that educational reform is a prerequisite of social transformation in its universal meaning? Robert Manners seems to provide an answer to the question, saying, "If you introduce change in any part, contingent changes of varying intensity will make themselves felt throughout the venture. The very change which may be welcomed by the group in power as a desirable innovation may be resented by those who feel oppressed by society because they feel that such change has been introduced to strengthen the status quo."[4]

This seems to indicate that social change in different conditions of development may be interpreted as reform for an imperative of the times rather than for the good of the individual. That is, it means different things to different people. Nations need to operate and function by the recognition of the need for social reform. Many were unwilling to do that, and it is not surprising that most of them have been in trouble. The fact of the matter is that the nations of the world could not afford to operate by Churchill's definition of social reform.

Change becomes transformation when it is designed with the main objective of seeking improvement in the existing system to serve the needs of all the people. After the war, the colonial governments in Africa faced the challenge of defining a new theory of educational reform from a broader perspective that was being articulated by the international community. Today, the nations of southern Africa, like the colonial governments they replaced, have to take historical precedence into account in defining elements of their theory of educational reform.

THE SAN FRANCISCO CONFERENCE AND A NEW THINKING ABOUT THEORY

The outbreak of the war in 1939 was an event that not only changed the thinking process among the people of the world but also demanded an appraisal of old values cast in new international relationships. What was at stake was not that the Axis powers sought to rule the world, but how human relations of the future would be determined and how social institutions would operate. The outbreak of the war was, in a sense, a conflict between old and new values. The use of the atomic bomb to end the war created new problems in human and international relationships that required an articulation of new theoretical considerations to address them.

The fear of atomic destruction was combined with the concern of the victorious Allies to pose new questions about the extent to which nations were prepared to use this destructive power to protect their national interests. The fact of the matter is that the existing world had been altered by questionable theoretical perceptions about the future. Instead of ensuring world peace and security, the use of the atomic bomb compounded old problems and created new ones. These were the realities that delegates to the San Francisco Conference took into account in attempting to formulate new theoretical considerations to make the world safe.

Before nations endeavored to reshape the fabric of a new order in the presence of this immensely destructive power, they decided to engage in a collective effort to examine the past in order to understand the present and plan the future. As the war came to an end, both the victorious and the vanquished nations decided to form an organization known as the United Nations (UN). The Dumbarton Oaks Conference of October 1944 produced the international climate that was needed for the formation of the UN. Following discussions that had been started in August, representatives from the Soviet Union, Great Britain, China, and the United States agreed on conditions for the founding of the UN. Meeting at Yalta in February 1945, Churchill, Roosevelt, and Joseph Stalin went further to articulate new theoretical principles relative to the structure of the UN itself. They agreed to convene a conference in San Francisco to begin on April 25, 1945, to prepare a charter for the formation of an international organization called the UN. In this task, they were mindful of the enormous consequences of the demise of the League of Nations in 1920.

Exhausted by the war, and unsure of the future, these four nations agreed to invite forty-one other nations to the San Francisco Conference. By the time the UN Charter came into being on June 26, 1945, delegates representing fifty nations had signed it. With its ratification in October, the UN Charter was poised to alter the character of the relationships between nations. In 1946, John D. Rockefeller, Jr., believing in the cause for world peace, gave $8.5 million to the UN to buy the builder's site in New York City. Construction of the building began in 1949 and, when it was completed in 1952, had cost $67 million. The cooperation, enthusiasm, and support that came from all over the world suggest that the international community was now ready to accept the challenge of constructing a new world order.

The preamble[5] of the UN Charter was meant to ensure that all members of the UN understood and accepted a new theoretical perception that reminded them of their collective responsibility to ensure peace. The preamble stated,

We the people of the United Nations, determined to save succeeding generations from the scourge of war, which twice in our life-time, has brought untold sorrow to mankind, and to reaffirm our faith in fundamental human rights, in the dignity and worth of the human person, in equal rights of men and women, and of nations, large and small, and to establish conditions under which justice and respect for the obligation arising from treaties and other sources of international law, and to promote social progress and better standards of life in larger freedom, wish to practice tolerance and live together in peace with one another as good neighbors and employ international machinery for the promotion of the economic and social advancement of all people. Accordingly our respective governments have agreed to the present Charter of the United Nations and hereby establish an international organization to be known as the United Nations.[6]

The excitement with which nations supported the inauguration of the UN was tempered by the equally nagging feeling that in spite of the claimed commitment by nations to embrace its principles, global conflict was likely to break out again in the future. For this reason, the delegates assembled in San Francisco decided that, before they asked nations to embark on the collective task of reshaping the future, they needed to take a journey into the past to examine developments that had brought the world to the brink of self-destruction twice in the century. The belief in the theory that one must study the past to understand the present and plan the future was a central component of their action. Painful as this exercise was, they felt it had to be undertaken in order to take all relevant dimensions into account in planning that future.

The first step toward this rendezvous with the past was to make an assessment of what had caused the war in 1939. Beyond articulating the popular view that the war was caused by the reckless policies of the Axis powers, the delegates to the San Francisco Conference went much further to look for a broader field from which to understand human behavior in order to deal with all relevant aspects of their efforts to plan for the future in a more realistic and comprehensive manner. To do this they reached three basic theoretical conclusions regarding what they identified as causes of the war. The theoretical conclusion was that the war had three causes: ignorance, poverty, and greed.

These three pillars of human weakness had often combined to create a climate of conflict, both national and international. Ignorance of the needs and feelings of other people, of what it takes to build a peaceful and happy society, and of the conditions that control the universal person often becomes a prime factor in selfish behavior. Selfish behavior itself leads to greed. Once one has the power, one can use greed to exploit those who are in a vulnerable position in society. Exploitation breeds resentment, and resentment eventually leads to conflict. Was it possible for the colonial governments in Africa to understand the significance of this line of thinking about human relationships?

The recognition of these three factors as causes of human conflict means that mankind must assume the responsibility of eliminating them to create a new climate of peace. It is ironic that coming out of the Industrial Revolution of the nineteenth century, ignorance, poverty, and greed are the very negative features of society that technological advancement was expected to eliminate.

But, on the contrary, they have intensified in contemporary global settings. The recognition by the delegates to the San Francisco Conference that these negative features of human existence had been a major cause of the war meant that a new effort had to be made to eliminate them if the future was to be different and more meaningful than the past. But they fully recognized that they needed to utilize new theoretical strategies to achieve this objective.

The second theoretical conclusion was that nations and their people prior to 1939 failed to understand each other because neither their leaders nor their citizens were sufficiently educated to understand human issues fully and the conditions that controlled relationships between them. Remembering that up to 1939 educational opportunity was the privilege of a few, the recognition of this reality led to the conclusion that if nations were to avoid conflict in the future, a new collective effort had to be made to educate people, both national leaders and citizens alike, to help them understand their respective responsibilities in developing democratic societies. This endeavor required rethinking the goals, objectives, and content of education itself. Educational theories of the past had to give way to educational systems based on new theoretical considerations.

The third theoretical conclusion was that discrimination and prejudice based on race, gender, and religion had always been a scourge that marred relationships between nations and their people. Nazi efforts to exterminate the Jews were the ultimate manifestation of racial hatred and prejudice. This negative aspect of human behavior was found among all nations, although it was more pronounced in some more than in others. It was not until the 1950s that the international community concluded that society needed to make a new thrust to eliminate discrimination in all its forms. Nations such as Great Britain and the United States, which had often been considered the citadels of democracy and the beacons of freedom, suddenly found themselves at the center of controversy generated by the various forms of discrimination and prejudice. In 1944, Gunnar Myrdal (1898–1987), a Swedish sociologist and researcher, appropriately called the situation in the United States an American dilemma.

The delegates to the San Francisco Conference took these realities into consideration in reaching the conclusion that discrimination of some people, whether it was based on race, religion, or gender, was repugnant to the principles of national development. Such programs as affirmative action and positive discrimination have been demonstrated efforts to eliminate this scourge in human experience following the civil rights movement in the United States in the 1950s. But the fact that discrimination has continued to exist in all nations underscores the importance of finding solutions to it, so that nations can put it behind them as they endeavor to chart a new course in their search for a *safari* to a destination of human fulfillment. This is the only viable means to national development and international peace and security. The recognition that discrimination and prejudice were the prime cause of inequality in society led to the conclusion that they were the basic cause of conflict both among people of the same country and among nations.

While the delegates to the San Francisco Conference readily recognized that discrimination and prejudice have always been two features of human existence that have persistently retarded efforts toward national development and often cause untold misery, they did not have a formula to eliminate them. The horrors caused by the Nazi perpetration of discrimination and prejudice are only a small part of the evidence showing that a society based on these two adverse conditions, created by man himself, robs itself of the opportunity to build a progressive social system. A society that enables its people to recognize the vitality and dignity of every person in it is the democratically progressive way. Idealistic as they were in engaging in this painful rendezvous with the past to plan the future, the delegates were not aware that problems of discrimination and prejudice would continue to ravage the beauty and glory of the human person potentially far into the future.

In Africa, the situation is no better. As soon as African countries began to gain political independence, beginning with Ghana in 1957, corruption by government officials, nepotism, and other irregularities have become the order of things. In a letter dated March 14, 1991, addressed to us, a bright, hardworking, and ambitious student in Sierra Leone expressed the problems that he and other students in a similar position are facing:

You see, sir, in Sierra Leone education has become a matter of privilege, not of right for the citizens. Scholarships are only awarded to the children and relatives of top government officials or civil servants. A system of nepotism and corruption has taken over the operations of the government. Because I do not have a relative working for the government I have no means of continuing my education beyond what I have done. God only knows if I will ever have the opportunity I desperately need. The government has abandoned its responsibility to its own people, and we are paying the price. Sir, I need your help![7]

EFFORTS TO DEFINE THE ELEMENTS
OF A NEW THEORY

The San Francisco Conference concluded that the development of education throughout the world was the only viable means to end inequality in society. This conclusion led to the belief that a thrust for educational reform would help eliminate the problems that society faced, especially poverty and ignorance, prejudice and discrimination, and political oppression. For the first time in human history people began to place hope in the realization that ending inequality of educational opportunity was possible only when educational reform had been effected. This belief also meant that other sociatics such as origin of birth, social class, health, education, and other considerations that had perpetuated inequality in society would no longer be used to determine who received an opportunity for education. The theoretical belief that a little black girl of humble origin in a remote rural area of Africa and a little white boy in an exclusive suburban neighborhood in a Western country stood on an equal plane to launch their educational *safaris* led to new endeavors to formulate new theoretical elements that address the task of initiating reform in education to realize national purpose through the fulfillment of basic human rights.

To make this belief a reality, nations began to make plans based on three theoretical beliefs. The first belief was that because existing systems and programs were insufficient to meet the projected needs of a changing society, educational reform must become a national commitment. The second theoretical belief was that economic development was needed during the critical stage of the new thrust for educational reform. The third theoretical belief was that educational opportunity was essential to seeking an improvement in the quality of life of all the people and that this objective would be met by initiating, at the political level, fundamental reform of the educational system itself.[8]

The theoretical belief that popular democratic participation in the political process is essential to political stability as a condition of social transformation leads to the conclusion that this participation is not possible without adequate education. Understanding the basic tenets (rights and responsibilities) of popular democratic participation principles, citizens are uninformed about the political process designed to improve the sociatics of the country. Without political stability, a climate of national social transformation could not be created. This was how educational reform made the practice of democracy possible. The idea of political elites who had controlled and exploited the dispossessed and oppressed masses had to give way to a new theoretical perception that political stability was possible only within a national environment of popular participation under the principle of freedom of expression. This makes educational expansion an imperative of hope for the future whether it is 1945 or 1996.

The delegates to the San Francisco Conference also concluded that collective rendezvous with the past, as a theoretical perception of the future, would have little meaning unless all nations took specific action in setting goals and making concerted efforts to fulfill them. Among these goals were six that are critical to educational reform. The first goal was that nations must invest in educational reform to ensure their economic development with specific reference to seeking an improvement in the curriculum and making it comprehensive enough to allow students to learn about other people in the world. It was believed that knowledge of other people was essential to global peace and security.[9] Global peace and security have an economic price as well as benefit.

The second goal was for all nations to set 1960 as a target date for achieving 100 percent literacy.[10] The reason for this goal was that basic literacy was the only viable theoretical basis for the development of the individual as an essential component of national development. The development of the individual was considered to manifest itself in a variety of ways that would constitute elements of national development. These elements include economic well-being, freedom of political expression, and participation in national affairs. This was so that no group of individuals would have a monopoly on political power at the expense of other groups. The generation of new theories and ideas, the creative activity of the human mind, the ability to see oneself as an essential and viable element of society—all of these emanate from an ability to envisage oneself in terms of a global and futuristic society.

The third goal was to develop adequate educational facilities, such as classrooms, improved teacher-training programs, and the supply of adequate educational equipment. When combined and properly applied, these activities constitute an essential form of educational reform. Prior to the outbreak of the war in 1939, these facilities were totally inadequate or altogether wanting. The training of teachers was considered especially essential to providing adequate educational facilities. Teachers who were trained to understand the purpose of education would inspire their students with confidence for the future. They would also understand the problems of human existence in general and the nature of relationships that were intended to improve the human condition. These conditions also constituted important elements of educational reform.

The fourth goal was to extend educational opportunity to both men and women, boys and girls, on the basis of equality. The reality that, due to cultural traditions, some nations had a bias for educational opportunity in favor of men and boys had to be discouraged because a nation where only men were educated was like a cake baked on only one side. The thinking that society needed both men and women to make progress suggested the need to end all forms of bias against the educational advancement of women. It also suggested that bias had to be eliminated in both education and society itself. The fundamental consideration relative to the need to end all forms of bias against the educational development of women was that, as long as this bias continued, educational opportunity offered on the basis of gender would inhibit the ability of schools to discharge their proper responsibilities to their students.

The fifth goal was to encourage families to do their best to enable their children to go to school. In many countries of the world, it had been the practice before the outbreak of the war for parents to depend on their children to make a contribution to the family's economic well-being. It was stressed that parents must adopt the attitude that encouraging children to go to school was the best way of preparing for the future. Parents actively enabling their children to go to school, combined with the commitment of national leaders to stress education, made it possible to plan for a future quite different from the past. Parents who had missed an opportunity for education now began to see its value for the future of their children in an entirely different way.

The dramatic change of attitude toward the importance of education was the ultimate manifestation of the critical assessment or appraisal of the meaning of the past to the present to plan the future. In Africa, this dramatic change of attitude toward education was fully recognized by the colonial governments. In colonial Zimbabwe, for example, a high-ranking colonial official acknowledged it in 1961, saying, "The rather apathetic prewar outlook of the African masses towards education was rapidly being transformed into a general and urgent realization that education was the essential tool for gaining a foothold in a competitive civilized world."[11] Tragic as it was, the war had transformed Africans' thinking from accepting the colonial condition as inevitable to questioning its assumed values. They now began to see colonial systems not as something that they had to accept to ensure their survival, but as institutions that entailed negative features designed to engulf their existence and that they felt had to be eliminated to plan the future.

The sixth goal was that all nations must initiate carefully planned campaigns to provide adult literacy programs. The conclusion that adult education was important was a result of the view that those who had missed the opportunity for education earlier in their lives must make a contribution to national development without waiting to complete their education in the way regular students were expected to do. The approach to the question of adult literacy was also an outcome of a theoretical belief that those who had missed an opportunity for education earlier must not endure the perpetual life sentence of illiteracy, because every adult person has a critical contribution to make to the development of society.

The preceding discussion helps to explain why the search for a new theory to address the thrust for educational reform in southern Africa had to be initiated from a broader perspective than the colonial governments wished. But a problem that nations had addressed at the end of the war was the fact that while the delegates to the San Francisco Conference addressed issues of global importance, the colonial governments in Africa saw these issues from a narrow perspective that had serious limitations in their application. Churchill's response to the wider interpretation of the *Atlantic Charter* explains the extent of this conflict. Nevertheless, the task of formulating a new theory to address the imperative of educational reform had to be undertaken.

THE EVOLVEMENT OF A NEW THEORY IN COLONIAL SOUTHERN AFRICA

A discussion of the theory of education in southern Africa must, by its very nature, be divided into two sections: theory during the colonial period and theory after it. The important thing to remember about theoretical considerations of the colonial governments is that each colonial power formulated a policy it considered suitable to meet *its* objectives. From these objectives emerged a set of theories consistent with colonial goals, and these goals were different. For example, Germany formulated a policy known as *Deutsche Kolonialbund*. Portugal initiated a policy of *Estado Novo* (new state). The Dutch formulated a theory known as *apartheid*,[12] France and Belgium had a policy of *evalue*, and Britain formulated a policy known as *indirect rule*.[13]

Why did the colonial governments formulate policies that seem to be in conflict with those of other governments? Kenneth Knorr argued that these policies were based on common theoretical considerations that were needed to serve a common objective: to "convert the Africans into a commodity or raw materials to be employed in the service of the white man. The Africans were not allowed to decide for their own future because they were considered incapable of doing so. It had therefore to be decided for them to serve the white man as their master."[14] Paulo Freire of Brazil, a leading writer from the Third World, concluded that this is a situation that creates conditions of oppression and the task of the oppressed is not merely to liberate themselves from the conditions of oppression but also to liberate their oppressor.[15] There is no question that the main objective of the colonial governments was a product of a Victorian theoretical speculation that "The brain of an adult African looks very much like the brain of a European in its infant stage. At puberty all development in the brain of the African stops and becomes more ape-like as he grows older."[16]

What came out of this perception of the intellectual capability of Africans is the thinking that, because they were less intelligent than whites, their major function was to serve in an inferior capacity than that of the white man in every respect. This is the kind of theory that the colonial governments used to design education for Africans consistent with this view. This is a theoretical perspective that a senior colonial official in Zimbabwe took into consideration to argue in

1912, "I do not consider it right that we should educate the Native in any way that will unfit him for service. The Native is and should always be the hewer of wood and the drawer of water for his white master."[17] This is also the perspective that James Oldham used to conclude in his study in 1930 that the colonial governments operated under the theoretical assumption that "The most natural and obvious way of civilizing Natives is to give them employment. This is their best school. The gospel of labor is the most salutary gospel for them because the Negroid people have shown little capacity to establish a fully developed civilization of their own."[18]

A study of the activities in Europe leading to the colonization of Africa would support Manners's conclusion that change, which can be interpreted as transformation by those in power, may be regarded as designed to sustain the status quo by those who are powerful for those who are powerless. While Europeans regarded the Great Industrial Revolution as a technological transformation that meant the improvement of the standard of living, Africans considered it an improvement in the machinery of oppression. This phenomenon represents the first phase in the colonization of Africa.

We present a few examples that substantiate the accuracy of this conclusion. The formation of the Dutch East India Company in 1602 was an event that gave the Dutch an advantage in the competition in which major nations in Europe were engaged in the spice trade with the East. When the Dutch East India Company dispatched Jan van Riebeeck to the Cape in South Africa in 1652, Europeans thought that this was a great breakthrough in facilitating trade between Europe and the East. However, when Riebeeck began to formulate policies to govern the company's relationships with Africans, it became evident that while company officials saw the white man's action as an improvement in relationships between the white man and Africans, Africans themselves saw those policies as a machinery of their oppression. From its inception in South Africa, the Dutch East India Company created an environment of conflict between itself and the Africans. This is the environment that the apartheid system was not able to resolve until the escalation of that conflict in 1990 forced F. W. de Klerk to make a new thrust to find a solution before it was too late.

While the effects of the Industrial Revolution of the nineteenth century were profoundly felt in industrial production, it was in the area of reform in transport and communication that gave a new meaning to entrepreneurial adventure in Africa by Europeans.[19] The ability to transport large amounts of materials, numbers of people, and information to and from distant places and the knowledge of the distribution of products on a larger scale than had been done in the past combined to play a critical role in the quest for colonies in Africa. The completion of the trans-Atlantic cable in 1866, made possible by the work of an American inventor, Samuel Morse, radically transformed the system of communication with profound implications for the colonization process in Africa.

The knowledge among Europeans that they had become masters of what they considered technological feats boosted their own sense of superiority over people in distant lands. They also began to associate their accomplishments with the blessing and rightness of their goals, objectives, and endeavors in a larger context of human interactions. In this environment, they regarded the colonization of Africa as a blessing that only the colonial governments were capable of extending to Africans. In return, Africans must be grateful for receiving the blessings of Western civilization. The question of what was right or wrong for the colonized people could only be answered by the colonizers themselves. In this setting, any resistance by the colonized, especially Africans, was regarded as an act of rebellion against properly constituted authority. The sad part of this is that technological reform did not translate into the transformation of interactions between people of vastly different cultures within the political boundaries of their own countries.

The knowledge that Africa contained large amounts of new materials motivated European nations to launch an entirely new entrepreneurial adventure there. This was the beginning of the second phase in the process of the colonization of Africa in what became known as the *scramble for Africa* beginning in 1875. By the time the Berlin Conference of 1884 began, European nations recognized that it was not in their national interests to go to war over resources and colonies in Africa. The idea of convening a conference came from Otto von Bismarck (1815–1898), the charismatic chancellor of Germany, at the conclusion of the Franco-Prussian War in 1871. Bismarck decided to convene the conference to enable European nations to resolve their differences over the procedures of claiming colonies in Africa. Bismarck himself chaired the conference, suggesting the extent of the power and influence he had acquired over the course of developments both in Europe and in Africa.

What is important to recognize here is that the structure of colonial policy was based on many theoretical considerations. One of them was that European colonial governments believed that colonization would result in the advancement of Africans because they would begin to see the value of accepting Western culture. But in the course of implementing their policies, the colonial governments went much further than Africans would tolerate. The introduction of the system of passbooks, the practice of registration, the introduction of forced labor, and strict segregation laws were conditions of colonial theories and policies that forced Africans to feel the weight of colonial power in a way they could no longer bear.[20]

While the colonial governments felt secure as a result of implementing their theories and policies, they had a false sense of security because when the conditions were right, Africans set out to prove that the theoretical basis of colonization was wrong. Was the response of Africans to these theories and policies a deliberate outcome of their application by the colonial governments? Courtland Cox suggested an answer when he wrote in 1972, "At the base of the colonial political assumptions was the absolute belief in the inferiority of the African people and the certainty of chaos if their subjection was eased in the slightest."[21]

Kenneth Knorr adds that while the formulation of colonial theory by the colonial governments was intended to improve the effectiveness of the colonial administrative systems to benefit the colonial governments themselves, the ultimate effect of its application was that it "converted the Africans into a commodity or raw materials to be employed in the service of the white man. The Africans were not allowed to decide for their own future because they were considered incapable of doing so. It had, therefore, to be decided for them to serve the white man as their master."[22]

The theories formulated by the colonial governments, especially that Africans were incapable of making decisions relative to their own development and that a national chaos would result if their subjection was eased in any way, combined to create a need for change. Fundamental change was needed, not only in the attitudes of the colonial governments, but also in seeking ways of improving the effectiveness of the structure of colonial administrations themselves. Indeed, arrest and imprisonment for political activity considered incompatible with colonial politics, denial of voting rights, discrimination in economic and educational opportunities, and the administrative systems themselves became demonstrated evidence of the application of the theoretical belief of the colonial systems. All Africans could do was hope that the colonial governments would treat them humanely.

While Africans were at a loss to understand why colonial governments were so set against giving them any opportunity for development, the colonial establishments themselves were totally convinced of the correctness of the Victorian eighteenth-century theoretical notions. These theories would not accommodate the aspirations of the colonized Africans. This is also the kind of setting in which reform was intended to do only one thing: to improve the power of the colonial governments themselves. Until Africans began to demand equal rights, the colonial governments made no effort either to modify this theory or to change their strategy to initiate the process of developing the Africans for the manual labor market.

There are plenty of examples to substantiate this conclusion. In 1952, for example, Godfrey Huggins (1883–1971), the prime minister of colonial Zimbabwe from 1933 to 1952, argued during a political campaign speech, saying,

We must unhesitatingly accept the theory that our superiority over the Africans rests on the color of our skin, education, and cultural values, civilization, and heredity. We must be sufficiently realistic to appreciate the fact that we have a paramount monopoly of these qualities. It would be outrageous to give the Native a so-called equal opportunity when he is likely to ruin himself as a result.[23]

Huggins's own protégé, Ian Smith (born in 1919), the last colonial prime minister who served from 1964 to 1979, added to this melodramatic theoretical perception when he attempted to explain in 1965 why his own government resorted to mass arrest and imprisonment of Africans to control their political aspirations. Smith said, "We have had to resort to certain forms of political restriction and arrest of the Africans because when you have a primitive people such as the Africans of this country are it would have been completely irresponsible of the government not to have done so."[24]

As one seeks to understand the theories used by the colonial governments as a basis of strengthening themselves in Africa, one needs to understand first some reliable theoretical considerations in order to understand and put them in their proper context. Two examples come to mind. The first example is that in his theoretical study, *Education for Liberation,* Adam Curle concludes that the effect of an educational theory in societies in which education is controlled to sustain the interests of those in power creates serious problems. Rather than promote the advancement of those who need it, those who oppress create conditions in which habits of thought and action make those who are subjected to it an imposition, and they are forced to feel less than human.[25] Curle concludes that this objective is accomplished in two ways.

The first way is the formulation of a set of quasi-theories that, in effect, is a result of myth. The second way is by repeatedly trying to psychologically condition the controlled into believing that they are primitive because they are members of a primitive culture and society. Repetition of this myth often diminishes the self-worth of the controlled to the extent that they lose their self-esteem. Curle also suggests that this type of brainwashing strategy negates the real purpose of education, to create an environment of mutual respect between the people of different cultures who live in the same society. Instead, it creates self-doubt, fear, and a feeling of inadequacy.[26] The feeling of inadequacy and self-doubt leads to further strengthening of myth and control by those in positions of power.

The second example is that in his own study, *The Colonizer and the Colonized*, Albert Memmi of Tunisia, a professor of philosophy at the Sorbonne, reaches interesting conclusions about the relationship between the colonizer and the colonized. He says that the extent of control exercised by the former on the latter is done by utilizing the myth about their culture and intellectual potential.[27] Memmi goes on to add that after conditioning the colonized to believe in the superiority of the colonizer, they lose their sense of self-pride and motivation so essential to their development. This is the environment in which the colonizer formulates and strengthens a mythical theory about the inferiority of the colonized to strengthen their control because they are presumed to come from a primitive culture. Under this condition, any change in programs purported to promote the development of the colonized is, in effect, designed to promote the interests of the colonizer himself.[28] Therefore, any effort, apparent or real, made to improve the position of the colonized forces the colonized to see it in the context of a desire on the part of the colonizer to sustain his own interests.[29]

What has been discussed so far in this chapter leads one to accept Curle's and Memmi's theories about the character of the colonial governments in Africa. What the colonial governments considered reform, Africans considered a strategy to enhance the power of the colonial governments to control them. It was therefore not possible for the Africans to believe that the colonialists who had gone to Africa in search of fortune were now genuinely trying to train Africans to function in any other capacity than as cheap labor. Once this element of doubt on the part of Africans became part of their modus operandi in their relationships with the colonial governments, there was nothing that could be done to salvage the rapidly deteriorating situation caused by mistrust and doubt. This situation ultimately led to conflict between the two sides when the time was right. Thus, educational reform, or the appearance of it, initiated during the colonial period had a peripheral meaning.

It is quite easy to see why colonial officials shared the view expressed by Ethel Tawse Jollie in 1927 that Africans must not be educated in the same way the whites were being educated because they would be expected to play a different role from that of whites. Jollie's central argument, which she made during a debate in the colonial legislature in Zimbabwe in that year, was that since the colonial government did not intend to hand over the country to the Africans or to admit them to the same social and political position that the colonialists themselves enjoyed, there was no point in making a pretense of educating them in the same way whites were being educated.[30] This theoretical argument had a powerful influence on the structure of colonial policy. By the end of the Second World War, it was quite evident to Africans that the colonial governments were using their theory of educational reform to deny Africans equal educational opportunities purely for political reasons. But political development was what Africans wanted to achieve as a result of educational reform. How would this conflict be resolved?

The realization that the colonial governments were using their theory of educational reform to stall the political advancement of Africans is precisely why the Africans themselves launched a campaign for political independence at the conclusion of the war. Their demand for better educational opportunities as a condition of seeking improvement in other conditions governing their lives ushered in a period of intense struggle for independence. Africans did not begin by demanding political independence; they began, instead, by demanding improvement of those conditions within the colonial system. It was only after they realized that the colonial governments were unwilling to consider their demands that they altered their strategy from seeking improvement within the colonial settings to demanding political independence. The victory that Africans eventually scored in their struggle for political independence now set the stage for a new and more challenging struggle for national development through new endeavors in education.

The theoretical consideration utilized by the colonial governments as a strategy of making it look as if they were trying to promote the political, social, and economic advancement of Africans was not limited to that aspect of national life. It extended to the educational process as well. Four examples in Zimbabwe, the Portuguese colonies of Angola and Mozambique, Namibia, and South Africa furnish evidence to substantiate this conclusion. In colonial Zimbabwe, the government considered the enactment of Ordinance Number 18 of 1899: The Appointment of Inspector of School, commonly known as the Education Ordinance of 1899, a milestone in its efforts to control education to suit its own purpose.

There is no doubt that the government was trying to eliminate the effects of the war of 1896 to give the whites a new sense of security and hope for the future. For this reason, Section A of the ordinance provided for an academic education for white students and Section B provided for practical training and manual labor as a form of education for Africans.[31] In exercising control of the education for Africans in a manner provided for by the ordinance, in a different manner than the way it exercised control of education for white students, the colonial government operated on the theoretical consideration that this would force Africans to come into line with civilized behavior, meaning acceptance of the colonial culture.

This belief was so strong that by 1903, the colonial government amended the Education Ordinance of 1899 by enacting Ordinance Number 1 of 1903, which specified that African education must be of a simple and practical nature to inculcate habits of cleanliness and discipline.[32] Without even waiting to measure the effectiveness of this ordinance, the colonial government amended it four years later by enacting Ordinance Number 133 of 1907. The theoretical rationale that the colonial government used in these amendments is that they represented innovation in the education of Africans to help them accept the value of what government officials called work ethics. In short, the colonial government was trying to persuade Africans to accept its argument that the amendments were intended to promote their educational advancement.

Perhaps what the colonial government considered the best reform in education was Ordinance Number 7, promulgated in July 1912, the Ordinance to Control Native Education. This ordinance had far more serious implications than any previous ordinance, as is demonstrated by the restrictive nature of its provisions. While the colonial government considered this ordinance a means to promote the advancement of the Africans,[33] the effect that it had on Africans is that it implied serious limitations that meant, in effect, their inability to make any real progress. The ordinance's principal objective was to direct "the director of education to order the closure of any school if he is not satisfied as to the manner in which it is being conducted."[34]

One can see that, throughout the colonial period in Zimbabwe, the government claimed it was doing what it was doing because it was trying to improve education by changing it to improve the education of Africans. If this were true, post-colonial Zimbabwe would not have faced the enormous problems that it is facing now.[35] In 1939, Huggins admitted that the educational amendments were "essential if the white students are expected to keep their position of influence in society. Therefore, they will prevent the creation of a poor white class."[36] Huggins's statement substantiates the accuracy of the conclusion that whatever the colonial governments claimed to be a reform in the education of Africans, the Africans themselves believed that it was designed to safeguard the social, economic, and political interests of the colonial establishment or of the colonial governments themselves at the Africans' expense. One can also see that the theoretical assumptions of the colonial government in Zimbabwe, as elsewhere in colonial southern Africa, were carefully formulated to conceal their actual intent.

In the Portuguese colonies of Angola and Mozambique, what appeared to be a theory of reform in education came in various ways. For example, the Colonial Act of 1930 was designed to ensure that Africans received only the rudiments of education to ensure their acceptance of the Portuguese culture.

The late president of Mozambique, Samora Machel, understood the harmful effect of this line of thinking and action as a result of theoretical assumptions when he wrote, "Claims of educational innovation during the colonial rule was a strategy to sustain the fossilized structure of the African culture."[37]

But by relating the educational process to the labor code of 1928, the Portuguese colonial government theorized that the development of manual skills formed an essential component of the educational process for Africans and that this, more than any other form of education, was essential to their training so as to help them have new perceptions of an emerging social order.[38] It is therefore not surprising that the Portuguese national residents in Angola and Mozambique saw this change as an innovation to benefit Africans. The colonial governments were never without a theory of innovation. After the war in 1945, the Portuguese colonial officials felt so secure that they ventured into new areas of strengthening their own positions by claiming that whatever they did represented innovation.

Thus, in 1948, Antonio Salazar launched what he called the first six-year national developmental program in which he presumably established development priorities. Increased economic productivity; the building of national railways, ports, and harbors; and improved education for white students, were all high priorities in that so-called educational reform and plan of national development. Salazar outlined his theoretical reasons for placing the education of Africans low on his priority list to emphasize to them his position that self-help was a critical element of their collective development. The main objective of Salazar's plan of national development, however, was to make both Angola and Mozambique ideal for Portuguese settlers. Of course, he would not say that openly.

When the war of liberation broke out in Angola and Mozambique in 1961, Salazar was shocked to learn that the leadership of the liberation movement came from the ranks of the assimilados, for whom he thought the government's policy of *Estado Novo* had been designed to isolate from the African masses. It was then that Salazar was forced to reassess his own theory. He had to acknowledge the fact that he did not have actual understanding of its intent. Salazar admitted his failure, saying, "A law recognizing citizenship takes minutes to draft and can be made right away. But a citizen that is a man fully and consciously integrated into civilized political society takes centuries to achieve."[39] When Gulf Oil discovered substantial new oil deposits in Angola in 1966, Salazar immediately dispatched troops to protect the area. Hundreds of Africans were evicted with no provision made for their relocation.

When Salazar argued that the education of Africans would be in the form of employment offered by the oil fields, he was actually stating a new educational policy. Their education must be of a practical nature. He saw the involvement of his government as being limited to the investment of facilities to make practical training and manual labor viable. This was clearly a reversal of his earlier theory. His disappointment with the policy of *Estado Novo*, evident in the ability of the assimilados to provide the leadership of the liberation movement, created an entirely new climate that forced him to restrict the education of the Africans to practical training and manual labor. These were the elements of the original policy that the Portuguese colonial government formulated in 1898. By the time he suffered a massive stroke in 1968, Salazar had, in effect, invested more than a hundred million dollars in the education of Portuguese nationals and less than half that amount for the education of Africans.[40] The promise of improved educational progress he had made at the beginning of the Second World War in 1939 was never kept.

When, in 1967, UNESCO expressed serious concern about the lack of meaningful educational reform in both Angola and Mozambique, the farce of educational reform that Salazar had hailed as a blueprint of national development and as the envy of other colonial governments in southern Africa became clearly known. When Salazar argued that his government had increased spending for educational reform from 5.4 percent in 1964 to 9.5 percent in 1967, he neglected to mention that the bulk of this increase benefited the white students and the children of a few assimilados. The benefit to the average African student was quite negligible. It was only after both Angola and Mozambique had achieved full independence in 1975 that the full extent of the educational malaise under Portuguese colonial theory became known. Therefore, the notion of educational reform during the colonial period in southern Africa was not compatible with the universal purpose of reform because it was intended to benefit the political, social, and economic status quo, not to serve the educational development of Africans.

In South Africa, the purported educational reform began at the inception of independence in 1910 under the Afrikaners. Prior to that date education had been the responsibility of the church because the South African government had been quite indifferent to the educational development of Africans other than promoting practical training and manual labor. Because the church wanted Africans to be able to read and understand religious literature, it offered them religious education based on different theoretical considerations from those used by the government. For this reason, the church-related schools became more popular than government schools among Africans. This explains why, by 1945, there were 4,400 church-related schools compared to only 230 government schools.[41]

The governments were failing to reform the education of Africans for political reasons. In response, the government named a commission to supposedly investigate the question of education. When the commission submitted its report in 1936, it made no effort to hide its bias in supporting the theory of the government, saying, "The education of the white child must prepare him for life in a dominant society and the education of the Native child for a subordinate society. The limits of Native education must form part of the social and economic structure of society."[42]

That the government was pleased with this report suggests its unwillingness to seek a genuine improvement in African education, and it advanced a theoretical reason for its policy, saying, "The South African Native does not have the learning ability to be able to compete on equal terms with the average white student, except in tasks of an extremely simple nature."[43] It is therefore not surprising that by 1947 new theoretical perspectives were being expressed in an effort to uphold ideas of apartheid. In that year, the *National Educational Manifesto*, a private organization made of conservative Afrikaners who unreservedly supported the government of South Africa, issued a statement of new theoretical considerations, saying, "Education for Natives should be based on the principles of trusteeship, non-equality and segregation. Its aim should be to inculcate the white man's view of life and society."[44]

Peter Molotsi, an eminent South African scholar, concluded that the purported educational reform that the Bantu Education Act claimed to bring about was, in effect, a farce. Molotsi said,

Although the Bantu Education Act was hailed by the South African government as an improvement, it was persistently opposed by the African people because it was introduced in the name of reform. But it soon became apparent that it was actually guided by the bigotry of the Afrikaner Nationalists. The mission and sustained rejection of Bantu Education will render the whole diabolical scheme a self-deceiving exercise and futility, a misguided mission.[45]

The character of colonial educational reform in southern Africa leads to the conclusion that while the colonial establishment based its claim of educational reform on the theoretical assumptions that meant, in effect, an improvement of education for white students, it entailed elements of underdevelopment of education for Africans. What appeared to be an improvement in the educational structure was, indeed, a curtailment of the educational opportunities for Africans. This situation, therefore, demanded a new approach to the concept of reform after political independence was attained. But for South Africa, the agony of underdevelopment through a lack of genuine effort to reform education continued to take its toll. The development of the human resources it needed for the future was genuine political change, which took place in 1994. Until that year, it was unlikely that the Afrikaners would see the need for reform from a different angle.

THE NEED FOR A NEW THEORY

To accomplish their newly defined goals and objectives, the nations of Africa found it necessary to formulate entirely new theoretical considerations. In suggesting that the struggle for political independence entailed basic theoretical considerations about the role of education in enhancing the role of the individual in society, Dzingai Mutumbuka, who became Zimbabwe's first minister of education and culture after independence, expressed some ideas that were fundamental to the formulation of the elements of a new theory. In 1979, Mutumbuka said, "A new alternative system of education has been developing along a new theoretical perception that education must produce a new man richer in consciousness of humanity. This is the only way a new nation can make life better and more meaningful for all."[46]

The recognition by Africans that national development is impossible without an education designed to promote critical thinking and development of the individual has led to the formulation of a theoretical perspective to suit the demands of new conditions and times. This endeavor has taken on powerful dimensions, not only in Africa but also throughout the Third World. When Paulo Freire argued that all human beings, no matter how oppressed, are quite capable of engaging in constructive interaction with other people,[47] he is actually suggesting the elements of a new theory in the Third World that education should help define new forms of relationships between the individual and society. This relationship must not be assumed, but must be regarded as coming out of the application of a new theory that addresses the importance of educational reform.

To structure this kind of relationship properly, a theory of educational reform must be evolved to shape the direction of national development. Mutumbuka's concept of a person richer in the consciousness of humanity corresponds to Freire's idea of an education designed to promote human interactions intended to shape the emergence of a new social, political, and economic system. In that context, the position of the individual takes precedence over all other considerations. Increasingly, the nations of Africa are beginning to realize that without ensuring the position of the individual in a larger social context, it is virtually impossible to ensure the development and the security of the nation. This is why in 1990 there were widespread demonstrations throughout Africa against one-party or one-man forms of government.

In 1987, the Conference of Catholic Bishops in Zimbabwe outlined critical theoretical elements that appear to define the relationships between the individual and society, saying,

It is important for Third World nations, especially those of Africa, to recognize that the individual cannot find educational fulfillment without freedom to choose his own course of study. Where there is no clear orientation toward choice in education, educators are like the blind leading the blind. In this kind of setting society itself pays the ultimate price—underdevelopment.[48]

A high school principal in Zimbabwe seemed to agree when he said in 1983,

Educational reform must be designed to give all students the freedom to choose their own course of study. Freedom of choice translates into freedom to earn a decent income, to own a home and to be self-sufficient. These are the elements that construct a foundation upon which a good political, social, and economic system must be built. Without recognizing the freedom of the individual, society remains without a vision for the future. Without vision, social transformation is lost. This means that it is building its future on quicksand.[49]

One can see that the need felt by the African nations for a theory of educational reform to ensure the advancement of the individual as a prerequisite of national development suggests the need to embrace democratic principles, values, and practices. Unless African nations recognize the importance of operating by these values, any definition of national development they may try to utilize in their efforts is bound to have little meaning. Under these conditions, the entire endeavor may fail. The African nations face the enormous task of defining new theoretical elements to ensure their own development. To succeed in their endeavors, the African leaders must engage in a rigorous exercise of self-examination in which they put their nations' interests above those their own.

The responsibility of building nations must not be relegated to the political interests of the leaders. Rather, the task demands the total confidence of the people, and the people must not give their government their total confidence if they have reason to believe that the government is less than sincere in its efforts. The process of formulating a new theory of educational reform must go hand in hand with the process of formulating a new political theory under the principles of democratic behavior. Many African leaders still have to learn this simple basic principle. Until they do, their nations will continue to pay the price of underdevelopment characteristic of one-party government.

The attainment of political independence by Namibia on March 21, 1990, meant that of all the countries of southern Africa only South Africa was still under the influence of colonial forces as of that date.[50] The attainment of political independence in southern Africa also means that a new hope can emerge among Africans for real progress rooted in the dreams and aspirations that had been eluded by the unwillingness of the colonial governments to do something real in trying to reform the educational systems to serve the needs of all people. Although the nations of southern Africa soon recognized that it was relatively easier to fight to bring the colonial systems to an end than to initiate the much needed reform in education, they also recognized the imperative of such reform to ensure social change consistent with their aspirations. This recognition demanded the formulation of a new approach.

One sees that emerging nations of the Third World, especially southern Africa, are increasingly becoming aware that without education to sharpen the individual's consciousness of himself in order to enable him to acquire the skills that he needs to fulfill his own ambitions and aspirations, society itself remains unfulfilled and so underdeveloped. In 1977, the Education Commission in Botswana took this line of thinking to address the importance of enunciating elements of new theory of educational reform, saying, "The principal aim of education is to ensure the development of the individual. The individual is of unique value to society, and it is only through developing his capacities that society changes, not for change's sake, but to serve the needs of all people and so improve the quality of human life."[51]

One major reason why the nations of southern Africa are placing emphasis on having education focus on the development of the individual as a prerequisite of national development is that it enables the individual to play an important role in a collective endeavor to promote the development of society itself. It also helps the individual in defining and understanding what he needs to realize his own aspirations. Therefore, the importance of the individual in a larger social context has become the focus of the theory of educational reform in developing nations, because they believe that national development is possible only when individuals are fully developed. This perception represents a fundamental change from the theoretical perspective of the colonial governments.

The importance of the educational development of the individual in developing nations as a new theoretical consideration has been addressed in a context broader than southern Africa. Paulo Freire concludes that all human beings, no matter how oppressed, and so presumed ignorant, are capable of engaging in constructive interaction with other people. In this perspective, Freire is actually suggesting that without educational reform defined to promote the ability of the individual relative to his relationships with other people, society itself pays the ultimate price of underdevelopment.[52] Freire also seems to suggest that while the struggle for national liberation entails collective strategies and endeavors, its origin is an outcome of individual endeavor.

Similarly, the outcome of the collective struggle must, by its very nature, afford the individual the opportunity to set individual goals. Therefore, Mutumbuka's concept of a new educational theory to enable the individual to have a "richer consciousness of humanity" corresponds to Freire's theory that any education that fails to respond to the needs of the individual cannot possibly respond to the needs of the nation. If the colonial governments had operated under the premises of this theoretical consideration, an environment would have been created for finding solutions to the problems that developing nations are now grappling with.

When the Conference of Catholic Bishops decided that the educational development of the individual is the best way to ensure national development, they were addressing the fundamental importance of the educational development of the individual as a new theoretical perspective. In 1983, the principal of a high school in Harare expressed this perspective, saying,

Every state stands to benefit more than anyone else from its educated citizens. All governments have therefore a stake in the education of their people as individuals. The more the people are educated, the more they help create a happy society. Progressive governments recognize that by educating their people as individuals, they are actually creating conditions for social and political stability. Therefore, educational innovation must afford all students freedom to choose their own course of study. This will mean freedom to earn a decent income, to own a home, in essence, self-sufficiency. These are the elements that constitute a foundation upon which a good political and socioeconomic system must be built.[53]

President Robert Mugabe himself took this same line of thinking of theoretical perception of educational reform in the new era when he launched a national literacy campaign in July 1983, saying,

To set the mind free, to make observation and analysis accurate, to make judgment informed, objective and fair, to make imagination creative, are as important a cause of struggle for individual educational development as the collective struggle for political emancipation. Individual mental emancipation through educational innovation is both the major instrument and modality of political and economic emancipation, and cannot be taken for granted.[54]

This is also the line of theoretical perception that the late President Machel of Mozambique took into consideration when he argued in 1981 that a theory of educational reform in postcolonial southern Africa "must seek to strengthen social institutions by focusing on educational reform to meet the developmental needs of the individual"[55] as a prerequisite of national development.

The reader must not have a misconception that a new theory of educational reform in the nations of southern Africa is designed to promote the individual as an end in itself, because it is not. In this chapter, we have advanced the argument that the best route to national development is through the development of the individual. When the individual is able to meet his own needs, he is able to meet the needs of his society. The Conference of Catholic Bishops in Zimbabwe argued that a theory of educational reform must seek to make it possible for the nations of southern Africa to educate the individual so that he can respond to the needs of his society. It is true of many people in various societies that the individual should be educated to utilize his talents to meet the needs of his society because he is able to meet his own needs first.

It is the role of the governments of southern Africa to provide education to develop the competencies of each person. These will be compatible with the needs of the community as a whole. Conventional wisdom suggests that this cannot be done in the context of existing systems of education. Therefore, educational reform is the crown jewel of national development because it ensures the development of the individual.[56] What this perception of the theory of educational reform seems to imply is that the thrust for social transformation must result from carefully considered elements that must undergird the essential theoretical considerations of educational reform in terms of both focus and expected outcome.

SUMMARY AND CONCLUSION

The discussion in this chapter makes a clear distinction between the purpose of educational reform during the colonial period and theory of educational reform in southern Africa in the postcolonial era. The former stressed the development of Africans as a group who were educated to serve the needs of the colonial status quo. The latter must stress the importance of educational reform to serve the needs of the individual as a prerequisite of national development. Three basic conclusions arise from differences in the theoretical perceptions of these two. The first difference is that by emphasizing the importance of sustaining the colonial status quo, the colonial governments created a society in which, in the words of Bernard Chidzero, Zimbabwe's minister of finance and economic planning, "inequality was the very foundation of its structure underpinned and sustained by an inadequate educational system."[57] In this setting education, especially for Africans, became a mechanical exercise, void of any real meaning for the people whose needs it was intended to serve.

The second difference is that the inadequacy of the educational system during the colonial period created a critical demand for educational reform as an imperative condition of national development in postcolonial southern Africa. This reality has also demanded that the nations of southern Africa formulate new theoretical perspectives on educational reform to place emphasis on the development of the individual. To approach this task with a faint heart or without a clear focus would harm the very purpose for which reform must be initiated. The fact of the matter is that nations of southern Africa cannot afford not to initiate educational reform. Preserving colonial educational status quo would be tantamount to committing a national developmental suicide. Nations that fail to realize the importance of educational reform also fail to realize the importance of the educational development of the individual. This can submerge the aspirations of the people, and thus, of the nations themselves, to perilous depths of underdevelopment.

The third difference is that some Third World nations have yet to realize that educational reform is meaningless without a corresponding freedom of choice. Freedom to choose is itself an important component of democracy. Because the colonial governments did not allow freedom to choose, they did not practice democracy, contrary to their claim. In the nations of southern Africa, the recognition of the right of students to choose their course of study consistent with their needs and aspirations must translate into the practice of democracy in society itself. This is the context in which the nations of southern Africa must see the importance of theoretical consideration of educational reform from its proper perspective. In this regard, most emerging nations of southern Africa still have a long way to go, although some have made a good start. Chapter 6 presents some suggestions of the methods of initiating educational reform in contemporary southern Africa.

NOTES

1. The *Atlantic Charter*, August 14, 1941. Courtesy of the British Embassy, Harare, 1989.

2. King George VI (1895–1952), who was on the British throne from 1936 to 1952.

3. Martin Meredith, *The First Dance of Freedom: Black Africa in the Post-War Era* (New York: Harper and Row, 1984), p. 35.

4. Robert Manners, "Functionalism, Reliability, and Anthropology in Underdeveloped Areas," in Thomas Weaver [ed.], *To See Ourselves: Anthropology and Modern Social Issues* (Glenview, Ill.: Scott, Foreman and Company, 1973), p. 117.

5. Ironically, Jan Christiaan Smuts, the prime minister of South Africa, a country that would soon become notorious for its racial policy of apartheid, is credited with drafting the preamble.

6. Preamble to the UN Charter, June 26, 1945. New York: United Nations, 1991.

7. Letter dated March 14, 1991, from a student in Sierra Leone.

8. Philip H. Coombs, *World Crisis in Education: The View from the Eighties* (New York: Oxford University Press, 1985), p. 31.

9. Ibid., p. 32.

10. As of 1996, no nation had reached a 100 percent literacy. This does not mean that the goal cannot be reached.

11. Southern Rhodesia, *The Report of the Commission of Inquiry into Discontent in the Mangwende Reserve* (James Brown, Chairman) (Salisbury: Government Printers, 1961), p. 77.

12. Historians tend to argue that the policy of apartheid came into being in 1948 when the Nationalist Party came to power in South Africa. However, Dickson A. Mungazi argues in his study *The Struggle for Social Change in Southern Africa: Visions of Liberty* (New York: Taylor and Francis, 1989) that this policy was introduced in 1662, ten years after the Dutch settled at the Cape.

13. Ibid., p. 43.

14. Kenneth Knorr, *British Colonial Theories* (Toronto: University of Toronto Press, 1974), p. 378.

15. Paulo Freire, *Pedagogy of the Oppressed*. Translated by Myra Bergman Ramos (New York: Continuum, 1983), p. 28.

16. Charles Lyons, "The Educability of the Africans: British Thought and Action, 1835–1965," in V. M. Battle and C. H. Lyons, *Essays in the History of African Education* (New York: Teachers College Press, 1970), p. 9.

17. A letter to the *Rhodesia Herald*, June 28, 1912.

18. James Oldham, *White and Black in Africa* (London: Longman, 1930), p. 11.

19. Mungazi, *The Struggle for Social Change in Southern Africa: Visions of Liberty*, p. 23.

20. Dickson Mungazi, "The Change of Black Attitudes Towards Education in Rhodesia" (Ph.D. dissertation, the University of Nebraska, Lincoln, 1977), p. 52.

21. Cortland Cox, *African Liberation* (New York: Black Education Press, 1972), p. 82.

22. Kenneth Knorr, *British Colonial Theories*, p. 378.

23. Godfrey Huggins, "Partnership in Rhodesia," a political campaign speech, Ref. 12/03/51, March 13, 1951. By courtesy of the Zimbabwe National Archives.

24. Quoted in George Sparrow, *The Rhodesian Rebellion* (London: Brighton, 1966), p. 25.

25. Adam Curle, *Education for Liberation* (New York: John Wiley and Sons, 1973), p. 58.

26. Ibid., p. 60.

27. Albert Memmi, *The Colonizer and the Colonized* (Boston: Beacon Press, 1965), p. 9.

28. Ibid., p. 11.

29. Ibid., p. 12.

30. Ethel Tawse Jollie during a debate in the legislature in Southern Rhodesia, *Legislative Debates*, 1927.

31. Southern Rhodesia: Ordinance Number 18 of 1899: The Appointment of Inspector of Schools.

32. Southern Rhodesia: Ordinance Number 1, 1903.

33. Southern Rhodesia: Ordinance Number 7: Ordinance to Control Native Education, July 12, 1912.

34. Ibid.

35. Dickson A. Mungazi, "Educational Innovation in Zimbabwe: Possibilities and Problems," in the *Journal of Negro Education*, Vol. 54, No. 4 (1985), pp. 196–212.

36. Godfrey Huggins, "Education Policy in Rhodesia: Some Notes on Certain Features," campaign speech given in Salsburg, Rhodesia, 1939.

37. Samora Machel, *Mozambique: Sowing the Seeds of Revolution* (Harare: Zimbabwe Publishing House, 1981), p. 34.

38. Mungazi, *To Honor the Sacred Trust of Civilization: History, Politics, and Education in Southern Africa*, p. 95.

39. *New York Times*, May 31, 1961.

40. Mungazi, *To Honor the Sacred Trust of Civilization: History, Politics, and Education in Southern Africa*, p. 29.

41. Trevor Huddleston, *Naught for Your Comfort* (New York: Oxford University Press, 1956), p. 24.

42. South Africa, *The Report of the Inter-Departmental Commission on Native Education*, 1936.

43. T. M. Jansen van Rensburg, "The Learning Ability of the South African Native," in Nicholas Hans, *Comparative Education and Traditions* (London: Oxford University Press, 1958), p. 35.

44. Dennis Herbstein, *White Man, We Want to Talk to You* (London: Oxford University Press, 1979), p. 84.

45. Peter Molotsi, "Educational Policy and South African Bantustans," a paper presented at New York Association of African Studies, Empire State Plaza, Albany, NY, October 29–30, 1981. Mungazi attended this conference.

46. Dzingai Mutumbuka, "Zimbabwe's Educational Challenge," paper presented at the World Universities Services Conference, London, December, 1979. In the Zimbabwe National Archives.

47. Freire, *Pedagogy of the Oppressed*, p. 39.

48. Zimbabwe, Conference of Catholic Bishops, *Our Mission To Teach: A Pastoral Statement on Education* (Gweru: Mambo Press, 1987), p. 6.

49. A high school principal during an interview in Harare, Zimbabwe, August 8, 1983.

50. South Africa gained political independence in April 1994 when Nelson Mandela replaced F. W. de Klerk as president.

51. Botswana, *Report of the National Commission on Education*, 1977, p. 23.

52. Freire, *Pedagogy of the Oppressed*, p. 39.

53. A high school principal during an interview in Harare, Zimbabwe, August 8, 1983.

54. Robert Mugabe, "Literacy for All in Five Years," a speech given in launching National Adult Literacy Campaign, July 18, 1983. Quoted by permission of the Zimbabwe Ministry of Information.

55. Machel, *Mozambique: Sowing the Seeds of Revolution*, p. 35.

56. Zimbabwe, Conference of Catholic Bishops, *Our Mission to Teach: A Pastoral Statement on Education*, p. 7.

57. Bernard T. Chidzero, *Education and the Challenge of Independence* (Geneva: IEUP, 1977), p. 13.

6

Approaches to Educational Reform

The basic concept of change represents a powerful approach to educational reform.

Samora Machel, 1970

Educational reform must aim at first at sustaining the educational interests of the individual student as an approach to promoting national development.

Zambia, *Educational Reform: Proposals and Recommendations*, 1977

CONSIDERING CHANGE AS REFORM

In discussing the thrust for educational reform in southern Africa one must keep in mind that the concept of change as a method of seeking improvement in the existing system has always been an operative concept of human experience and endeavor. One can see that the concept has been essential, from the age of Nero through the religious reformation movement of Martin Luther, to the struggle for political independence in Africa and of the civil rights movement in the United States, both in the twentieth century. Human society has always embraced the concept of change, not for change's sake, but as a method of seeking improvement in the conditions that control human life and shape the character of society. The American author Philip H. Coombs suggests that any approach to change is meaningless unless it is directed toward seeking improvement or at making efforts to correct a situation that is less than adequate in serving human needs.[1]

The relationship that exists between the concept of change as a method of initiating reform and social transformation is the line of thinking that President Samora Machel took into consideration in urging his fellow Mozambicans in 1970 to recognize the critical nature of change as reform. He suggested that an effective approach that he regarded as the enormously important question of basic literacy must constitute a viable method of initiating educational reform to benefit the individual student as a condition of ensuring the development of the nation.[2] In the nature of the struggle that nations of southern Africa are engaged in, it is important to understand that without designing a set of approaches to educational reform, its entire structure and content may be lost. Approaches to educational reform require a deliberate articulation of basic operational themes to ensure desired outcomes. Machel seemed to understand this well.

In 1970, Machel addressed this importance, saying,

The main battle in the field of education is against illiteracy. If we are to succeed in our efforts to change and so improve our educational system, we must mobilize the masses in this battle, making them aware of the need to gain literacy and showing them the catastrophic consequences of illiteracy. This basic concept of change represents a powerful approach to educational reform, and we must approach it with all the urgency and the importance it requires. Without the active participation of the masses as part of the strategy for change in the battle against illiteracy, it will not be possible to wipe it out.[3]

The purpose of this chapter is to discuss some approaches that the nations of southern Africa can employ in initiating reform in their systems of education.

OPERATIONAL PRINCIPLES OF EDUCATIONAL REFORM

There are two essential elements of the approaches to educational reform that Machel discussed in his address in 1970 that require more than a casual discussion. The first element is that recognition of the problems constitutes an important approach to the concept of reform. That recognition enables the national leaders to make an accurate assessment of all the relevant problem areas of the existing system of education. This diagnostic exercise makes it possible to pinpoint the areas that need attention. This enables the nation to design appropriate approaches to finding solutions. For example, in many countries of Africa, the conflict between rural economy and urban economy presents a difficult problem of designing approaches for dealing with the resulting conflict.

To find solutions to this problem it is important to consider the problems posed by the rural economy, because nearly 80 percent of the entire population is rural. Philip H. Coombs suggests an approach to this problem, saying, "Rural children and youth in developing countries still have many essential learning needs. For them learning reading, writing, and arithmetic is especially important and can stand them in good stead throughout their life, wherever they end up."[4] Coombs goes on to argue that the recognition of the relationship that exists between the rural conditions of life and an urban setting forms a basic approach to educational reform.

The second critical element is the involvement of the people in seeking improvement through meaningful change. Without popular support and participation in any national endeavor, success cannot be assured. George Watson argues that success in seeking improvement in any national endeavor must entail the ability of national leaders to arouse a popular passion for meaningful change.[5] Therefore, the thrust for educational reform, as a major national endeavor, depends on the demonstrated commitment of the national leaders to inspire their people with confidence for the future and the enthusiasm they embrace in recognizing that they are an important part in the national effort to bring about change for the good of all. The national leaders must never underestimate the ability of the citizens to rise up and accept a challenge in a national cause, provided that this is done within the spirit of democracy and the free expression of ideas.

As one examines the thrust for educational reform in southern Africa, one sees seven basic principles that underlie any strategies to initiate it successfully. A brief discussion of each principle and the contributions they may make to any approach to successful educational reform follows. The first principle is that once the reform process has been initiated, it must be continued until positive or desired results begin to show. This suggests that educational reform must be a continuous process because conditions of human life continue to change. The continuous nature of educational reform must also take into account two principal aspects of it. The first aspect is that it must be initiated with specific objectives to determine success or failure. The second aspect is that it must entail graduated stages to ensure success of one stage before the next is attempted.

The second principle is that educational reform must originate from within, rather than from without. This means that the reform process must not be initiated by duplicating educational programs in other countries, because conditions are fundamentally different. Outside considerations, such as demands made by developed nations that nations receiving aid must abide by certain requirements as a condition of that aid, have the effect of minimizing the proper purpose of educational reform. In this setting, educational reform is undertaken with the express purpose of receiving the needed financial aid. For this reason, the fundamental goal of reform itself is lost in the conflict that emerges between the purpose of outside pressure groups, such as the World Bank and International Monetary Fund (IMF), and the intentions of the nation itself. Therefore, educational reform initiated as a response to outside pressure or demands loses its value and direction. Nations that offer assistance to developing nations in their effort to improve their systems of education must respect local national goals and objectives to retain their relevance.

The third principle is that reform must be initiated from a perspective of considering the best educational interests of the students as a prerequisite of promoting national development. This means that expediency and political benefit must never come into the picture. Along with this approach, those who initiate reform must operate under conditions of absolute honesty and conviction that what is being initiated reflects the express will of the people and the needs of the students. Once consideration of expediency and political benefit have been removed from the process of reform, the people and their government join hands in mutual trust and confidence, because a collective effort has gone into the decisions surrounding the thrust for reform, and the people do not feel exploited politically. This approach ensures that the best educational interests of the students have been taken into account.

The fourth principle is that an approach to reform is more effective and may yield tangible results if it is the product of an integrated approach. This ensures that cumulative effects are measured more accurately than those of a disintegrated approach. The integrated approach to reform eliminates haphazard methods so that one form of success may be recorded in one aspect of reform, while limited success may be recorded in another aspect. For example, an effort made to attain universal primary education leading to an improved literacy rate may disrupt efforts to reform technical or secondary education. An integrated approach would ensure that no aspect of reform is accomplished at the expense of another. Educational reform as a whole would suffer a setback if it is directed at some aspects and neglects others. An integrated approach would help take all relevant aspects into consideration.

The fifth principle is that reform demands national leaders who are well informed about the issues surrounding that reform. They must also know the environment in which it is cast. The system initiated by the colonial governments of appointing members of commissions to study ways of improving education from overseas[6] was a practice initiated under the assumption that the local people did not know the educational needs of their country as well as people in Europe did. Some nations of southern Africa have perpetuated this practice to the detriment of their efforts. We do not take the position that outsiders have nothing positive to contribute toward meaningful change in education, but that emerging countries ought to exercise more care than did the colonial governments in resorting to people outside the country to carry on major tasks because, no matter how good they may be, their knowledge of all the important conditions of the country is limited. This is likely to undercut the effect of their task.

The sixth principle is that reform must be undertaken at a basic or fundamental level. That is, to have the desired effect in its critical aspects, educational reform must begin at the beginning. If reform is sought at the college level, for example, it is a futile exercise to ignore the need for reform at the primary and secondary levels, because doing so would negate the integrated approach. Similarly, if reform is sought at the secondary level, it becomes meaningless if it ignores the need for reform at the technical or college levels. The concept of a basic or fundamental level also has two added advantages. The first advantage is that it makes it necessary to examine all the facts of reform from the integrated perspective. The second advantage is that it makes it possible to measure results. In this manner, superficial considerations of reform are eliminated.

The seventh and final principle under consideration is that the primary concern of reform must be to improve the system, rather than to see the promotion of individuals in one way or another. It is quite common in human nature to have an ulterior motive behind a national program. The programs initiated by the colonial governments in southern Africa often carried a hidden agenda to promote the political fortunes of those who were involved in them. This is why the Africans in Angola, Mozambique, and South Africa reacted negatively to national policies that were thrust under this environment. In Mozambique and Angola, national policies were designed to promote the political fortunes of Antonio Salazar, Marcello Caetano, and other colonial officials. In South Africa, the Bantu Education Act of 1953 had the effect of promoting the political stars of Daniel Malan, Hendrik Verwoerd, and John Vorster instead of ensuring the development of the African population.

The conclusion suggested is that the nations of southern Africa must remember that an approach to educational reform undertaken from the perspective of seeking to meet the needs of students, rather than to promote the political interests of certain individuals, is best designed to meet the developmental interests of the nation. Once this perspective becomes a modus operandi, it is possible to design a set of goals and objectives that are compatible with larger national goals. Therefore, directing the thrust for educational reform to national goals and objectives creates a national climate in which the formulation of purpose in the educational process itself carries a much more meaningful intent. The relationship between seeking improvement in the educational system and providing an opportunity for students to realize their own ambitions must remain the balancing rod of educational reform.

APPROACHES TO EDUCATIONAL REFORM

The observance of these seven principles does not, in itself, constitute educational reform, but when considered properly, they combine to form a set of approaches that would enable the nations of southern Africa to undertake that task with a clear direction toward intended outcomes. However, the nations of southern Africa must not assume that there is only one approach to educational reform, because a variety of them that can be adopted to suit different conditions and to meet specified objectives.

The adoption of any approach is determined by a combination of factors that must be put together to accomplish those objectives of national importance. In this chapter, we present seven approaches to educational reform, not suggesting that they are the only ones, but used only as examples. These are making an assessment of needs; formulating national and educational objectives; developing human resources; stabilizing and making education equitable; assessing existing education; seeking an end to the urban-rural conflict; integrating the curriculum; establishing priorities; and coordinating regional and national priorities.

INITIATING AN ASSESSMENT OF NEEDS

The initial stage of designing a method must involve a thorough assessment of needs before the reform process is undertaken. It is not feasible to undertake reform without conducting an assessment of needs. This exercise constitutes an important approach to educational reform. In undertaking this assessment of needs, it is necessary to determine exactly why reform must be initiated, the objectives to be accomplished, the time and resources needed to complete it, the expected outcomes, and the problems to be encountered and how they will be resolved. Unless all these factors are taken into consideration, the reform exercise has a potential for failure, and failure leads to frustration, and frustration poses serious national political implications. Therefore, an assessment of needs is an exercise that must be undertaken with absolute care. Once reform is undertaken as a result of conducting an assessment of needs, it must not be allowed to fail.

From the assessment of needs objectives can be formulated. An assessment of needs must also indicate the magnitude, the complexity and, indeed, the risk of having national interests subordinated to those of the individual learner because the entire reform process is initiated for the sole purpose of improving the quality of education for the individual. On the one hand, in succeeding to protect the educational interests of the individual, the educational process will protect national interests. On the other hand, seeking to protect national interests as the first priority does not necessarily protect those of the individual. Assessment of needs must take this reality into account if successful reform is to be initiated. In 1977, the Educational Reform Report of Zambia cautioned against the consequences of ignoring this fact, warning,

It is against this background that there have been many examples in the world of educational reform which did not succeed even though the idea behind it seemed valid and promised many benefits. Educational reform must aim first at sustaining the educational interests of the individual in order to promote national development. If educational reform aims at national development first, it fractures the wheel on which it must run, the importance of the individual.[7]

A fundamental principle of undertaking an assessment of needs must focus on the theory that behind every example of successful educational reform is an understanding that quite often, without taking all aspects of assessment of needs into consideration, efforts aimed at reform itself become a comedy of errors. This does not ensure success. The Lagos Conference of 1976 urged African nations to ensure that the needs assessment exercise was carried out with specific objectives in mind. The Lagos Conference stated, "In its content structures, operations, methods, costs, as indeed in its alternative aims, the educational system must remain close to the needs of the students before it can meet the needs of the nation. The assessment of needs must not seek to maintain the educational status quo, but to improve it in the way that the resulting education meets the needs of the students."[8]

A critical component of this assessment of needs must include some specific aspects of the educational process itself. Among these aspects must be determined the adequacy of facilities, especially the use of technology. They must also include the extent to which financial resources are available to meet the needs. They must also include an adequate supply of teachers who are adequately trained to meet the needs of students in a variety of settings. These include social, emotional, psychological, the role of the people, and, of course, academic settings. It is important for those who are responsible for educational reform to remember that problems of society are becoming more complex and that they can no longer be resolved by traditional methods. They must remember that making an assessment of educational needs is an inclusive process that demands detailed articulation of all factors related to the educational process of the learner. The social, emotional, spiritual, intellectual, and economic welfare must be modeled in the classrooms.

ASSESSING THE EXISTING EDUCATIONAL SYSTEM

It must also be remembered that assessment of needs as part of a strategy for educational reform entails evaluation of the existing system of education. In all countries of southern Africa, the emphasis that is placed on universal primary education has yielded limited results for a number of reasons. The increase in population has translated into an unprecedented increase in enrollment at the primary level. This has not produced a corresponding increase in financial resources and facilities to accommodate the increase. While the cost of providing primary education is less than that of providing secondary and higher education, the enrollment figures themselves place heavier demands on financial resources at the primary level than at the other two levels.[9] Therefore, an evaluation of the existing system of education would help facilitate understanding of political national priorities and economic support of the process of planning financial resources to be allocated to different levels of education to undertake successful reform. In 1977, the Botswana Commission on Education concluded that failure to make an accurate evaluation of the existing system of education as an approach to educational reform "is similar to the farmer who eats his seed corn now. He may be fed today, but he will be hungry tomorrow."[10]

An essential component of conducting evaluation of the existing system of education as a part of an approach to educational reform is to view the educational needs of students in terms of the manpower needs of the country. Conditions direct attention from the need for developing national resources to conditions that dictate the nature of approach to the educational reform in response to basic considerations of educational development of the students, which defines the direction that the reform itself must take. This approach is often based on the assumption that it provides useful guidelines to the country in its initial stage of reform and stresses the importance of focusing on the fundamental importance of placing control of the process under collective responsibility. Collective responsibility ensures that all relevant facts have been taken into account in planning effective reform action.

The manpower approach also requires making projections about the number of trained teachers required by a given time. In the same way, it is important to know the needed number of medical people, the needed number of medical institutions, and the level of competency required to operate various institutional infrastructures. Having this information must be taken into consideration to initiate educational reform. This can be done on the basis of improving existing facilities while new ones are being created so that inadequacies that currently handicap development are eliminated without creating a break in the flow of the educational process. This approach has the advantage of not confusing students about the direction that their education is taking. In 1977, the Botswana Commission on Education saw this approach as offering advantages to the educational system, observing, "Areas of employment, political decision, teaching and medical services afford manpower planners an opportunity to estimate the future demand for staff with different types of specialized training."[11]

Another important feature of evaluating the existing system of education to initiate effective reform is to practice openness and candor in this exercise of national self-examination to allow full participation of the people. Openness will encourage interaction by politicians, professionals, and ordinary people in the community. This consultation process has advantages that are not fully understood as an approach to educational reform. It creates a climate of mutual trust and acceptance of new ideas. It implies the decision to observe democratic principles. It makes it possible for citizens to understand and appreciate the national efforts to improve education by having educated decisions made by literate citizens. It creates an environment of trust between the people and the government in their mutual desire to cooperate. It enables the people to have the sense of belonging so crucial to the success of national endeavors and programs. It generates a new level of confidence and esteem, because the government remains committed to democratic principles in its relationships with the people. The painful exercise in self-criticism, which an evaluation of the existing system entails, must be shared by all to have its desired effects recognized.

Assessment of the existing system of education must also include an examination of the impact of the problems that national development might have on reform. Among these problems is resistance to change by some people, especially for political reasons. Therefore, taking political considerations into account is an important approach to educational reform. One way of resolving the problem of resisting reform is creating a constitutional provision that makes political accountability part of the duties of those who hold public office. They have to discharge accountability to their constituencies. In 1984, the World Bank suggested that it also makes it possible for "all parties to discuss key issues, whether or not there is an immediate requirement for legislative action and assures that politicians are exposed to the analysis of professionals and members of the public, and that the constraints and opportunities the nation faces are fully discussed."[12] This approach ensures politicians do not exercise veto power or undue controlling influence over the processes of innovation, change, or reformation.

Any assessment of the existing system of education that does not take into account the projected rate of economic growth in relation to projected population growth rate can give a false picture of critical factors surrounding educational reform. The rate of economic growth enables the nation to make appropriate budgetary allocation to the various items related to national growth rate, such as gross national product or per capita income. Important factors related to the rate of economic growth include the rate of inflation, foreign trade to facilitate foreign currency flow, and the rate of unemployment. All these factors indicate that the nations of southern Africa must remember that they simply cannot afford a haphazard approach to educational reform because it is crucial to efforts directed at national development.

Taking the rate of economic growth as an approach to educational reform demands demonstrated fiscal responsibility in two critical areas of national development. The first area is exercising expenditure control so that the citizens are not overtaxed. This implies that as soon as funds have been released as a result of budgetary allocation, an efficient and properly structured process of spending must be initiated in a prudent economical manner and a sociatically generous distribution in grades K to adult. A national finance unit must be instituted to assist the accounting officials in discharging their fiscal responsibility and to ensure proper collection and disbursement of revenue in the first place. This would make sure that accurate financial records are kept to reflect equally correct expenditures designated by the legislature itself.

The system of checks and balances that this process provides also acts as a deterrent to corruption, a serious problem among Third World nations. It should be a standard procedure in all the countries of southern Africa that, by the constitutional nature of his duties and responsibilities, the auditor-general be required to ensure that the financial books are audited regularly. The responsibility of overseeing finances and the responsibility of implementing strategies must be shared among several high-level government departments. The introduction of this system would ensure that actual payments are made and records kept in more than one department.

Any liabilities or costs for services rendered or goods delivered would be entered in the ledger books of each department and receipts would be kept by each department involved in the transaction. When auditing is carried out, a careful check of all records would be made to see that they matched exactly. If they do not, it becomes relatively easy to trace where the error is. The net result of this process is that if the system is stalled at the time plans are being formulated, it provides clear knowledge of expectations. Furthermore, the temptation for corruption is reduced when those who hold large sums of money are charged with the responsibility of discharging them. Therefore, the processes of reform, innovation, and change can have a much more reasonable chance of success.

The second area relates to monitoring expenditure, not only in the cost of educational reform but also in all areas of national fiscal responsibility. With reference to how economic growth determines whether or not educational innovation succeeds, the World Bank concludes that the efficiency of a national system of management of finances as a measure of the rate of economic growth gives a clear picture of the overall financial situation that must be carefully watched to ensure that cost overruns do not occur.[13]

Another critical consideration in the process of financial management is the nature of the relationship that exists between two components of the national budget. These are the recurring budget and the development budget. In many Third World nations, a deficit occurs when expenditure exceeds revenue. This often arises from unexpected increases in expenditures on new projects or expenditures caused by extended drought, refugees, or major civil strife, all of which most nations of southern Africa have experienced. Therefore these nations need to be conscious of the fact that to accommodate the rate of economic growth so that a steady flow of finances is sustained for national developmental projects, recurring budgetary items pose financial implications that must be assessed accurately at the time they become noticed and they must become part of the national expense.

It is equally important for the nations of southern Africa to be aware of the fact, as the World Bank put it in 1984, that "While the critical constraint upon national development is the lack of trained manpower,"[14] the lack of manpower itself is a consequence of failing to make an accurate projection of the rate of economic growth. This failure inhibits the ability of nations to ensure adequate fiscal management. If the thrust of educational innovation is to be a successful national endeavor, it must take all these financial implications into consideration. As an approach to educational reform, an assessment of manpower needs must take into account projections of population increase, gross national product, and educational outcomes and national objectives.

RECOGNIZING THE NEED TO DEVELOP HUMAN RESOURCES

A major approach to educational reform in southern Africa is embracing the concept of human resources development. All governments need to recognize that an important component of the educational process is the acceptance of the importance of developing the technical and scientific skills of the people. This must be done under the assumption that nations need trained people to run institutions. In essence, this represents a different approach to innovation from what is intended by the formal educational process. Zimbabwe appeared to recognize the essential character of this approach when it concluded, "The nature and character of practical experience that the individuals acquire in the course of their daily economic activities are an important factor of human resources development and form a critical component of a strategy for improvement."[15]

One must add, however, that the various dimensions in which people gain such experience depend, to a very large extent, on the level of their involvement in the formulation and implementation of development plans, such as the formulation of their constitution. This suggests the conclusion that at the initial phase of formulating developmental plans, the knowledge of and proper attitude toward institutional operational process constitutes an ideal environment that helps emerging nations appreciate that the change that is being initiated is intended for their own benefit. This level of understanding makes education far more meaningful than placing emphasis on formal educational innovation alone.

It is true that all levels of formal education transmit experiences and knowledge of the real world and so enhance the ability of citizens to understand the human condition from a proper perspective. But it is the concept of human resources development that enables students to accept change as an imperative of national development. It molds their attitudes toward the world of work and so helps them accept the concept of change in a manner that translates into a realization of larger social conditions that must not be taken for granted. The development of adequate health conditions, proper nutrition, proper housing, agriculture, sanitation, and a healthy work environment must all be understood as essential components of human resources development.[16] Their acceptance also means acceptance of important features of an approach to educational reform.

SEEKING TO END URBAN-RURAL CONFLICT

In southern Africa, as in most Third World nations, differences in educational facilities and economic opportunity form the basis of social and economic conditions that translate into differences between rural and urban areas. What many nations do not seem to understand is that neglecting the development of rural areas is tantamount to neglecting the development of 80 percent of the population. The question is, What strategies can the nations of southern Africa adopt to solve the problems of rural-urban contradiction? To find the answer to this question it is necessary to discuss the problem of land holding during the colonial period. Throughout southern Africa, the best land for the conditions of human settlement were reserved for white farmers who employed Africans as cheap labor. A network of urban centers, such as Bulawayo and Harare in Zimbabwe, Johannesburg and Cape Town in South Africa, Maputo and Beira in Mozambique, Lusaka and Ndola in Zambia, was developed to facilitate transport and distribution of agricultural products in markets that the colonial entrepreneurs controlled.

To have this land, the colonial legislatures passed laws that made Africans in both urban and rural areas foreigners who had to depend on the white man for economic survival. In the urban areas, they were employed in factories, and in the rural areas, they were employed as laborers. Such laws as the Land Act of South Africa of 1913 and the Land Apportionment Act in Zimbabwe of 1929 effectively deprived the Africans of any land rights. They were forced into crowded patches of desolate land that "consisted of poor land with a generally less favorable natural environment, inferior possibilities for development of productive infrastructures, demographic densities, and a suboptimal settlement pattern. This inferior socioeconomic space was forced upon the Africans by the colonial governments."[17]

Because the colonial farmers were interested only in the profit that came from their agricultural enterprise, they did not endeavor to develop the land or the Africans in any way. Therefore, they neglected education, health services, and other social and economic aspects of their life. It was not surprising, for example, that during the rainy season, all family members, including children, were forced to work on tobacco farms. Any educational activity was suspended and the teacher became a supervisor of students working on the farm. The colonial governments enacted laws to protect the farmers who became managers of schools on their property. The establishment of schools on farms owned by the farmers was itself a strategy for enhancing the supply of cheap labor. This is how tobacco farmers became wealthy landowners. In Zimbabwe names like B. D. Goldberg, A. M. Tredgold, Ian D. Smith, Winston Field, and Godfrey Huggins became synonymous with the political power that wealth accrued to the white farmers.

In urban areas, tobacco auction sales floors captured the imagination of business enthusiasts who made a fortune by taking risks. Investment in building industry boosted the romance and the adventure of many whites to the extent that laws were soon passed to make Africans foreigners also in urban areas.[18] Godfrey Huggins, the prime minister of colonial Zimbabwe from 1933 to 1953, explained in 1937 why such a law was necessary, saying, "Our municipal areas must not be polyglotted with a mixture of black and white. We must proceed with the policy of segregation to keep our urban areas as white as possible. The Native is a visitor to our cities for the purpose of serving the whites who live there."[19]

One unfortunate outcome of the rural-urban contradiction that emanated from the policies of the colonial governments in all of southern Africa is that in neglecting the development of both the rural and the urban areas, rural Africans suffered from a systematic stagnation in their advancement efforts and urban Africans suffered from an array of social dysfunctions that the colonial governments failed to foresee. Beginning with the influenza of 1917, the problems of sanitation, food supply, transport, housing, and deterioration in health care all combined to create a sociatic environment that made urban areas unpleasant and unsafe places for Africans to live and work.

By 1923, conditions all over southern Africa had deteriorated so badly that church leaders took it upon themselves to warn, "The whole life is a scourge of disease. Every epidemic flourishes and until there is a meeting of the minds between the officials and the Natives about what must be done to improve the situation and solve the handicapping differences between the rural areas and urban areas hope cannot be held for an improvement. This situation threatens the entire population."[20] The rural Africans were faring no better.

A. J. Wills aptly described the problem, the dilemma of choice that the educational policies of the colonial governments forced Africans to encounter in being denied the opportunity for adequate education and rural training programs, saying, "By assuming that African agricultural produce was inferior to white produce the colonial officials created a bias against rural development. At the same time it expressed displeasure for an academic education because the qualified Africans would be knocking at the doors of society which would not find suitable employment opportunity for them."[21]

Due to years of neglect, the rural-urban contradiction that the policies of the colonial governments created became an accepted sociatic, economic, and systemic problem. When new independent nations were born, their leaders found the problems so complex that they decided not to try to do anything to solve them. "They felt that this was better than trying to do so and create an impression among the people that their governments were incompetent because they would not be able to solve problems of national development."[22] But by failing to grapple with a major national problem, the independent nations of Southern Africa compounded it. They preferred to blame the colonial governments rather than to accept the reality that the responsibility had to be placed squarely on their shoulders to solve it now rather than blame and shame the past.

The strategy for resolving rural-urban contradiction to ensure educational reform evolves around the application of simple principles. These include a thorough assessment of needs, especially those of the rural areas, because they have been neglected for many years. They also involve formulating objectives, not only to ensure their educational development but also to restructure the entire socioeconomic system itself. This will enable them to become viable. The fact of the matter is that the problems of rural-urban contradiction are so severe that nothing less than a radical approach will do. But a radical approach does not in any way mean a predawn revolution. Rather, it means a steady process of the complete transformation of the system because it has inhibited the ability of the nations of southern Africa to initiate meaningful reform.

The application of these principles also means that the nations of southern Africa must recognize the importance of regional cooperation as a strategy for solving rural-urban contradiction to initiate innovation and design reform. Regional cooperation would generate sufficient resources, both human and financial, needed to initiate reform. This also makes it possible to consult each other on investment and development policies, because the problems of development are quite similar. It would also offer incentives to the local people for participation. In this process, three considerations are critical. These are: ensuring that the need and all aspects of reform are fully understood and accepted by the local people, assessing the necessity of national assistance to rural areas to enable them to reach a functional level of eventual autonomy, and developing sufficient technological manpower and know-how to tap resources needed for development.[23]

There is no question that the sociatic aspects of society, that is, educational opportunity, health services, and community development, are at the center of the rural-urban contradiction. It is equally true that these pose one of the most serious challenges to efforts directed at national development. As long as African nations bend under the weight, or the price tag, of solving these problems, the entire movement for educational innovation and national development itself loses both its purpose and the direction it must take. For nations of southern Africa, therefore, this is a call it must answer, a challenge they must accept. The result of evading that challenge will inevitably perpetuate the scourge of underdevelopment that has been inherited from the colonial period and perpetuated by a self-determined postcolonialism.

Among the areas of national focus is an effort to resolve problems of rural-urban contradiction as part of an approach to educational reform. The land resettlement programs, reform and expansion of structures of supplementary services including research, and extension of agricultural development are areas receiving national/political and economic attention. These would create local markets, create a new credit system, and facilitate the flow of capital,[24] all of which are essential to local development. Educational innovation that is initiated under these conditions stands a much more improved chance of success than in other settings of rural life.

Other areas of focus in the rural-urban conflict include improving the production of free cooperative enterprise, the development of water resources, reformation of local industries to generate internal capital flow, and capital investment, which is be needed to support educational reform. One must conclude that the ability of the nations of southern Africa to seek solutions to problems of rural-urban conflict constitutes an important component of approaches to educational reform. This approach indicates the necessity to coordinate efforts on a national level to ensure success, not only of educational reform but also of the thrust for national and regional development as a whole. Without this coordination, those efforts will be fragmented and flow along worn, polluted economic and sociatic paths of the past.

SEEKING REFORM OF THE CURRICULUM

Educational reform is meaningless unless it takes some critical factors into account; this is now apparent. An important additional consideration is that educational reform is also meaningless unless one of its major purposes is to transform the curriculum so that it is in accord with the demands of the times. This is one of the major tasks of innovation that the nations of southern Africa have either failed to accomplish or have simply not attempted to initiate because they are afraid to fail. This is why they have found it easier to maintain the curriculum designed by the colonial governments with only cosmetic alterations than to initiate fundamental reform. But the nations of southern Africa fail to realize that however difficult the task may be, it is one that must be undertaken.

There are six basic principles that must guide efforts toward innovation of the curriculum. The first is that a new curriculum must reflect an environment structured to facilitate the emergence of a set of dynamic ideas intended to ensure progressive education suited to the needs of the students and of a new era. This means that an educational system designed to meet the needs of students, their need for fundamental education, also meets the needs of the country. The two objectives, career choices and opportunities for personal growth, become compatible only when the educational interests of the students come first. In this kind of setting, the educational process makes it possible for its recipients to express "the values and aspirations of all the people based on the principle of total equality."[25]

The second principle is that the fundamental objective of education is to enable the individual to function fully in his environment, to be secure in his personhood, to see himself as an important contributing member of society, and to help shape the direction of its development. Only the individual who is secure in his personhood is able to see the problems of his society from a broader perspective than is otherwise possible. Only a curriculum that provides an education to the individual to ensure his security will eliminate the elements of national conflict. Therefore, to adequately prepare the individual to play this important role, reform must be initiated based on this principle.

The third principle is that the new curriculum must entail essential elements of innovation that would mean, inter alia, the ability of all students to comprehend the diversity of human interests and aspirations. Without taking this diversity into consideration, society loses the emergence of new ideas and a variety of perceptions necessary for its own development. This demands that the curriculum become flexible enough to accommodate this important diversity of interests. Once the opportunity is there, it offers different people an opportunity to pursue different professional goals. This is how society benefits from the education of its members. To enable it to accomplish this objective, the curriculum must be innovated.

The fourth principle is that because education in the colonial period was designed to sustain the colonial status quo, a fundamental change must now occur to redirect its development along the lines that lead to a new era of human endeavor and interaction. The elitist character of the colonial educational policy must be replaced by the application of the principle of equality of educational opportunity. This is essential to the development of the talent that manifests in every student and that the nation needs as a critical resource to ensure its development. Maintaining a curricular status quo hurts the purpose for which education exists.

The fifth principle of curriculum innovation is that because the colonial educational system had the effect of divide and rule, the aim of the new educational system must be to enable all students to realize the concept of unity of purpose. The educational objectives of the individual students and those of the nation must be compatible. The only way in which this essential balance can be achieved is by designing a curriculum that is different from that of the colonial period. It is important for the nations of southern Africa to remember that an effective implementation of this kind of curriculum demands deliberately careful collective action. It must never be imposed. The excuse that many national leaders in Africa give for imposing new programs is that the people are not sufficiently educated to understand the process of change. This merely hides their real intent and their paternalistic behavior. This behavior undercuts the very purpose of the endeavor for meaningful change and must be avoided at all costs.

The sixth principle of reform in the curriculum is that because the capacities of students to learn and muster concepts in general develop at different rates,[26] the new curriculum must be reoriented toward suiting this reality. The application of this principle can be achieved by individualized instruction, selecting classes, counseling methods, group or cooperative learning activities, informal instruction, and placing less emphasis on learning to pass public examinations. The challenge of the nations of southern Africa is to accept these principles as essential components of educational innovation lest they inflict harm to the educational process by failing to recognize the imperative of innovation.

The acceptance of these principles would assist in designing a new curriculum that has the components of the objectives of a new era. Instead of teaching misconceptions such as "Cecil John Rhodes was the founder of Rhodesia," "David Livingstone was the first man to discover the Victoria Falls," or "the Africans were uncivilized until the white man came," the new curriculum would help students reach conclusions such as "although the colonial governments invaded the African society on the assumption that it was primitive and uncivilized, the Africans themselves refused to be what the colonial government officials said they were, primitive and uncivilized."

This simple approach has wider implications as a method of educational reform than appears on the surface. It revives the essence of a new sense of pride and positive self-image that were distinct characteristics of Africans before colonization. Even the age of slavery could not destroy these two human qualities. Once these qualities are instilled in students, a new breed of people will emerge to help chart a new course in the struggle for national development. This new thinking about the curriculum would seek to create three new conditions that promote educational reform more efficiently than the colonial condition created. The first condition is that it would transform the educational system from seeking to produce a new elite to providing a broad-based education that makes realization of the concept of equality possible. The second condition is that it would help students in relating the educational process to real-life situations. The third condition is that it would help strengthen a new cultural and national identity.[27]

RECOGNIZING THE NEED TO ESTABLISH PRIORITIES

Important features of any approach to educational reform must of necessity involve the establishment of national priorities. This is a very difficult task in light of the fact that there are great educational needs that must all be met in southern Africa. Without priorities, however, any efforts directed toward meaningful change may be futile because the implementation of reformation plans may lose direction if they are spread too thin. The nations of southern Africa need to consider the following questions in determining their priorities: What is the greatest educational need right now? Is it primary education, secondary education, adult education, higher education, or vocational and technical education? What are the consequences of failing to establish priorities in the first place? What is the best method of financing reform, and how much would it cost? What agents can be used in implementing reform plans? What other national resources are needed for successful reform? How long will it take to implement these plans? What objectives must direct the course of reform? What are the outcomes of reform?

Finding answers to these questions suggests two critical aspects of educational reform itself. The first is that detailed plans must be made before reform is attempted. The second aspect is that the formulation of such plans demands collective action. This means that plans cannot be worked out overnight, but must take a considerable amount of time and energy to complete. The danger is that if too much time elapses, people will lose their enthusiasm, and the whole plan may go down the drain. It is therefore important that leadership of tested ability and integrity be part of the planning exercise of the strategy for an innovative approach to educational reform.

Because the establishment of national priorities varies from one country to another, this aspect of educational reform may be harder to coordinate at the regional level than other aspects. The needs are so divergent that trying to coordinate programs may yield only marginal results. But with a comparatively low rate of literacy, it seems that all nations may need to place both adult education and universal primary education at the top. This is why the National Commission on Education in Botswana stated in 1977, "Of all the levels and types of education it has been asked to consider, this commission feels bound to accord the highest priority to the improvement and reform of the primary level. Despite the expansion achieved, the sizable resources allocated to it, and the untiring efforts of many devoted teachers and administrators, this sector of the educational process is in disarray."[28]

In reaching this finding, the Botswana Nationaal Commission on Education deliberately examined the evidence that suggested the conclusion that primary education, considered from any perspective, was the most important level of education because "it is the foundation on which further learning is based, and opens up to the young person a range of opportunities for further study and work which are closed to the uneducated."[29] Indeed, under proper influence, the students' characters, their study and work habits, attitudes, and potential begin to form at the primary school level.

In addition to this, the concept of nation-building so important to all nations, begins to take shape at the primary level as the school process helps implant in the students a sense of belonging to a wider social order so that they come to understand and appreciate the full meaning of what it means to be part of a national endeavor to sustain national development. But this is not to suggest that primary education must be placed at the top of the priorities, but only to advance an argument in favor of doing so. One can make a similar case for adult literacy or vocational and technical education. Priorities must be established also by considering all possible options and through a collective process; they must not be imposed.

COORDINATING NATIONAL AND REGIONAL PROGRAMS

The inauguration of the African Economic Community (AEC) in 1980 was a development that boosted the morale of the Organization of African Unity (OAU) in the struggle for political and economic independence.[30] In April 1980, the black-ruled countries of southern Africa created an organization known as the Southern African Development Coordination Conference (SADCC) in accordance with the guidelines of the OAU, not only for the purpose of ensuring economic independence from South Africa but also to sustain the momentum in the continuing effort to create new conditions for their development. The SADCC drew its authority and initiated its sociatic, economic, and political programs from the authorization of the OAU, under-scoring the importance of the OAU's original objectives. SADCC had four essential objectives:

1. To eliminate economic dependence on South Africa.
2. To build an operational and equitable infrastructure and integration of the various segments of the economic system.
3. To mobilize national resources and cooperate with other black-ruled countries in their developmental efforts.
4. To engage in joint action to secure international support to isolate South Africa economically.[31]

The OAU and the SADCC believed that the realization of these objectives would hasten the creation of the new conditions of social reform. This suggests the extent to which both organizations were committed to the concept of change as reform. South Africa's fear of this possible isolation explains its acceptance of the so-called Sullivan principles and its efforts to attract foreign investments, especially from Western nations. Realizing that South Africa's refusal to see reform in the way the African nations did, both the OAU and the SADCC refused to cooperate. In this regional endeavor to coordinate their own programs outside the control of South Africa, both organizations put in place a new and powerful approach to reform.

Whereas South Africa believed that the SADCC posed no real threat to its economic power, this approach to the problems of southern Africa had aroused an international outcry against any action by any member of the international community that could be interpreted as helping to sustain the last vestiges of the colonial system that South Africa represented. The OAU and the SADCC had achieved a major part of their objective of bringing about an understanding of the need for reform. A critical aspect of the SADCC is that it was designed to function as a supranational structure that would handle issues related to the restoration and preservation of that distinctive African cultural and economic identity uniquely structured to accelerate the end of the colonial system. In cooperating with both the OAU and the AEC in advancing the cause of national sovereignty in the subcontinent enshrined in political independence and social and economic development, SADCC was trying to sustain a fundamental tenet of its charter and to fulfill its task of creating a regional climate for social change to occur.

Regardless of the enthusiasm with which it approached its responsibilities, however, the SADCC faced the major problem of trying to minimize differences in the level of national development of its members. By 1985, some countries of southern Africa, such as Tanzania and Zimbabwe, had a sound educational base; others, such as Mozambique and Angola, did not.[32] The countries of southern Africa fully recognized that unless they made collective efforts to coordinate programs at the regional level, any efforts made toward reform would yield marginal results.

The SADCC was also important in the struggle for initiating change as an approach to reform in another vital respect. The development of trade policy and self-reliance among all the black-ruled countries of the region ushered in a phenomenon that had not been tried in the past. Efforts to cooperate in building infrastructures, to engage in economic planning, to develop a viable agricultural policy, to overcome competition from the multinational corporate enterprises, and to pose a threat to surrogate states of South Africa at the time, such as Malawi and Lesotho, only occurred when members of the organization demonstrated a complete understanding of its purpose and when they had proved their commitment to the success of its mission. Therefore, the creation of the SADCC was a milestone in the struggle to bring the colonial system to an end.

For the SADCC to recognize the importance of its role in promoting change in individual countries the region as a condition of their development meant that coordinated efforts had to be made. Financing development projects had to be done on a bilateral basis. To this end, we believe that a new regional development bank needs to be established with sufficient flexibility to allow the development of national monetary policies. This is important in giving coherence to regional monetary policies that may facilitate efforts to meet the cost of educational reform. Such a development would do two things. The first thing is that it would do would be to serve notice to countries still in the state of civil strife, such as Mozambique and Angola, that, unless they directed their efforts toward a national purpose, they would be left out of regional developmental planning and programming.

The second thing is that it would offer a viable alternative to foreign investors who derive huge financial profit from their entrepreneurship in the region, especially the extraction of minerals. The additional investment would ensure social, financial, and political stability. This would allow a greater rate of educational reform and would strengthen the economy of the region as a whole. Combined with investment in the economic development of the region, which all nations wish to sustain, this would accelerate the reform process itself. The essential question that must be answered is: To what extent would the SADCC hope to exercise control of the economic development of the region? Such international agents as the IMF and the World Bank may not permit competition from a group of developing countries that they have helped. Indeed, if the SADCC would have a positive influence on the economic development of its member states and if it can succeed in convincing foreign investors that investing in developing programs entails careful planning, the IMF and the World Bank would be persuaded to recognize it as a viable alternative to programs that yield high profit by exploiting the resources of the region for the benefit of foreign investors.

If the SADCC were successful in this endeavor, then it would place itself in a position to respond to a more challenging call. Educational reform in the region is an imperative. Educational reform can be costly in terms of resources, both financial and personal, but a start has to be made with existing resources. No country on its own has sufficient resources to bring about the reform that it may be seeking. Then, every effort must be made to resolve duplication and wastage. Before reform is initiated, the SADCC can play a critical role in laying the groundwork and forming a clearinghouse of information in the form of making detailed plans of action. It can help in coordinating the reform programs themselves. It can make sure that the resources of one region or national agent are sufficient to finance the projects. It can make it possible for all the parties to sustain their level of energy. It can make it possible to offer advice on the need to exercise constraints or control on spending and avoid cost overruns. Finally, the SADCC can help in ensuring that reform plans are implemented within a reasonable time frame.

SUMMARY AND CONCLUSION

The discussion in this chapter leads to two basic conclusions. The first conclusion is that there is a variety of approaches that the nations of southern Africa can take to educational reform. This chapter did not exhaust them all, it discussed only some specific examples as options that can be used to suit the specific needs of different countries. The fact that has been stressed in this chapter is that educational reform cannot be initiated without careful planning and coordination. That planning constitutes a specific approach to reform is a critical factor of its success. Because reform is so crucial to national development, it must be a product of careful consideration of all the relevant factors.

The second conclusion is that whatever approach is adopted, or is a combination of a number of them are utilized, it is essential to take all factors into account in planning and implementing educational reform. No matter how adequate an approach is, it is ineffective if inadequate considerations or conditions surrounding it are forced to surrender to other factors. Designing approaches to successful educational reform takes two critical elements into consideration. The first element is a collective approach to ensure that it has the support of all people. Without that support success in implementing reform plans cannot be ensured. The second element is that reform must be accomplished within a reasonable amount of time. This is where a regional agent such as the SADCC can play a crucial role. These two elements must supplement each other to make sure that implementation is not hurriedly put in place. Once these two elements become operative components of educational reform, they can help reduce the possibility of failure because every other aspect will have been accommodated.

NOTES

1. Philip H. Coombs, *World Crisis in Education: The View from the Eighties* (New York: Oxford University Press), p. 117.

2. Machel, "Educate Man to Win the War, Create New Society, and Develop a Country," September 1970.

3. Ibid.

4. Coombs, *World Crisis in Education: The View from the Eighties*, p. 55.

5. George Watson, *Change in School Systems* (Washington, D.C.: National Training Laboratories, NEA, 1967).

6. For a detailed discussion of this practice and the problems it created in the educational process in Africa, see, for example, Dickson A. Mungazi, *Education and*

Government Control in Zimbabwe: A Study of the Commissions of Inquiry, 1908–1974 (New York: Praeger Publishers, 1990).

7. Zambia, *Educational Reform: Proposals and Recommendations*, October, 1977.

8. UNESCO, "Education in Africa in the Light of the Lagos Conference," Paris, France, 1976.

9. This is the reason why Zimbabwe, for example, provided free primary education from 1981 to 1992, but was unable to continue beyond that date. This has created serious problems. A letter that we received on February 21, 1996, from the Ministry of Education Culture in Zimbabwe states that the average cost was about Z$500 per year at the primary level, an amount many families could not afford.

10. Botswana, *Report of the National Commission on Education*, 1977, p. 38.

11. Ibid.

12. World Bank, *Public Sector Management in Botswana* (Washington, D.C.: Author, 1984), p. 20.

13. Ibid., p. 31.

14. Ibid., p. 35.

15. Zimbabwe, *Transitional National Development Plan*, Vol. 1, November, 1982. By the Zimbabwe Ministry of Information.

16. Ibid.

17. Ibid.

18. Dickson A. Mungazi, "The Educational Policy of the British South Africa Company Towards Rural and Urban Africans in Zimbabwe: A Dilemma of Choice, 1899–1923," *African Urban Quarterly*, Vol. 2, No. 1 (February, 1987), p. 8.

19. Southern Rhodesia, *Legislative Assembly Debates*, April 2, 1937.

20. Ralph Diffendorfer (ed.), *The World Service of Methodist Episcopal Church* (Chicago: Methodist Council on Benevolences, 1923), p. 115.

21. A. J. Wills, *An Introduction to the History of Central Africa* (London: Oxford University Press, 1964), p. 285.

22. An interview with a rural African leader, in Mutare, Zimbabwe, July 15, 1989.

23. Zimbabwe, *Transitional National Development Plan*, Vol. 1, November 1982.

24. Ibid.

25. ZAPU, *Zimbabwe Primary Syllabus*, August, 1978.

26. Roger Riddell, *From Rhodesia to Zimbabwe: Education for Employment* (Gweru: Mambo Press, 1980), p. 52.

27. UNESCO, "Education in Africa in the Light of the Lagos Conference," 1976, p. 17.

28. Botswana, *Report of the National Commission on Education*, p. 53.

29. Ibid.

30. Claude Phillips, *The African Political Dictionary* (Santa Barbara, Calif.: ABC-Clio Information Service, 1985), p. 159.

31. Dickson A. Mungazi, *The Struggle for Social Change in Southern Africa: Visions of Liberty* (New York: Taylor and Francis, 1989), p. 91.

32. Dickson A. Mungazi, *To Honor the Sacred Trust of Civilization: History, Politics, and Education in Southern Africa* (Cambridge, Mass.: Schenkman Publishers, 1983), p. 16.

7

Results of Educational Reform

> The underlying result of educational reform is the improvement of the
> structure of relationships between citizens and their society. These rela-
> tionships represent the transformation of society itself.
>   Zimbabwe, *Transitional National Development Plan*, 1982

EDUCATIONAL REFORM AND THE
TRANSFORMATION OF SOUTHERN AFRICA

Reporting on the results of educational reform in Botswana in 1977, the
Botswana National Commission on Education observed,

Education is close to the center of life of any society because it is intimately involved
with its culture and values, its political system and its economic situation. For this reason
a fundamental result of any educational reform does not only concern itself with the
overall change in the operation and benefits of the school system, but also with the basic
improvement of the conditions of human beings in important areas of national life.[1]

What the Botswana National Commission on Education was suggesting is that
the improvement of a national culture, the political system, and socioeconomic
conditions as a result of the effectiveness of the educational system can result
only from an educational system that has been reformed.

   In November 1982, the *Transitional National Development Plan* of Zimbabwe seemed to reiterate the importance of this outcome of the educational
reform, stating,

The underlying result of the educational reform is the improvement of the structure of relationships between citizens and their society. These relationships represent the transformation of society itself. This means achieving the correct relationship between the people and the level of economic production, not as an end in itself, but in order to provide qualitative dimensions to enhance the transformation of our society.[2]

What these two reports seem to suggest is that educational reform cannot be undertaken for its own sake, but must focus on its structure and content as a major approach to seeking social and economic change to serve the needs of all the people. In this context, therefore, the nations of southern Africa need to examine broader national implications as a result of educational reform before it is initiated. This would require an assessment of the direction it is taking and the contribution it would make to the development of the individual as a condition of ensuring the development of the nation.

The purpose of this chapter is to discuss some results of educational reform in light of what it is intended to accomplish. The fundamental consideration that will become its focus is the question: How does educational reform benefit the individual in order to benefit the nation? It will be seen that educational reform cannot be initiated without full understanding of all factors that influence it to improve conditions of human life in a larger social order. Also, critical considerations of how educational innovation benefits the individual as a prerequisite of benefiting society are presented. These prerequisites are the concept of self and freedom of choice.

EXPECTED RESULTS OF EDUCATIONAL REFORM

Nations of southern Africa need to undergo a much faster rate of social change than they have experienced in the past. They can accomplish this objective if they direct their efforts toward meaningful change made possible by educational reform. It is certain that conditions of both regional and national life quite different from the past must emerge. In the form of a dramatic political change that translates into national and regional development, urban and industrial transformation must come about as a result of meaningful educational reform. This leads to the conclusion that when reform becomes a factor of social change, national institutions are profoundly affected in such a way that the nations of southern Africa, as nations everywhere, cannot cling to traditions of the past and hope to ensure their development and contribution to a global society.

On February 22, 1996, Afrikaner parents in South Africa took their children out of integrated schools. This is an example of an effort to hold on to the traditions of the past. These parents must realize that they are hurting the future of their children by refusing to accept the concept of reform. They should also remember that it is not within their power to foil the process of reform. It is unfortunate that such an action shows the behavior of those who wish to live in the past. This is not to suggest that maintaining traditions of the past has no place in the future. However, it represents a caution to those Afrikaners who are still living under the shadow of apartheid. It is in their own interest to put that sad chapter behind them and look to the future by seeking to cooperate with the African majority.

Social change in southern Africa will therefore mean, inter alia, the emergence of new cultural practices and attitudes that are adapted to new conditions to enable the people and their society to respond to an evolving social order. Against this background, linkages must be created between the reformed educational process and the character of social change. If linkages are broken, or if they do not function in terms of seeking an improvement of education as a condition of seeking improvement of society, one must conclude that those responsible for educational reform have failed. Unless politicians, educational planners, and economic supporters fulfill their assigned tasks, a new start will perpetually remain imminent.

The nations of southern Africa realize that initiating educational reform can be expensive. But a more important result is that educational reform enables the nation to do self-examination to initiate creative planning, to develop new social and technical personal skills, to initiate efficient management of national resources, to redesign competent administrative structures and effective delivery systems so that persons responsible for their operations become more sensitive to human needs than was the case in the past. Educational reform also creates a new environment of motivation and an improved level of performance in the educational process and in society. It also provides people an opportunity to discover new levels of potential as a reservoir of national service.

Another important result of educational reform must be a realization by national leaders and the people alike that, in the age of self-consciousness and self-actualization, human development is precious to the sustenance of national character and that providing a good education must be a fundamental national objective.[3] Unless educational reform is initiated with this objective in mind, its effects are likely to be more negative than positive, more detrimental than progressive, more inhibiting than promotional. Where would this lead the nations of southern Africa?

RESULTS OF EDUCATIONAL REFORM ON THE INDIVIDUAL

An important conclusion reached in this study is that unless educational reform serves the developmental interests of the individual and elevates him to a new level of self-actualization, it cannot possibly serve the interests of the nation. If this happens, educational reform must be considered a failure. The question now is: How does educational reform serve the developmental interests of the individual as a prerequisite of serving the developmental interests of the nation? To furnish an answer to the question two complimentary aspects pertaining to educational reform must be discussed as conditions of the development of the nation. The first is the concept of self. The second is freedom of choice.

THE CONCEPT OF SELF

The thinking that the individual has value and worth to his society only when it is recognized that he has value to himself demonstrates the importance of education. Success of education for an individual is a result of the supreme act of creation. This suggests the very essence of the human being. Although the colonial society failed to build human institutions on the importance of this fundamental principle, this belief had its origin in the African heritage itself. In designing strategies to give meaning to the concept of self, the African traditional society was wise enough to help its members understand a basic truth. By utilizing it in its original form, the concept of self would yield limited results.

However, seeking to improve self-concept through education, Africans understood that the human person was quite capable of attaining a higher level of performance than a limited environment would allow him. Therefore, Africans rejected the Western notion that perfection could not be reached. Aiming at reaching perfection through educational reform was evident in the ability of the individual to base his life on moral and spiritual values and the manifestation of the positive attributes that distinguish man from other living species. The philosophy of humanism in Zambia is based on this fundamental tenet.[4]

In recognizing the emergence of a new concept of self as a result of educational reform, the nations of southern Africa must build into the new educational system a strategy that enables students to appreciate their individuality. This grows out of an environment that enables them to eliminate the negative features of human existence. Individuality cannot come out of a narrow curriculum, nor does it result from a narrow definition of the purpose of education or the rigidity of instructional methods. The teaching of the importance of individuality as a critical component of self must begin simultaneously with the beginning of the educational process itself. It must start as soon as the learner is aware of his environment and his relationship to it. This environment, by its very nature, must include providing the student the tools that he needs to develop his unique talents and to realize his interests and needs.

One sees six critical principles that are essential to the realization of the concept of self as a result of educational reform. The first principle is that both the curriculum and the educational process must be broad and flexible enough to enable the student to choose his course of study carefully. It is important for a person to have the ability to design his own unique strategies, which are essential to serve his needs and interests. Out of this environment, the student learns to attain a level of intellectual excellence that gives him a set of new experiences needed for success in both his educational endeavors and in life.

The second principle is that the student inculcates in himself the discipline that he needs to carry out learning tasks that elevate the spirit of human endeavor to new heights. The third principle is that the student learns techniques of problem solving in his unique way. A method of learning that weaves the problem solving of traditional society with the methods of problem solving utilized by the Western rational method would be beneficial.

The fourth principle is that the student will learn to apply logic and human reasoning to show that he is not controlled by emotion. This is the setting from which moral and spiritual values have a new meaning to the individual. This is how these values benefit society. The fifth principle is that the student must learn to appreciate his cultural values as he demonstrates his aesthetic appreciation of its content. This gives him a new sense of his identity and individuality. The sixth principle is that the student learns to develop the spirit of self-reliance, not only to learn what he must learn, but also in developing a sense of independence, both in thought process and in integrating his action consistent with his individuality.

The application of these principles leads to an important conclusion regarding the strategies of seeking to accomplish the concept of self as an outcome of educational innovation in southern Africa. It enables the student to ask the question: Who am I? The answer defines the concept of self. This approach was explained to us by a fifteen-year-old high school girl in Harare, Zimbabwe, in August, 1989, saying,

The advent of political independence to Zimbabwe in April 1980 meant a tremendous opportunity for the rapid reform of the system of education to enable all students to realize their unique individuality. The essential element of this reform is the realization that before the student learns about the characters of William Shakespeare, or the principles of Archimedes, or the theorem of Pythagoras, or Edward Gibbon's interpretation of history, or the theories of John Dewey, or the political philosophy of Thomas Hobbes, or of Godfrey Huggins, she must learn to understand herself in relationship to her needs and interests. This entails an understanding of the concept of self. This, then, means that the student must have a thorough grasp of the concept of self in order to set goals, to determine priorities, to design learning strategies, and to motivate herself. These are essential elements of success because they demonstrate the concept of self at its best. Unless the student has a clear understanding of the concept of self, her educational endeavor is meaningless. Therefore, any change in the educational system that does not envisage the emergence of a new concept of self cannot be regarded as reform, and has therefore failed.[5]

Indeed, in addition to enabling the student "to set goals, to determine priorities, to design learning strategies, and to motivate herself," the concept of self, as a result of educational reform, entrenches the basic principle that differences between people constitute manifestations of the importance of their individuality. In southern Africa, where differences between men and women and between boys and girls determine the kind of opportunity one gets,[6] both in school and in society, educational reform that enables the student to realize the concept of self acquires an added importance.

The recognition of this problem has become a guiding light in young women's search for self in more meaningful ways than they did in the past. This is why this fifteen-year-old high school girl went on to add,

As an African girl struggling to carve a new concept of self in a set of changed circumstances, I find myself caught between cultural traditions that force me to accept an inferior position in society and the need to raise myself above the level of mediocrity to assert my own definition of self in order to realize my individuality. I am caught between the need to strive to attain academic excellence as a measure of my own understanding of the concept of self and strengthen that male mystique that my culture says a woman must always try to preserve by allowing boys to do better in school. I hope that change in the educational system will allow me to strive towards excellence without threatening that male mystique. I hope it will mean change in the attitudes of my society towards the education of women so that the curriculum will no longer compel girls to take home economics and reserve mathematics and science for boys. Any educational system that enables all students to realize their own goals as a distinct feature of individuality and self, is a manifestation of the result of its reform.[7]

This argument suggests the conclusion that the concept of self goes far beyond the school activity as a result of educational reform. It elevates one's image of self to the extent that one refuses to be controlled by the weaker side of human existence. It enables a girl to refuse to become pregnant if she does not want to. It enables a boy to see himself as someone who has value to himself and his society beyond the social conventions and designations he must respect. It enables the school and the community to see students in the way Edgar Allan Poe defined as their prime reason for being.

The concept of self enables the government to reevaluate educational programs and policies in order to respond adequately to conditions that demand new approaches to national problems. It demands that students become the center of the educational activity because their needs and interests supersede any other consideration. In short, the concept of self is of paramount importance to the entire educational process. It also becomes an instrument of eliminating negative features of the African culture, especially the practice of placing group interests above those of the individual.

The concept of self, when fully comprehended and embraced as a result of educational reform, becomes a major motivating instrument of preserving personal growth. It helps to provide a potent incentive to determination and perseverance in efforts to overcome learning problems. It generates resourceful energy in seeking to master concepts that are essential to further learning. It provides continuity and the unity of purpose in endeavors that are related to the learning process. Its arouses curiosity and strengthens the pursuit of goals that are critical to successful human enterprise. It makes it possible for students to pose new and relevant questions in the process of learning. It influences the formation of new attitudes needed to engage in purposeful activity. Therefore, the concept of self, as a result of educational reform, stands out larger as a social entity. It also gives the student something far more important than the educational process itself. This is why the colonial governments could not possibly conceive of educational reform from this perspective. Colonial education provides a sense of self in terms of employability as a laborer.

In 1989, the principal of a high school in Mutare, Zimbabwe, explained what he considered to be the concept of self as an outcome of educational innovation, saying,

The change of educational system from what it was during the colonial period to what it must be following independence demands a corresponding change in both content and purpose. A fundamental product of education in the postcolonial period must be to promote the concept of individuality. Individuality means self-concept. Self-concept means independence of thought process. This means freedom to grow, to set goals, to ask searching questions, to pursue the fulfillment of goals consistent with the spirit of inquiry, to formulate appropriate attitudes that put the student in the frame of mind that enables men and women to be themselves and be proud of their accomplishments. Unless these are results of reform in education, it cannot be regarded as reform. The colonial governments never thought of education from the perspective of its inclusive quality. This is the challenge that many nations of Africa face. Can they rise to meet it?[8]

Freedom to grow suggests two critical elements as an outcome of education directed toward fulfilling the concept of individuality and the student's own definition of self. The first element is that it cultivates an environment of intellectual growth. The potent force in human existence that distinguishes the individual who has good self-concepts as those who have motivation and purpose. An individual who does not possess motivation and purpose has little inspiration toward an enlightened vision of himself.

The second element is that a healthy concept of self provides an individual with the ability to comprehend the world of reality so that he can function in it without having to make major adjustments or to relearn essential factors to function in society. John Dewey, an American educator, takes this line of thinking in discussing the importance of individuality as a product of education, saying, "He is lucky who does not find that in order to make progress, in order to go ahead intellectually, he does not have to relearn much of what he learned in school."[9]

What all this seems to suggest is that the concept of self is central to the pursuit of a career, whether or not one sees oneself as possessing abilities that lead to success in life. Success in life includes a decent standard of living, a decent income, ability to provide for one's family, security in one's person, good medical care, and good educational opportunity for one's children. Because, by their very nature, these outcomes of self are individual, the educational process has meaning only if it is so designed that each student gets from it the opportunity to fulfill his own definition of its purpose. This is a critical dimension of the challenge of educational innovation in southern Africa.

Paul Hirst, a British author, concludes that a good educational program creates an environment from which the concept of self and the search for individual fulfillment combine to generate a knowledge of reality about how one seeks to relate to it to attain a higher level of achievement than would otherwise be the case.[10] In the concept of the struggle for individuality in southern Africa, it is not so much the fault of the student that the educational process becomes a flaw, but the failure of those in positions of responsibility to structure it in such a way that it elevates the individual to the utmost level of performance to which he is entitled.

This is the line of thinking that the Educational Reform Commission of Zambia took into consideration when it concluded,

Educational reform must involve change in direction, in depth, and in breadth. It should include a substantial change to mean acceptance of the intrinsic value of individual enterprise, not only in education, but also in society itself. It must take into account the various factors which are the basis of the interplay between the educational system and the individual student's search for fulfillment.[11]

It is for these reasons that educational reform must reflect the "components and the structure intended as a framework of the vehicle which will carry the essential elements of developing individual character so important to the dynamics of building a nation."[12] A guiding principle in this endeavor should be the knowledge that every student possesses a potential to be his best and in his own way. For this human endeavor to yield tangible results, there must be two ingredients. The first ingredient is the support that comes from the entity called the school, without which the student cannot succeed. Support is crucial in the teacher's work to help the students to set goals, to design strategies to fulfill them, and to identify those areas of both potential and interest that the student may not be fully aware of on his own. The second ingredient is cooperation among all levels of the school system, from the principal to the teacher, the parents and the community, and the government and the people. This demands a close study of the student's environment, both home and community, to see if there are detracting influences that must be eliminated.

The many students who try to function under a deprived environment or background, or in a dysfunctional organization, a common feature among many nations of southern Africa, must not be regarded as having been sentenced to their educational deaths. Rather, their situations must be viewed as a challenge to be overcome, a factor of motivation that can be utilized to attain new heights of personal achievement. Once these ingredients are in place, the student can place himself in a position that he understands. He must envisage himself as an individual human being with a unique potential for making a contribution to the development of his society. This is what the concept of self, as a product of educational reform, means: being able to identify one's goals within the sociatic framework of one's society and having the opportunity to actualize one's goals and aspirations.

EXERCISING FREEDOM OF CHOICE

One major reason why United Methodist Church Bishop Ralph E. Dodge[13] was deported from colonial Zimbabwe by the Rhodesia Front government in July 1964 was his persistent call for the recognition of the concept of the freedom of choice in education and in the national political arena. In 1963, convinced that freedom of choice was a fundamental human right, Dodge argued,

We hold governments responsible for the promotion and protection of the rights of all people as part of the fundamental freedoms of speech, choice in education and in society itself. The elimination of political mistreatment of persons for any reason is the first step towards granting all people freedom of choice. Freedom of choice in the educational process cannot be exercised in situations in which the educational system is controlled to suit the political purpose of those in power. Reform of the system of education is needed to ensure that freedom of choice combines with innovation in the curriculum to form a major factor of the advancement of the individual.[14]

For Dodge to expect the colonial government to respect the principle of freedom of choice was to expect the colonial government to accept the concept of self for all people. This was a tenet that any colonial government rejected because accepting it would undercut the basis of its own survival. But it was the concept that Dodge and Africans felt must be expressed to shape the direction of their development. The refusal of the colonial government to accept this principle did not invalidate it. This suggests that the principle of freedom of choice is an aspect of education that most nations of Africa have found difficult to implement because they are fearful. The influence of the colonial period is stronger in this regard than many nations would like to admit.

The concept of change as an approach to reform was understood by only a few colonial officials relative to the struggle for social change in southern Africa. For example, Harold Macmillan, British prime minister from 1957 to 1963, recognized change in Africa as a condition of the survival of the colonial governments themselves. This is why he made a historic speech to the joint session of the South African parliament in Cape Town in February 1960. Macmillan warned the colonial systems in Africa of the consequences of resisting change, saying, "The wind of change is blowing through the continent of Africa. Whether we like it or not, the growth of nationalistic consciousness is a political factor. We must accept it as a fact. Our national policy must take account of it."[15]

Because of the crisis caused by apartheid in South Africa and Namibia over many years, and the continuing civil strife in Angola and Mozambique, it would seem that the elements of reform are still being put together in the region. For the reform to be complete there must be two elements. The first element is reform in the educational system that would make it possible to create and develop human resources to provide future service to the nations. The second element is the development of experienced leadership to administer the government efficiently and properly. This can mean only the true and genuine practice of democracy. The rush of many African nations toward one-party governments is, indeed, reentrenchment of the old colonial systems. Only when these two essential elements are in place can meaningful educational reform and social change take place to initiate social transformation.

The problem of freedom of choice in southern Africa is compounded by three basic factors. The first factor is that with a rapid population increase, it is more difficult to cater to the educational needs of all the students. The second factor is that many children who are ready to begin primary schooling do not have the opportunity to actually enroll because there is simply not enough space. Although the children in rural areas experience more educational problems than those in urban areas, the problem of enrollment has created serious national concern in all nations of southern Africa. The third factor is that many parents try to enroll their children in school at a younger age than they did in the past because they want to introduce them into the school environment early to protect them from detracting influences around them. Parents also believe that the earlier the students are introduced to the educational environment, the better are their chances of remaining in school.

Indeed, in these three factors lies the fabric of the challenge of educational innovation in southern Africa. In 1977, the Educational Reform Commission of Zambia recognized this challenge when it observed,

The shortage of space in the lower primary school is greater in urban areas than in rural areas. In some urban areas the shortage is so serious that one-third of the number of children cannot go to school. This is because the urban child population has increased faster than new classrooms have been built. The rapid rise in population, the desire of parents to send their children to school earlier than usual have come to cause problems that demand a corresponding rapid reform of the school system to enable all children to receive the education they need.[16]

An important factor for the nations of southern Africa to remember in these difficulties relative to the freedom of choice, as the Report of National Commission on Education of Botswana noted, is that "Students need help in identifying their own talents and abilities. They also require exposure to different opportunities in the adult world. Much better information on career options should be provided to students so that they exercise their freedom of choice."[17] But for the students to exercise this freedom of choice the school authority must recognize that the educational system itself has to be reformed because the educational process, as it existed during the colonial period, was out of pace with the needs of the students. The fear that change represents some risks of failure that may damage the credibility of the government must be substituted for by the knowledge that it is better to risk failure through change than to try to maintain a system that is out of date.

This is a situation that demands the exercise of freedom of choice in education by all students. For this to happen, two considerations must be central to its application. The first is a broad and diverse curriculum that eliminates the narrow perception of education. Broadening the curriculum would allow students an opportunities to exercise all their options. The second is the availability of adequate educational opportunity so that students carry out an educational activity that is consistent with their own objectives and interests. Unless these two considerations are present, the concept of freedom of choice may have a shallow meaning.

A serious problem that may arise relative to the concept of the freedom of choice in southern Africa is the disparity that still exists between opportunities to exercise it between boys and girls. Clearly, this is one of the negative legacies of the colonial period, and the nations of southern Africa should recognize that to resolve this disparity is to meet the challenge to their efforts toward educational innovation. In July 1989, Faye Chung, Zimbabwe's minister of primary and secondary education, acknowledged this disparity. Speaking during the opening of a seminar on rural women's access to education held at Kadoma, Chung noted,

Enrollment in schools and other educational institutions indicate that there is a higher percentage of boys than girls despite the fact that women constitute 51% of the population. This disparity increases with increasing levels of education. The inadequacy of proper facilities and financial resources coupled with negative aspects of outdated traditions and culture militate against women's access to education.[18]

The fact is that this kind of educational disparity impinges heavily on the students' freedom of choice. It is shown in the disability that women suffer in both education and in society itself. However, like many African politicians in the postcolonial nations of southern Africa, Chung elected to blame other factors, such as cultural traditions and limited financial resources, for her inability to resolve a serious national problem. She was not likely to recognize the reality that government policy itself is essentially responsible for many of the problems that these emerging nations are facing. The fact of the matter is that educational innovation has not been carried out in bold and decisive fashion because many governments fear that failure may reflect negatively on the government itself. The fear that initiating change is risky inhibits the ability of the nations of southern Africa to initiate the much needed change that would serve the interests of all students. Until these nations face this reality and become resolved to do something to improve the situation, they will always experience the scourge of underdevelopment.

While Chung went to considerable lengths to argue that, "My government introduced free and universal primary education on attaining independence,"[19] she did not address the real cause of the problem, failure to initiate reform. She may not have been aware that Africans are quite capable of understanding the need for change if there are clear leadership, clearly stated objectives, strategies to fulfill them, and if they are directly involved in the process of formulating and implementing change. Chung's recognition that "For many decades women have been left out in most development plans and activities"[20] is precisely the reason why reform must be initiated to ensure that the problem is fully resolved. What good does it do the people to acknowledge the existence of a problem and then do little to resolve it?

Most nations of southern Africa seem to recognize the importance of freedom of choice in the educational process as a critical outcome of reform. In 1988, for example, Dzingai Mutumbuka, then minister of education and culture in Zimbabwe, addressed this aspect when he argued that the emerging nations of Africa must recognize that it is in their own best interest to give the students an opportunity to select their own course of study with the assistance of the school. Dzingai Mutumbuka argued that the nations of southern Africa, as nations all over the world, must allow students

to develop as skilled persons who can adopt to changing technological development. This applies to the types of courses, the levels of the courses, and their depth and breadth. It is important to realize that the training the students receive is only a basis on which to develop further knowledge and skills to enable the learner to develop as a good craftsman and good technician, to substitute self-doubt with self-confidence, to balance the concept of collective identity with that of the individuality. This allows freedom of choice as a distinct outcome of reform of the educational system.[21]

Mutumbuka recognized that without reform, education cannot fulfill this critical objective.

But in all his enthusiasm to put the concept of freedom of choice in education into practice, Mutumbuka, like other national leaders in southern Africa, may have missed an important consideration, and that is, before it can be put into practice, the concept of the freedom of choice must be realized only as a result of educational reform. The reason why it has not been realized up to now is that educational innovation itself has not been established. In 1979, the ruling ZANU of Zimbabwe issued an election manifesto in which it outlined thirteen freedoms that it said every citizen was entitled to. Among these freedoms was the freedom of choice in the educational process.[22] But, in 1990, eleven years later, this form of freedom looked as distant as it had in 1979.

National leaders of southern Africa, like Faye Chung did in July 1989, argue that limited financial resources are the cause of many of the problems their nations experience in education. It would be erroneous to place blame on limited financial resources without taking other important considerations, such as the inability of national leaders to initiate innovation, into account. In any event, limited financial resources are often a result of a faulty fiscal policy or mismanagement. A dimension of freedom of choice that only a few nations of Africa fully understand has to do with special education. That kind of education must be provided students with special needs because they are mentally or physically impaired.

Before the educational process can attempt to meet the needs of these students, it is necessary first to clearly identify the causes of their impairment and then determine the interests and goals of the individual students. Once this is done, full attention must be given to the physical, emotional, social, and mental development of each student as an individual. The fact that some students are handicapped must not be a reason to deny them any opportunity to exercise their freedom of choice.

The Educational Reform Commission of Zambia took this line of thinking into account when it went on to add,

All handicapped students are entitled to adequate education in the same way that other students are. They should receive basic and further education as any other students. Since the handicapped students are a special case, there should even be *positive discrimination* [affirmative action] in the provision of facilities and amenities for purposes of ensuring their educational development.[23]

The commission warned that realizing the educational needs of students with special difficulties requires basic reform as its prerequisite. In recognizing the fact that "Special education is not yet fully developed for a long time because it has not been properly organized,"[24] the Educational Reform Commission of Zambia was warning against the consequences of further delay in facing the challenge that this problem presents in the thrust for educational innovation.

This is the line of argument we have been advocating, that the nations of southern Africa must overcome their fear of failure in initiating educational innovation because the consequences of maintaining the educational status quo are more devastating than those of failure to initiate change for both the student and society itself. Freedom of choice, as a critical outcome of educational innovation, must be accepted as such if the educational process must have meaning to national development.

THE EFFECT OF EDUCATIONAL REFORM ON SOCIETY

This study has argued that for education to serve its real purpose, it has to be reformed to suit the conditions of the time. It has also argued that before educational reform benefits society, it must demonstrate tangible benefits to the individual. This chapter has discussed two critical elements of the individual that educational innovation must focus on: the concept of self and freedom of choice. Once the individual secures educational benefits as a result of realizing these two elements, then society itself stands to benefit from properly educated individuals in it.

This study has also argued that because national leaders in southern Africa focus on their own definition of national development, they tend to neglect the educational development of the individual as a foundation on which any concept of national development must be built. The leaders of nations of southern Africa must be reminded that any definition of national development is virtually meaningless if it is not based on the educational development of the individual. The question now arises: How does educational reform designed to benefit the individual also benefit society? This section provides some answers to the question.

When leaders of nations of Africa speak of the need for national development, they are thinking essentially in terms of political unity. In their enthusiasm to achieve this objective, some leaders adopt methods that entail dictatorial action. In doing so, they become intolerant of those who hold different political views from their own. Thus, to ensure their political insulation, they institute one-party systems that rob the citizens of their right and freedom of political dissent. They advance four reasons for turning a country into a one-party system of government. The first is that the people are not sufficiently educated to understand the complexities and responsibilities in a democratic system. The second reason is that democracy is expensive, it takes a lot of money, energy, and time. The third reason is that because attempts to practice democracy are related to tribal or ethnic affiliation, they become divisive and national unity is substituted by national conflict due to a lack of understanding and cooperation. The fourth reason is that democracy is a Western imposition and so it is alien to African culture. We reject all these opinions as totally invalid for a very simple reason: democracy is universal, and its application is not in any way the prerogative of any particular culture. The fact that the colonial governments did not practice democracy is no reason why nations of southern Africa should not practice it.

The truth of the matter is that what the leaders of African nations who take this line of argument seem to neglect is that with proper education these problems need not exist in the first place. The character of educational innovation that this study has discussed would help create an entirely new political environment that would eliminate doubts and suspicions of any one group of citizens against another. The freedom that citizens have as students to choose their course of study must translate into freedom of expression of ideas in the national political arena.

The nations of southern Africa regard freedom of expression as a forum for criticizing the government, and so they are not aware that it is an essential component of national political stability. The government is best served by advancing logical arguments to defend itself rather than by silencing opposition because, once the government resorts to this method of eliminating opposition or criticism, the political stability it hopes for is seriously threatened. Government leaders must also have educational reform that teaches them how to handle adversity and diversity. When people are properly educated, they fully understand the importance of exercising political responsibility in a way that does not threaten the government. This is how educational innovation designed to serve the needs of the individual serves society.

Another important outcome of educational innovation relative to national political development is that it negates the creation of one-party systems because citizens come to understand the importance of true democracy and will contribute to its development in a way that eliminates the fear that dominates the thinking and the behavior of leaders, the fear of military coups, of one form of political violence or another, and of political disintegration. When citizens understand the need for political stability based on the genuine practice of democracy, they help create a national climate from which emerges a realization that one-party systems rob nations of the vitality that manifests and sustains itself in the minds and hearts of the people. They destroy the creativity, the emergence of new ideas, and the resources that all nations need to sustain the momentum for national development.

Indeed, one-party systems strengthen the notion that political wisdom is a prerogative of the party in power and the individuals who are in government know more about national issues than any one else in the country. Nothing is more dangerous to efforts directed toward national development. When citizens are educated as a result of educational innovation, they help to eliminate the myth that a one-party system represents national unity. They endeavor to create a multi-party system as the only form of true democracy. Under these conditions, how can one-party systems be justified? When there is no democracy or constitution to ensure equality, the needs of the people become overshadowed by the needs of the government leaders. The world has seen the results of world leaders whose self-will has run riot.

There is yet another important outcome of educational reform that the leaders of the nations of southern Africa must understand as playing an important part in the national political arena and development. This is, citizens will help create open government operations through participation. This gives people a sense of belonging. It also creates an atmosphere of mutual trust. It protects the government from the temptation of engaging in corruption. It helps to eliminate the veil of secrecy so common when corruption becomes part of government operations. Open government operations afford nations the courage to face their problems in an honest manner. This is how confidence, mutual trust, and cooperation between the government and the people develop in the interest of national development.

Perhaps one example of efforts to create a national climate of open government operations is evident in what Zimbabwe has tried to do during the past few years. Not only is Zimbabwe the first country in southern Africa to enact legislation making corruption a criminal offense, but the government has also enforced it. Whenever there are reports of impropriety by any government official, the president is required to name a commission of inquiry that carries out its investigation in public and its proceedings are reported fully by the media. In 1988, after receiving reports that a number of government officials were engaging in corruption, President Mugabe used appropriate clauses of the legislation to appoint a high-level commission of inquiry under the chairmanship of Justice Sandura to investigate the charges.

In April 1989, the Sandura Commission reported that, indeed, six senior government officials were implicated in corruption. President Mugabe immediately released the report to the public and ordered that the officials stand trial in accordance with the law.[25] Subsequently one senior government minister, Maurice Nyagumbo, died under suspicion that the scandal had so tarnished his political career and his family reputation that he had come to the end of the road. The other five ministers were found guilty and sentenced to heavy fines in addition to losing their positions in the government. One senior official, Dzingai Mutumbuka, and his wife were fined a total of $105,000 in August 1989.[26] President Mugabe told his fellow Zimbabweans that his government would not tolerate corruption and he would enforce the law. While the efforts by Zimbabwe to have open government operations will by no means lead to the end of corruption, they demonstrate that it is important to stamp it out.

The outcome of this effort toward open government operations must be understood in the context of the reaction of the people. In May 1989, when reports of this corruption first surfaced, Edgar Tekere, an inner member of the ruling ZANU and a senior government official, resigned to form the Zimbabwe Unity Movement (ZUM) and charged the government with corruption, saying: "Zimbabwe's national leadership is already so thoroughly decayed by corruption that we are very close to the point of collapse of the executive. The ruling party is vigorously advocating the conversion of Zimbabwe into a one-party state and is seeking to entrench its undemocratic self as a dictatorship."[27]

Because President Mugabe had not tried to conceal the fact that some of his colleagues in government had, indeed, engaged in corruption, and because he often said that he would not tolerate it, Tekere's charges even helped him to "take a good deal of air out of his balloon by dealing with the corruption issue head-on."[28] One must remember that Tekere's remarks underscore the importance of preserving a multi-party democracy. It is quite possible that the extent of the corruption would not have been fully exposed to the citizens if there was a one-party system of government. Openness in government is therefore a critical component of the democratic system and cannot be practiced under a one-party system, no matter how much the government tries.

While the citizens were still displeased with the corruption by government officials,[29] they came to appreciate the efforts that Mugabe was making to have open government operations remain part of the system of government itself. It is for this reason that President Mugabe continued to enjoy a reasonable degree of popular support. The important thing to remember about political events in Zimbabwe is that because of the openness with which Mugabe has handled them, the citizens were pleased with the knowledge that his government had nothing to hide.

This view was expressed to Dickson Mungazi by the principal of a high school who said in August 1989,

While we were quite displeased with this Zimbabwean Watergate because it robbed the people of their trust in their government, the fact that the president himself was quite candid in acknowledging that some of his colleagues had engaged in corruption and allowing the media to cover the investigation on it suggests that he was concerned about the need to preserve the interests of the nation. I must say also that if there were a one-party system of government, there would never have been an Edgar Tekere to raise charges of corruption in the first place. This means also that Zimbabwe needs to educate its people so well that they can understand the process of government so that there is no reason to turn the country into a one-party state. This demands a basic reform of the educational system.[30]

This is precisely what this study has argued, and there is no question that the government of Zimbabwe has recognized the importance of respecting the democratic values for the good of the country. Allowing ZUM a political platform underscores this conclusion. Indeed, while this African form of *glasnost* is rare, it can provide a model that other nations of southern Africa can follow. The violent repressive force that the police in South Africa used against demonstrators against apartheid is hardly a climate of openness in government. When, on January 18, 1990, the police used naked force to suppress the people who were demonstrating against the visit of the British cricket team to South

Africa, the determination of the South African government to entrench both an oppressive system and rigidity became fully known.

Another important outcome of educational reform is the need to improve manpower to sustain the strength of the economy. Once educational reform has been established, an effort must be made to attract more students to become teachers. This can be done by improving conditions of service, including salaries and benefits. To achieve this objective, an increase in the number of training schools must be initiated. Short-term solutions to the problem of the supply of teachers must also be initiated, such as the one that Zimbabwe inaugurated at the time of its independence in 1980, when it recruited teachers from all over the world to fill the need.

To enable the teachers to fulfill their responsibilities fully, they must receive the support of other staff members and members of the community. All these factors combine to create a new environment that enables the teachers to prepare their students to enter employment. This is also how educational innovation plays an important role in the development of manpower. Indeed, in many countries of the Third World, one of the most critical constraints inhibiting economic development, which, in effect, will become more critical unless there are substantial changes in education, is the serious shortage of skilled manpower. The seriousness of the shortage of skilled manpower will be more profoundly felt with the passage of time unless educational innovation is designed to eliminate it.

To ensure adequate manpower as an outcome of educational reform two critical factors must be taken into consideration. These are supply and demand. To assess the adequacy of supply through knowledge of the existing system, political accountability is necessary. This demands ability to project the economic growth rate and the percentage of trained people required to man various sectors of the employment aggregate. The rate of unemployment, a serious problem in all countries of southern Africa, should offer some insights about which areas, of both educational development and economic development should receive more attention and emphasis. This creates demand.[31]

The balance between supply and demand is a factor of economic growth that is often a product of educational reform. The process of making these decisions requires political accountability because both are inseparable from the political process. This national endeavor can best be initiated through educational reform itself. This suggests the conclusion that without educational reform, there is no manpower, and without manpower there is no economic growth, without economic growth, national independence and development cannot take place.

Yet another sociatic outcome of educational innovation is the improvement of health services and housing. The important thing to remember is that the healthier the citizens, the happier they become, and the happier they become, the more productive they become. But it would be wrong to assume that good health comes on its own; it must be the result of careful planning. Proper nutrition requires education. Knowledge of the importance of a balanced diet and the proper care of food is the result of good educational programs. Health and education are important factors for sociatic advancement.

The disparity that exists between rural health care and urban health care and the inadequacy of medical facilities and technology are conditions that can be resolved by educational innovation. Housing problems have their roots in the problems of socioeconomic development of the nation[32] and the failure of meaningful educational reform. Granted it takes time to resolve the problems left behind by the colonial governments, but the nations of southern Africa must realize that reform of the educational system can go a long way in assisting to find solutions to many problems they face today.

SUMMARY AND CONCLUSION

The discussion in this chapter leads to two basic conclusions. The first conclusion is that the concept of educational reform is an underlying imperative of national development when it is directed toward the development of the individual. Without the development of the individual, there is no national development. Two critical factors have been identified and discussed in this chapter relative to the educational development of the individual as an outcome of educational innovation. These are the concept of self and freedom of choice. Unless these remain central to any effort directed toward seeking an improvement of education, it would lose the purpose for which it is initiated.

The second conclusion is that when educational reform is designed to benefit the individual, it is society itself that ultimately benefits more. Therefore, it is in the best interest of the nation to remain sensitive to the need to protect and promote the educational interests of the individual so that society may benefit. Economic self-sufficiency, manpower development, a decent standard of living, and political participation are the insurance policy that creates a happy and progressive society. The nations of southern Africa must endeavor to ensure educational reform to preserve these important pillars of their development.

NOTES

1. Botswana, *Report of the National Commission on Education,* April 1977, p. 9.
2. Zimbabwe, *Transitional National Development Plan*, Vol. 1, November 1982, p. 17.

3. Zambia, *Educational Reform: Proposals and Recommendations*, 1977, p. 15.

4. Ibid., p. 6.

5. A fifteen-year-old high school girl, during an interview in Harare, Zimbabwe, August 6, 1989. The principal of the school told Dickson Mungazi, "This girl is one of the brightest students I have ever had in my twenty-four years as a teacher."

6. See, for example, *Chicago Tribune*, October 1, 1981, sec. 1, p. 2 for a detailed discussion of this practice.

7. Fifteen-year-old high school girl, during an interview in Harare, Zimbabwe, August 6, 1989.

8. The principal of a high school during an interview in Mutare, Zimbabwe, August 7, 1989.

9. John Dewey, *Experience and Education* (New York: Collier Books, 1938), p. 47.

10. Paul Hirst, *Knowledge and the Curriculum: A Collection of Philosophical Papers* (London: Routledge and Kegan Paul, 1974), p. 30.

11. Zambia, *Educational Reform: Proposals and Recommendations*, 1977, p. 7.

12. Ibid.

13. Bishop Ralph Dodge first went to Angola as a missionary in 1936. He was then elected Bishop in 1956, and was assigned to southern Africa with his administrative office in Harare, Zimbabwe.

14. Dickson A. Mungazi, *The Honored Crusade: Ralph Dodge's Theology of Liberation and Initiative for Social Change in Zimbabwe* (Gweru: Mambo Press, 1991), p. 59.

15. Harold Macmillan, "Commonwealth Independence and Interdependence," an address to the joint session of the South African Parliament, Cape Town, February 3, 1960.

16. Zambia, *Educational Reform: Proposals and Recommendations*, 1977, p. 13.

17. Botswana, *Report of the National Commission on Education*, April, 1977.

18. Faye Chung, "Women Are Less Educated Than Men," a speech delivered during the opening of rural women's access to education in Zimbabwe. Ref. 230/89/CB/SM/SK, July 25, 1989. By courtesy of the Zimbabwe Ministry of Information.

19. Ibid.

20. Ibid.

21. Dzingai Mutumbuka, "Training Institutions Play a Vital Role in Educational Reform," a speech delivered at the Harare (Zimbabwe) Polytechnic College. Ref. 447/88/CC/ES/GS. October 7, 1988. By courtesy of the Zimbabwe Ministry of Information.

22. ZANU-PF, Election Manifesto, 1980. (For details see, for example, Dickson A. Mungazi, *The Struggle for Social Change in Southern Africa: Visions of Liberty* [New York: Taylor and Francis, 1989], p. 128.)

23. Zambia, *Educational Reform: Proposals and Recommendations*, October 1977, p. 23.

24. Ibid.

25. *Herald*, April 13, 1989, sec. 1, p. 2.

26. *Herald*, August 18, 1989, sec. 1, p. 2.

27. *New York Times*, May 7, 1989, sec. 2, p. 5.

28. Ibid.

29. Chapter 1 of this study presents the evidence of this displeasure as seen in August 1989. Students at the University of Zimbabwe were staging demonstrations against it.

30. Interview with a principal of a high school, in Harare, Zimbabwe, August 6, 1989.

31. Zimbabwe, *Transitional National Development Plan*, Vol. 1, November, 1982, p. 9.

32. Ibid.

8

Educational Reform and the Transformation of Southern Africa: Summary, Conclusions, and Implications

> The wind of change is blowing through the continent of Africa. Whether we like it or not the growth of national consciousness is a political fact. We must accept it as a fact, and our national policies must take account of it.
>
> Harold Macmillan, 1960

> This is a time of testing in Africa. The old signposts are being torn down. The hallmarks of colonialism are disappearing. In the crucible of social change new human formations are beginning to take shape.
>
> William H. Lewis, 1996

APARTHEID AND THE CALL FOR REFORM

On March 11, 1996, dramatic events began to take place in South Africa in an unprecedented way. Twenty white men who were among the most powerful in running the government were brought to trial charged with the crime of massacring Africans in 1987 as part of a conspiracy to preserve white minority rule. Former Defense Minister Magnus Malan and nineteen other top military officials were charged in December 1995 with murder, attempted murder, and conspiracy to commit murder in the most extraordinary case yet brought against top officials of the former apartheid government that F. W. de Klerk led from 1987 to 1994. These top officials were accused of planning and carrying out in 1987 a coordinated attack on the home of Victor Ntuli, an African member of the ANC. Although white leaders in South Africa have condemned the trial as a witch hunt initiated by the government that Nelson

Mandela now leads, black leaders were reported to see in the trial an element of the justice they said they were struggling for over many decades.[1]

To understand these tragic developments one needs to understand the events of the previous few years. On February 2, 1990, President F. W. de Klerk made an unexpected announcement in the South African parliament that Nelson Mandela, after spending twenty-seven years at Victor Verster Prison, the Alcatraz of South Africa, would soon be released unconditionally. De Klerk also said that the ANC, the African political party that was formed in 1912 to fight against the colonial system in South Africa, and other political parties would be legalized once more (they had been outlawed in 1964). Mandela's actual release occurred on February 11 after necessary preparation was made to ensure that there were no adverse effects on the government. What Mandela said in Cape Town soon after his release underscores the importance of what has been presented in this study: change becomes reform when it is directed toward seeking improvement of the conditions that affect society and human life in that society.

Making direct reference to the destructive influence of apartheid, Mandela spoke to the thousands who came to welcome him, saying, "I stand before you, not a prophet, but as a humble servant. Your efforts have made it possible for me to be here today. Our resort to the armed struggle in 1960 was merely a defensive action against the violence of apartheid. Our armed struggle still exists today. We have no option but to continue. We call on our white compatriots to join us in the process of eradicating apartheid."[2] There is no question that in saying what he did, Mandela was calling for a major change in South Africa, and that as long as the system of apartheid remained in place, the country was likely to endure an agony of conflict more serious than it had experienced in the past. By this time, the international community had also become aware of the harmful effects of apartheid and demanded its immediate eradication as a condition of creating a national and regional climate that would ensure the transformation of Africa as a whole.

An examination of the application of the policy of apartheid evinces the determination of the Africans to end it in all its forms. Not only was there complete racial segregation in both society and education, but the government of South Africa also believed from 1910 to 1994 that white students must be educated to fill positions of political power and economic dominance while the black Africans were still educated for "technical" or blue-collar jobs. As a result, in 1984, for example, the government of South Africa spent ten times as much on education for white students as it did for black students.[3] In the same year the student-teacher ratio was 24:1 for white students and 47:1 for African students. In 1979, only five thousand Africans were enrolled in institutions of higher education out of a total population of twenty-two million compared to 11,825 white students out of a total population of 4.3 million.[4]

It is no wonder that Africans were demanding nothing less than the eradication of apartheid in all its forms as a condition for the transformation of the country. For many years, this demand was only one of many conditions that Africans felt must be eliminated to set South Africa on the road to genuine social change and national development. Because they felt that it was not possible to initiate change under apartheid, its eradication would constitute the first step toward educational reform as a prerequisite of the transformation of South Africa. By the time Mandela was released from prison it was quite evident to all the people of South Africa that the die-hard Afrikaners would continue to resist this call at the peril their own developmental interests and perpetuating national strife. When change in the political system finally came with the elections held in April 1994 a new stage was set for the real task that all South Africans knew they had to face—initiating the process for the transformation of the country. The recognition of the fact that call for reform under apartheid must give way to the call for the end of apartheid itself translated into a major national endeavor to save a country from blowing apart.

THE NEED FOR REFORM TO SOLVE THE PROBLEMS OF SOUTHERN AFRICA

In deciding to release Nelson Mandela, de Klerk's government must have fully recognized that it was time for change, and that apartheid would be maintained at the peril of maintaining a devastating national conflict and isolation from the world community. Neither the world community nor Africans all over the continent could any longer accept the continuation of the violence of apartheid. Speaking in Soweto during the reception held in his honor on February 12, 1990, Mandela expressed the determination of Africans to end apartheid once and for all. With special reference to education, Mandela warned, "The educational crisis in our country is a crisis in politics. Education under apartheid is a crime against humanity."[5]

In Chapter 1, we reached the conclusion that the problems of national development in all of southern Africa cannot be resolved until solutions to the political and economic problems of educational reform are found. This is the reality and the perspective that a prominent South African in Cape Town had in mind when he concluded, "The thrust for national development in all of southern Africa cannot be undertaken without meeting the challenge of educational reform. Educational reform is the foundation upon which national developmental programs are built. No country can envisage meaningful change in its political, social, and economic systems without initiating educational reform first."[6]

The release of Nelson Mandela must also be seen in the context of fundamental change that has been taking place elsewhere in southern Africa. On May 12, Mobuto Sese Seko, the military ruler of Zaire since 1965, announced that Zairians were now free to form other political parties and to exercise freedom of speech, provided they operated under his control and direction as he had outlined in 1971. When the students at the University of Zaire demanded that Seko resign from office as a condition of initiating reform in education so as to bring about social change, Seko resorted to his characteristic repressive approach. It was not possible for both Seko and the apartheid government to come to terms with the call for fundamental change without recognizing that change is imperative for reform and reform is an imperative for national development. It is a symbiotic cycle; since both represented the status quo, both became major problems in a regional endeavor to initiate reform. There is no question that when the international community and the Africans recognized the violence of both apartheid and Seko's high-handedness as problems of regional development, they were actually acknowledging them as major handicaps to educational reform and social transformation of southern Africa.

From 1983 to 1993 South Africa's active involvement in the brutal civil wars in Angola and Mozambique, along with the opposition activities brought about by dissident elements in Zimbabwe, and its periodic raids into neighboring countries in military pursuit of ANC guerrillas combine to destabilize the region and place it at a crossroads. Also South Africa's successful efforts to weaken the SADCC so that the black countries in southern Africa would continue to depend on it for economic survival caused enormous difficulties for the region as a whole. From 1987 to 1990, the apartheid government was pressured to accept the UN's terms contained in Resolution 435 of 1978 for the independence of Namibia on March 21, 1990. Then came the realization that the South African government had to come to terms with the demands made by the Africans if the whites ever hoped to have a meaningful future in the country.

The fact of the matter is that de Klerk's government could not come to terms with the demands made by the Africans in South Africa without persuading the Afrikaners to come to terms with the demands made by their neighbors. But South Africa would not come to terms with the demands made by its neighbors without ceasing its destabilizing activity in the region. The increase in sales of firearms by 60 percent among the whites in April 1990 is an action that did nothing to resolve the problems caused by apartheid. South Africa's conscious decision to stop its aid to Afonzo Dhlamini's Renamo in Mozambique and to Jonas Savimbi's UNITA in Angola would constitute a set of elements that were essential to initiate social change to ensure regional peace and development. Above all, de Klerk and his government knew that they must persuade their fellow Afrikaners to accept the reality that it was in their own best interest to accept without further delay the principle of majority rule under the universal practice of one person, one vote.

This is the view that Dickson Mungazi expressed when he wrote a letter to de Klerk on February 15, 1990, saying,

It is very important for you to lift the state of emergency in order to allow the Africans to place their confidence in your sincerity to negotiate in good faith. To try to negotiate with them under the influence of the state of emergency is to try to have them function with their hands tied on their back. It is vitally important for the whites of South Africa to recognize that the principle of majority rule must prevail as a condition of social change which the people of South Africa must accept. History shows that whenever a minority rules over the majority, abuse of power and oppression become inevitable. This condition can only be perpetuated at the cost of increasing racial conflict. The support that South Africa has been giving to Jonas Savimbi and Afonzo Dhlamini's Renamo in Mozambique has also created a violent situation in all of southern Africa. Regional peace is important for South Africa itself and its action to stop periodic raids into frontline states can go a long way in resolving major problems the entire region is facing.[7]

The massive demonstrations that were staged throughout South Africa on February 17, 1990, the first time that political demonstrations had been allowed and in which thousands of Africans participated, were in demand of fundamental change to accommodate the aspirations of all people. That the demonstrators demanded educational reform, equal political rights, better housing, better salaries, better working conditions, and an end to apartheid in general underscored the need for rapid reform in South Africa. The refusal of the colonial governments to recognize the importance of extending these basic human rights is what placed the country and the region at a crossroads over many years. The simple fact that Africans were not allowed to vote in national elections in South Africa until 1994, that they could not hold public office outside the Bantustan Homelands, is the basis of their legitimate demand for rapid educational reform to ensure complete social change with political power and economic opportunity.

By coincidence, there were massive demonstrations in Washington, D.C., on the same day. It was not surprising that the demonstrators demanded that President George Bush ensure that the United States would not lift economic sanctions against South Africa until apartheid had been dismantled and a nonracial society had been created. Their demands of President Bush to withdraw his invitation to de Klerk to visit the White House for discussions suggests the conclusion that Americans understood the imperative need for fundamental change before South Africa was readmitted into the circle of the international community. There is no doubt that these events suggest only one thing: transformation in all aspects of national life in South Africa was necessary to avoid major conflicts that could result in disaster felt worldwide.

In 1996, the Afrikaners had still not recognized the important of accepting change and the need for educational reform. In January, a school controlled by a group of Afrikaners in Potgietersburg drew the attention of the international community when they refused any efforts made by an African family to enroll its children. This refusal was the most blatant challenge to the national efforts to bring about equal access and equality of educational opportunity to all the students of South Africa. Integration of schools was required by the laws promulgated in 1994. The Afrikaner parents opposed integration of schools on the grounds that it would erode away the culture of the Afrikaners. In response, government officials joined African parents in a court action to force the Afrikaners to accept African students.

When the court ruled in favor of integration, the Afrikaners threatened to appeal to the constitutional court.[8] Explaining the reason for her action in trying to enroll her daughter in the school, Meiki Kekan said, "I want my child to get a quality education, just like whites."[9] When asked for her reaction, seven-year-old Karaba Kekan, Meiki's daughter, simply responded, "I am not afraid."[10] She and sixteen other African students went straight into the office of the principal to enroll, forcing the Afrikaner parents to withdraw their children from the school. In a move reminiscent of the crisis caused by integration of schools in the southern United States beginning in 1957, dozens of police officers were placed in various positions to protect the African students at Potgietersburg school. Dozens of journalists were also on hand to record the activities surrounding the school. The Afrikaners did not appear to have learned anything from the experiences in the United States during the civil rights struggle or from those of Zimbabwe in 1980. This crisis shows that once the reform process has been initiated, it cannot be stopped or reversed. It gains momentum as it pulls out of the depression of oppression.

PURPORTED REFORM DURING THE COLONIAL PERIOD

The action of the Afrikaners at Potgietersburg in resisting integration of the educational process is quite typical of the action of the colonial governments all over Africa. This is why the decade between 1970 and 1980 witnessed a spiraling demand for more and better education in Africa than at any other period in the history of the continent. However, the decade between 1980 and 1990 witnessed the emergence of new attitudes toward educational reform to make fundamental change in the political, social, and economic system possible. There has now merged a sociatic need for the year 2000 that must be figured into the equation. During the decade before 1960 and 1970 the African nations were still struggling to shake off the effects of European colonial rule as they attempted to carve for themselves a new national identity. But the African nations quickly realized that the thrust for educational reform was more complex than they had thought, because the influence of the colonial period was stronger than they thought. Indeed, during that decade and beyond, the African nations were attempting to educate their people to fit into social structures that are no longer in existence today, that is, the social structure that accommodated apartheid. The difficult choices that the nations of southern Africa had to make in the educational systems and the priorities that they had to establish as a strategy for the future development of education were, in effect, forced on them by many economic factors. Most were factors beyond their control.

There is no question that the problems these nations have been facing can be traced to the establishment of the colonial governments in the nineteenth century. In this study we have concluded that as an outcome of the Berlin Conference of 1885, European nations placed more importance on securing raw materials than on the development of Africans to facilitate the creation of better human relationships for the future to suit the social conditions of a new era. For this reason, the colonial governments considered it essential to limit educational opportunity for Africans so that they could be more effectively controlled politically by training them to function as laborers.

This strategy suggests the conclusion that from their inception, the colonial governments did not encourage the development of education among the Africans because they knew that their ability to acquire it would enable them to acquire elements of critical thinking. With critical thinking skills they would recognize the injustice of the colonial systems themselves. Therefore, the denial of equal educational opportunities to Africans became the green pastures in which the milk cows of colonialism grazed. As the colonial governments became more solidly established, the need to train Africans to function as laborers became more profoundly felt. In southern Africa as a whole, the views that Cecil John Rhodes, Paul Kruger, Leopold II, Antonio Salazar, Daniel Malan, Hendrik Verwoerd, and John Vorster expressed toward the need to restrict the educational advancement of Africans suggest that as economic conditions changed, the need to change the system of education became apparent.

But, because the colonial governments considered change in the way that it was intended to ensure their effective control, Africans were trained to function only in terms of a desire among colonial officials to make them more efficient laborers. This kind of change cannot be regarded as reform, even though the colonial governments themselves considered it an improvement because it was an improvement in the effectiveness of the machinery of control. It did not ensure improvement in the conditions that controlled Africans. The denial of equal educational opportunities to Africans presented the colonial governments with a formidable problem. In colonial Zimbabwe, for example, when free and compulsory education was extended to white students in 1935, Africans struggled against great difficulties in their effort to gain meaningful education.

After the Second World War, a general political consciousness among Africans all over the continent created a new situation that the colonial governments did not anticipate. When Africans began to recognize the injustice of the colonial systems and demanded change, not only in education, but also in other important sociatic areas of their lives, the colonial governments were reluctant to respond affirmatively. The more Africans were denied equal educational opportunities, the more they demanded them, and the more they demanded them, the more the colonial governments repressed them. This is also how a climate of conflict was created in the friction between Africans and the colonial governments. The friction finally united the conflicts, and all countries in southern Africa freed themselves from colonial oppression. Ironically they now face oppression again.

That this situation was having implications beyond the educational process is evident in the new environment that emerged in which political manifestations of education became a new factor of the relationships between the colonial governments and Africans.[11] Once political manifestations of education became the new modus operandi of relationships between Africans and the colonial governments, the struggle for equal educational opportunities took a back seat to the struggle for political rights and independence, and their major efforts to create conditions of educational reform possible so as to make social change possible were frustrated.[12] This is precisely the strategy that was adopted by Africans of South Africa from 1976 to 1994. It is equally true that the educational policy of the colonial governments in southern Africa failed to develop a system of communication that would have become the basis of resolving national problems because the colonial governments saw the education of the Africans only as it was intended to prepare them to serve the purposes of the colonial society.

One reaches three conclusions about the formulation and implementation of the educational policy of the colonial governments in southern Africa. The first conclusion is that not only did these policies have the effect of trying to control the rise of African nationalism, but they also had an adverse effect on Africans' reactions to Western culture itself. The second conclusion is that the overall effect of the colonial educational policy is the emergence of an action that continued to isolate the colonial governments from a rapidly developing trend of thinking among Africans that equality of educational opportunities that includes development of the concept of self, economic opportunities, and political freedom of choice were essential to national development. The application of the policy of the colonial governments also made it unlikely for them to see the conflict that was emerging between the two sides from the point of view of Africans.

The third conclusion is that because the emergence of new attitudes among Africans against the policies of the colonial governments originated primarily as a result of their contact with missionaries, the colonial governments tried to enlist them on their side of the growing conflict. Indeed, in Angola and Mozambique, the Catholic Church supported the policies of the Portuguese government. In South Africa, the Dutch Reformed Church came out squarely on the side of the government. But by 1970, realizing that it was pursuing a wrong policy, the church decided to shift its policy from supporting the government to supporting the Africans because the Africans themselves had convinced them of the rightness of their cause. In that same year, the British Conference of the Missionary Society issued a statement condemning the policies pursued by the colonial governments in Africa and called for action to bring all colonial systems to an end. The statement said, "The struggle for justice in society means that there is a need for radical social change. But radical social change is not likely to take place without a revolution."[13]

This shift of position by the church was crucial in the ensuing struggle for independence. It added a critical dimension in the political landscape that would soon come into existence. The decision of some of the members[14] of the Dutch Reformed Church in 1985 to oppose apartheid is one major reason why de Klerk and his government decided to announce their intention to initiate the process of the transformation of South Africa. But when, in April 1990, de Klerk announced that the advent of an African majority government was not envisaged in the kind of change he had in mind, the course of reform that the people of South Africa had hoped would be initiated with his announcement of February 2 suffered a severe setback. This meant that while some members of the Dutch Reformed Church played a critical role in forcing de Klerk to see the imperative of major social change in South Africa, there were others who exerted on him strong pressure not to yield to demands for the kind of change that Africans wanted to see. In this context the action of taking sides in the controversy surrounded the need for major social change that added a new twist in the conflict between the Africans and the government.

This critical situation suggests that the claim and initiative for educational reform during the colonial period could not be accomplished without corresponding change in the political, social, and economic systems. The unrepresentative character of the colonial society, such as existed in South Africa until 1994, did not permit Africans to play a significant role in its operations and functions. What is even more disturbing is that in their resistance to efforts to help them perceive the need to bring about a genuine reform in both the social system and in education, the colonial governments themselves became the ultimate victims of their own policies. This is undoubtedly the fate that Afrikaners knew awaited them and the government of South Africa in their resistance to efforts to assist them to see the need to end apartheid. Those members of the Dutch Reformed Church who made a call for change cannot be blamed for supporting Africans in their struggle for political independence as a prerequisite of educational reform.

In 1963, William H. Lewis put the struggle for meaningful change in Africa in the context of the conditions created by the colonial systems, saying,

This is a time of testing in Africa. The old signposts are being torn down. The hallmarks of colonialism are disappearing. In the crucible of social change, new human formations are beginning to take shape. In some respects this is a supremacy of important transitional period, one signifying the end of innocence. Now, in the throes of national building and modernization, Africa is fashioning new values, identities and orientation.[15]

What is important in Lewis's observation about the need for change in Africa during the colonial period is that the need is still felt in the nations of southern Africa today. Based on the tenets of traditional African wisdom, the educated African of 1990 can define his values, traditions, and customs and create an identity. This is what students in other countries are doing; they are defining their concepts of self in terms of their past knowledge, current wisdom, and visionary future.

At this point in the history of southern Africa, if one looks back to the dramatic events of 1963, one would have to conclude that it was almost unquestionable that the closing phase of the colonial period would leave behind a legacy that, by 1996, would still stand in the way of meaningful change. Today, the practice of one-party systems of government, the system of president for life, and political repression are among the most devastating forms of that legacy. One-party government in perpetuity is stagnating to a democracy. In this kind of setting, the African leaders themselves must be aware of the damage they are inflicting on a national effort toward change by holding on to outdated institutional structures.

Apart from the cultural, political, and social consequences resulting from the policies pursued by the colonial governments in Africa, there have been serious economic consequences that have had an enormous impact on the efforts of nations of southern Africa to change the systems to ensure reform. Because the most important reason European nations embarked on a colonial adventure in Africa was economic, it would be unrealistic to think that after years of pursuing economic policies that placed the Africans at a disadvantage, the effect would suddenly disappear at the time African countries became independent.[16] It is this reality that the nations of southern Africa must take into consideration in their effort to improve the conditions of life of their people to ensure national development.

We have reached a conclusion in this study that economic development and educational reform are closely related. There is a belief among some leaders of the nations of southern Africa that the economic problems of their nations originated from the system of monopoly practiced during the colonial period. In essence, this meant that the colonial governments controlled major aspects of the economy. These leaders, therefore, have come to a wrong conclusion that nationalization of major industries is the answer to all their economic problems. They are not able to see all the adverse effects of nationalization. These include corruption by government officials themselves, rampant inflation, decline of the currency, stagnation in economic productivity, and a lack of incentives. These are only a few of the many problems of nationalization that leaders of the nations of southern Africa are not able to solve to invest in educational reform and development.

The leaders of the nations of southern Africa also fail to realize that the colonial governments were assured of markets and that exploitation of African labor sustained the economy. The substitution of the system of monopoly during the colonial period with a system of nationalization after it offers no viable alternative solution to the problems of economic development in southern Africa. The African governments cannot engage in either a system of monopoly or nationalization without oppressing their own people. The development of the economy is such a delicate operation that it has to be approached in a deliberate and careful manner. A balance has to be maintained between national policies that provide a dynamic advancement of the economy and the freedom of the people to engage in those economic activities that are central to their own interests as a prerequisite of national development. These are the elements that demand meaningful social change. Competition and capitalism are not major traditional African values that have to be learned.

In 1960, Harold Macmillan, the British prime minister from 1957 to 1963, put the case for fundamental social change in Africa in the context of the influence of events that had global implications. Speaking to the joint session of the South African Parliament in Cape Town, Macmillan warned the colonial governments of the consequences of refusing to accept change, saying,

In the twentieth century, especially since the end of the war in 1945, the process which gave birth to the nation-states of Europe have been replicated all over the world. We have seen the awakening of national consciousness among people who for centuries lived in dependence upon some other power. The wind of change is blowing through the continent of Africa. Whether we like it or not, this growth of national consciousness is a political fact. We must accept it as a fact, and our national policies must take account of it. Its causes are to be found in the pushing forward of the frontiers of knowledge in the service of human needs and in the spread of education.[17]

The importance of Macmillan's speech lay not in the results that he anticipated would ensue from the positive response of the colonial establishments, but in awakening a new level of consciousness among Africans that this was a period of fundamental social change. Africans, therefore, regarded the speech as an invitation to mobilize themselves in response to a popular call to initiate the process for fundamental change. For the Africans of 1960, the call for this kind of change signaled the beginning of a new era in their perception about themselves as a group of people with a destiny. They were free to take part in shaping new directions to the kind of future that they had always wanted and hoped for since 1945. Africans, therefore, regarded the colonial systems and all that they represented as something that must have no part in influencing that future except their own influence.

THE CAMPAIGN FOR EDUCATIONAL REFORM IN SOUTHERN AFRICA TODAY

In their struggle for political independence and self, beginning with the end of the war in 1945, Africans recognized the importance of shaping developmental policies despite the fact that the colonial governments argued that they were not yet ready to assume their full role in an industry-based economy. The major theoretical assumption of this approach was that national political independence was a necessary condition for their development. This strategy had the important feature of taking the increased political consciousness into consideration. It was quite obvious to Africans that no economic development could take place to benefit the people in countries that were still under colonial rule. The knowledge that political institutions must be transformed along lines that would serve the needs of the people to strengthen the economy and so make it possible to ensure their advancement is what Africans recognized as the basis of the challenge they felt must be met in educational reform.

But to ensure an effective educational reform to suit the needs of the emerging southern Africa, Africans also recognized that fundamental change had to be initiated in important features of education itself, such as objectives for the organization, administration, curriculum, and planning of educational systems throughout the country. Literacy had to become the number one political, economic, and sociatic priority.

In most countries of southern Africa, change in the system of the administration has not kept pace with rapidly moving events. The growth of the school population, increase in spending for education, and planning for the future are all aspects of the system of administration of education that must be taken into account to ensure reform.[18] It is important to remember that seeking to improve the system of administration of education does not mean increased bureaucracy. We have concluded that it is equally true to say that no country in southern Africa has sufficient financial resources to do all the things that need to be done to improve education. However, educational reform must be initiated at all levels if educational development is going to begin.

In seeking to improve the administrative component of educational reform, the nations of southern Africa must be aware of the need to ensure careful financial planning to avoid duplication and waste, but to utilize the best from existing systems and make those components indigenous that can be. To ensure an effective system of administration of education, the nations of southern Africa need to observe three basic principles. The first principle is that participation and consultation at all levels must form the thrust for basic change. This will help determine how the schools will be run, the courses offered, and the general conduct of the school personnel. There must be consultation in the formulation and the implementation of policy in all its dimensions to ensure that the people are involved in their own educational development. Unless those responsible for the thrust and trust for educational reform take this principle into account, their efforts may yield limited results.

The second principle is to regard education as a unified system that, while intended to serve the needs of local students and suit local conditions, must embrace the thrust for national development as a secondary objective. This involves taking national issues into account. This approach, when properly addressed by the educational process, will give breadth and new meaning to national purpose. A unified system will necessitate coordination of all school activity, formal and informal, academic and vocational. This approach to a unified system will enable those undertaking educational reform to set educational objectives that are consistent with larger national goals. It will also enable those in positions of responsibility to define arrangements to fulfill those objectives and to ensure proper progression.

The third principle is that the nations of southern Africa must endeavor to reform education, as the commission of education in Botswana stated in 1977, "in terms of both the learning outcomes and the efficiency with which they use resources."[19] To establish this objective, professional efficiency is needed in managing the course of reform to realize the relationship that must exist among investment, planning, and educational outcomes. The utilization of specialists in various segments of education, such as financial analysts, must not be delegated to individuals who have had no professional training and experience, because educational reform is far too important to be undertaken by amateurs. The wisdom of laypeople can be utilized to derive input into what traditional values and customs must be handed down through formal academic educators. It must be emphasized that in observing these principles, the nations of southern Africa must realize that they entail the practice of democracy in that those who are a part of the process in reform are intimately affected by a national program. They must, therefore, be a part of its formulation and implementation, but keep a pulse on the heartbeat of the people.

To serve the purpose for which it is designed, this principle must be built into the national constitution itself or into the fabric of the electoral and educational processes. While local bodies may, in their respective areas of responsibility, exercise proper authority and procedures in implementing policy, they must take national implications into account to ensure maximum benefits of the process of reform itself. It is only by observing principles of democratic behavior in all its dimensions that educational reform becomes meaningful. Naming a permanent body to oversee educational reform, to advise on planning, to coordinate programs, and to seek resolutions to problems would enhance the prospects of success in this national endeavor. The fact of the matter is that once reform has been undertaken, it must be carried out until positive results begin to show.

In embracing these essential elements of democracy in an endeavor toward educational reform, the nations of southern Africa must constantly remain aware, as the *Transitional National Development Plan* in Zimbabwe observed in 1982, that throughout human history, "it is actually the people who have constituted a dynamic motivation force behind cultural, social and economic development"[20] as a result of educational reform. This highlights the conclusion that the development of the people must become both the focus of educational reform and the major means of achieving it. Any national policy that does not take both considerations into account is void of any real meaning. This also suggests that the people must be educated in such a manner that makes them adequately prepared to utilize the educational opportunity that results from reform and understand the responsibilities and the privileges of being politically active in understanding and implementing change through education.

SUMMARY AND CONCLUSION

We have also concluded that the transformation of southern Africa must seek to reduce the enormous economic and sociatic differences that exist between rural areas and urban areas. Throughout the region the people fall into two groups: the rural people, most of whom are engaged in subsistence agriculture, and the people who reside in urban areas. About 80 percent of the people reside in rural areas. This means that without a viable means of economic activity, the development of rural areas is at best haphazard. With 80 percent of the population denied a viable means of economic development, the nations of southern Africa are forced to have a false sense of progress and resort to the ways of their grandfathers to sustain life. Lack of educational opportunity has kept them from knowing about health-related issues such as AIDS or the hazards of smoking. Lack of education and the lack of news keep rural people from knowing about birth control and crop rotation. Rural man's life was considered successful by the number of children he fathered.

When the national resources of the countries of southern Africa are directed toward the development of 20 percent of the population in urban areas,[21] national leaders must realize that they cannot prosper with this serious imbalance between urban and rural conditions. The fact of the matter is that government leaders tend to neglect rural areas because they are considered less involved in national politics. Change in this situation would demand fundamental change in the economic system. This would necessitate equalizing the educational system. Equalization would mean eliminating differences in the nature of conditions between urban areas and rural areas, such as schools, books, and teachers. Unless the nations of southern Africa make a concerted effort to eliminate rural-urban differences, their countries will continue to experience the scourge of underdevelopment.

It is also in the best interest of the nations of southern Africa to recognize that their societies are composed of people of different levels of educational attainment. In addition to the rural population consisting mainly of peasants, there are also the working class; intellectuals; and professionals, such as teachers, medical doctors, nurses, and writers. The important thing to remember is that educational reform will make it possible for people of varied talents and interests to choose their own careers and give their nations a widely distributed range of services. This is how nations everywhere ensure their own advancement.

As part of a developmental strategy the nations of southern Africa need to understand that the advancement of their interests and talents must entail mobilizing natural resources to finance educational reform. Because this cannot be done where the educational process is weak and objectives are poorly stated and plans inadequately outlined, the governments must provide an adequate institutional encouragement that is essential for the establishment of national organizations in which popular participation is open to all. This collective action enables participants to identify areas of focus to ensure success in reform. This would make it possible to create new sociatic and economic structures in which people can utilize national resources and harness new deposits of energy for the benefit of all. Educational reform, to serve its proper purpose, must be initiated in the context of these realities.

As a product of sociatic growth, with economic support, educational reform must at all times be anchored on principles that are related to the ultimate aspirations of the people in an environment of established democratic values "set in a dynamic framework of a developing economy"[22] cast in the setting of free trade with minimum or no government control. This provides motivation and incentives for the flow of capital that is needed for investment in diverse industrial productivity. The exploitation of national resources, however, must be undertaken in the context of national commitment to preserve the environment and a fair system of distribution of resources. Legislation must be passed, such as in Zimbabwe in 1985, to make corruption a criminal offense by government officials and the people alike. Free trade and private enterprise also enhance the flow of capital where there is no abuse or corruption. It is here that the government can play a critical role.

The citizens of any country who enter the labor force as a result of an educational system that has embraced principles of reform will understand and operate under the reality of the emerging relationships that must exist between and among different social and economic classes. They will also know how to exercise their freedom of choice of careers that add to sociatic, economic, and political brain bank of the nation. Again, this provides an opportunity for collective action to correct the inadequacy that exists in the present system of education without class conflict. While most nations of southern Africa have found it hard to remove the legacy of the colonial system of education, their persistent efforts to state new objectives would result in an education that would assist in removing adverse effects of the national efforts directed at national development. Acknowledging this situation provides an incentive toward educational reform as a prerequisite of social change and the transformation of the region.

IMPLICATIONS

Once this environment of change comes into existence, the citizens also begin to see the importance of four simple factors that are essential to the sociatics of the individual and critical for the formation of a concept of self. The first factor is the establishment of new levels of communication skills and adjustable minimum wages that must be undertaken with a clear purpose of providing incentives to the pursuit of education. The second factor is providing a healthy work environment. This not only increases productivity but also generates a healthy climate of collegiality among workers. The third factor is respecting the workers' demands for flexibility in scheduling work hours. This allows a degree of control and adjustment of time slots. The fourth factor is respecting the principle of collective bargaining. This allows both management and the workers an opportunity to understand the concerns and appreciate the problems that the other side is experiencing. This means that conflicts are resolved in mutually amicableness, and tension and periodic strikes, which disrupt productivity, are avoided. This suggests that educational innovation affords benefits that would otherwise be lost to efforts toward national development. Reformation must, by its nature, build in an avenue for conflict resolution. Conflict of opinion is a natural part of the democratic process.

To fulfill national objectives based on the observance of these principles, the nations of southern Africa must endeavor to restructure the national ministry of education to give it a new and innovative role. It must then provide real, not symbolic, leadership based on clearly identified educational objectives. It must try to recruit individuals with high moral principles, thorough knowledge of issues in education, and commitment to national values and purposes. When placed under proper leadership settings, these individuals collectively facilitate the process of formulating educational programs consistent with those objectives. In this context, staff development must be directed toward new teaching strategies, scheduling harmonious operations of all levels of education, and proper handling of all levels of school personnel. A special curriculum unit must be created to ensure that it continues to serve the needs of the students in order to serve the developmental needs of the nation and the traditional needs of the culture.

In 1988, Zimbabwe attempted to launch such an initiative. In that year, President Mugabe outlined some essential elements of that level of innovation when he stated,

A master plan for education will be unveiled to aim at expanding the facilities and the capacities of all existing institutions, as well as creating new ones. A total of forty million dollars has been set aside for expanding the facilities. Planning is in progress to inaugurate a special curriculum board which will involve experts from both the public and the private sectors in order to research and develop new courses of study which will be geared to meeting the whole spectrum of pupil abilities, aptitudes and interests.[23]

This new course of study, when fully in place, would prepare students to undertake courses at the college level to enable them to be productive citizens in post-school careers in different areas of national life. But in all his enthusiasm to bring about change in the educational systems that would mean innovation, Mugabe neglected to address some important related areas of that endeavor: the required trained personnel; strategies for implementation; expected outcomes; and the sociatic, political, and economic factors that must be taken into account to ensure success. For some reason, the government of Zimbabwe, like that of any other country in southern Africa, did not realize that for innovation to be successful it has to be initiated with all these factors in mind.

The failure of the government of Zimbabwe to take all relevant factors into consideration in making an effort to initiate educational innovation is perhaps why, in 1989, there was a political dark cloud in this educational silver lining, as the government faced new problems of credibility caused by a declining economy and charges of corruption by some government officials.[24] When members of the government renewed their talk of introducing a one-party system, the situation took on dimensions of a major national crisis, which put the plans for educational innovation that Mugabe had announced on the shelf.

The national crisis in Zimbabwe caused by a combination of political events and the announcement of new plans to reform education in 1988 must be understood in the context of the announcement of educational plans that the government made at the inception of independence on April 18, 1980. Speaking on May 18, 1980, during the opening of the first session of parliament, President Canaan Banana[25] went to great lengths to outline what he called a new educational program initiated by the government, saying, among other things, that the government would spend three hundred million dollars on educational innovation in the 1981 fiscal year. Banana went on to add, "In the field of education, it is the intention of the government to pursue vigorously the reopening of the many schools in the rural areas which were closed as a result of the war and to introduce free education on a phased basis beginning with the primary sector."[26]

Failure to take a number of critical factors into consideration led to the government's inability to meet the goals that Banana had outlined. When, in 1983, Mugabe outlined a new scheme to reach 100 percent literacy rate by 1988, there was an added loss of credibility because, while these programs cost a considerable amount of tax funds, there was little evidence to point to tangible outcomes. This is precisely why the announcement of new educational plans in 1988 was received throughout Zimbabwe with measured skepticism. This situation evinces the accuracy of the conclusion that was reached in this study that failure to initiate adequate planning to ensure successful educational reform would erode away the credibility and confidence of the people. However, this does not mean that Zimbabwe has failed in its efforts to initiate successful reform, rather, it means that it seems to understand its importance and will continue to work out a formula that will ensure its success.

The discussion in this chapter and in this study suggests three implications of educational reform for southern Africa. The first is that its primary intent is to ensure the individual's development of a concept of self for individuals in a larger social context. Development of the individual means self-actualization. This includes self-sufficiency, security in one's personhood, and fulfillment of those goals that are unique to the individual. It means the promotion of one's interests consistent with one's talent. It means freedom to set goals and objectives and to establish priorities. It means ability to generate an environment that gives one freedom of choice to pursue study programs of one's interests. It is only when one's educational needs have become fulfilled that one plays a role in helping one's society fulfill its needs.[27] This is how the elements of national development are put in place. The underlying principle in the relationship between these elements is that there must be a successful climate and educational environment for innovation to make it possible.

The second implication is that a truly independent nation can only arise from a truly independent population. A truly independent population can only emerge from educated individuals. Many nations of Africa, including those of southern Africa, have yet to realize this truth. Without an educated population, nations will always be oppressed by a combination of sociatic forces such as social ills, racial bigotry, tribal or ethnic conflict, and political dissent, all of which southern Africa has experienced. One reaches the conclusion, therefore, that educational reform is in the best interest of the nations themselves. The important thing for the nations of southern Africa to keep in mind is that educational reform cannot be imposed from outside, because it requires a collective action based on common interests and a system to communicate

ideas among the people. About this important principle of educational innovation, Paulo Freire concludes that the "ability to communicate ideas of
self-consciousness"[28] forms an essential part of an education designed to ensure
self-fulfillment as an important step toward creating an environment of
national development. This means that cooperative efforts at the political,
economic, and educational levels must constitute a viable channel to successful
educational innovation.

The third implication is that the greatest threat to successful reform in all
of southern Africa comes from the government decisions to institute one-party
systems of government. Government leaders seem to neglect the fact that in
Africa the philosophy of one-party government has shown evidence that it robs
the people of a genuine desire to promote ideas of individuality as a condition
of national development. It replaces their confidence for the future with an
abyss of despair. What has been discussed about Zimbabwe substantiates the
accuracy of this conclusion. In this kind of social and political setting, the
educational process has only peripheral meaning because individual incentive
and self-motivation, which are important characteristics of human achievement, are rendered meaningless by the government's desire to have its own
philosophy and policy prevail at the expense of the goals and objectives and
creativity of the individual.

Therefore instituting a one-party system of government is often an indica-
tion that the government has something either to hide or to fear from its own
people. Thus, the introduction of a one-party system of government cannot
be considered a step in the direction of national development. After forty-five
years in office, the Nationalist Party of South Africa has found this to be true
the hard way. While the Nationalist Party has ruled supreme since 1948, both
the educational process and human interactions suffered a severe setback. It is
therefore important that the nations of southern Africa that have adopted a
one-party system of government, such as Zambia, Malawi, South Africa,
Mozambique, and Angola, change course and that those nations, such as
Botswana and Zimbabwe, that are multi-party democracies never adopt it.

The sustenance of democracy is too important to be tampered with, because
the survival of nations and the course of educational innovation depend on it
if waves of national conflict are to be avoided. No matter how government
officials see it, a one-party system of government is nothing less than a
dictatorship. This is why, for example, massive demonstrations staged against
the government of Kenneth Kaunda in Zambia led to an attempted military
coup in June 1990 and his defeat in 1992. Since he assumed the office of
president in October, Kaunda not only instituted a one-party rule in 1971, but
he also alienated Zambians by creating a political environment that denied

them a role in the affairs of their country. This is hardly an environment that creates conditions of national development. The people of Zambia, like those of Malawi and South Africa, have come to recognize the fact that their development must not be compromised by government leaders who seek to realize their own personal ambitions. Nations of southern Africa, be well advised and be wise!

NOTES

1. "Twenty of South Africa's Once Powerful White Leaders on Trial in Massacre," *Arizona Republic*, March 12, 1996, p. A6.

2. Nelson Mandela, in a statement made in Cape Town soon after his release from Victor Verster Prison, South African Broadcasting Corporation, February 11, 1990.

3. United Nations, *A Crime Against Humanity: Questions and Answers on Apartheid in South Africa* (New York: Author, 1984), p. 16.

4. Ibid., p. 17.

5. Nelson Mandela, speaking in Soweto during a reception held in his honor, South African Broadcasting Corporation, February 12, 1990.

6. An African during an interview in Cape Town, December 22, 1994.

7. Dickson A. Mungazi, Letter to F. W. de Klerk, February 15, 1990. On March 12, 1990, S. P. Basson, de Klerk's Administrative Secretary, responded to "acknowledge receipt of your letter."

8. The installation of the constitutional court is usually an appeal court put in place by the British each time a country in Africa gained political independence. It was intended to protect the interests of whites when an African government was installed. Among the latest examples of this system was in Zimbabwe in 1980 where white parents resisted integration of schools and appealed to the constitutional court, but lost the appeal, allowing schools to integrate.

9. "Blacks Win Rights to Enroll at White School," *Arizona Daily*, February 22, 1996, p. 8.

10. Ibid.

11. Dickson A. Mungazi, *Education and Government Control in Zimbabwe: A Study of the Commissions of Inquiry, 1908–1974* (New York: Praeger Publishers, 1990), p. 69.

12. Ibid., p. 70.

13. The British Conference of the Missionary Society, "Violence in Southern Africa: A Christian Assessment," October 28, 1970. Old Mutare Methodist Archives.

14. Led by Rev. Bass Naude, these members of the Dutch Reformed Church rejected the biblical reasons on which the church supported apartheid, that black and white had nothing in common and so were unequal even before God. See the documentary film *The Cry of Reason* (Los Angeles, Calif.: California News Report Publishing, 1988) for details.

15. William H. Lewis, *Emerging Africa* (Washington, D.C.: Public Affairs Press, 1963), p. 5.

16. Ibid., p. 7.

17. Harold Macmillan, "Commonwealth Independence and Interdependence," a speech given to the joint session of the South African Parliament, Cape Town, February 3, 1960. The British Embassy, Harare, Zimbabwe.

18. Botswana, *Report of the National Commission on Education*, 1977, p. 185.

19. Ibid., p. 186.

20. Zimbabwe, *Transitional National Development Plan*, Vol. 1, 1982, p. 18.

21. Ibid., p. 19.

22. Ibid., p. 20.

23. Robert Mugabe, "Policy Statement Number 20," Zimbabwe Ministry of Information, June 28, 1988.

24. *New York Times*, December 10, 1989, sec. 2, p. 17.

25. Banana was titular president of Zimbabwe from 1980 to 1989 when Mugabe assumed the office of executive president.

26. Zimbabwe: Government Policy Number 5, a Presidential Directive, May 18, 1980. Zimbabwe Ministry of Information.

27. Dickson Mungazi, "Educational Innovation in Zimbabwe: Possibilities and Problems," *Journal of Negro Education*, Vol. 52, No. 2 (1985), p. 15.

28. Paulo Freire, *Pedagogy of the Oppressed*. Translated by Myra Bergman Ramos (New York: Continuum, 1983), p. 62.

Bibliography

BOOKS

Anglin, Douglas [ed.]. *Conflict and Change in Southern Africa. Papers From a Scandinavian Conference*. Washington, D.C.: University Press of America, 1978.

Banana, Canaan. *Theology of Promise: The Dynamics of Self-Reliance*. Harare: The College Press, 1982.

Battle, V. M., and Charles Lyons. *Essays in the History of African Education*. New York: Teachers College Press, 1970.

Bond-Stewart, Kathy. *Education*. Gweru: Mambo Press, 1986.

——— . *Education in Southern Africa*. Gweru: Mambo Press, 1986, p. 15.

Chidzero, Bernard T. *Education and the Challenge of Independence*. Geneva: IEUP, 1977.

Coombs, Philip H. *World Crisis in Education: The View from the Eighties*. New York: Oxford University Press, 1985.

Cox, Cortland. *African Liberation*. New York: Black Education Press, 1972.

Curle, Adam. *Education for Liberation*. New York: John Wiley and Sons, 1973.

Dewey, John. *Experience and Education*. New York: Collier Books, 1938.

Diffendorfer, Ralph E. [ed.]. *The World Service of the Methodist Episcopal Church*. Chicago: Methodist Council on Benevolences, 1923.

Dugard, John. *The Southwest Africa/Namibia Dispute*. Berkeley: University of California Press, 1973.

Eicher, J. C. *Educational Costing and Financing in Developing Countries: Focus on Sub-Sahara Africa*. Washington, D.C.: World Bank, 1984.

Evans, M. *The Front-Line State, South Africa and Southern African Security: Military Prospects and Perspectives*. Harare: University of Zimbabwe, 1989.

Fafunwa, Babs. *History of Education in Nigeria*. London: George Allen and Unwin, 1974.

Freire, Paulo. *Pedagogy of the Oppressed*. Translated by Myra Bergman Ramos. New York: Continuum, 1983.

Gelfand, Michael. *Diet and Tradition in African Culture*. London: E. S. Livingstone, 1971, p. 45.

————— . *Growing Up in Shona Society*. Gweru: Mambo Press, 1985.

Henderson, Lawrence. *Angola: Five Centuries of Conflict*. Ithaca, N.Y.: Cornell University Press, 1979.

Herbstein, Dennis. *White Man, We Want to Talk to You*. London: Oxford University Press, 1979.

Hirst, Paul. *Knowledge and the Curriculum: A Collection of Philosophical Papers*. London: Routledge and Kegan Paul, 1974.

Huddleston, Trevor. *Naught for Your Comfort*. New York: Oxford University Press, 1956.

Huggins, Godfrey. *Education Policy in Southern Rhodesia: Notes on Certain Features*. Salisburg, Rhodesia: Government Printer, 1939.

Jansen von Rensburg, T. M. "The Learning Ability of the South African Native," in Nicholas Hans, *Comparative Education and Tradition*. London: Oxford University Press, 1958.

Kaunda, Kenneth. *Zambia Shall Be Free*. New York: Frederick Praeger, 1963.

Kimble, H. T. *Emerging Africa*. New York: Scholastic Books, 1963.

Knorr, Kenneth. *British Colonial Theories*. Toronto: University of Toronto Press, 1974.

La Guma, Alex [ed.]. *Apartheid: A Collection of Writings in South African Racism by South Africans*. New York: International Publishers, 1971.

Lewis, William H. *Emerging Africa*. Washington, D.C.: Public Affairs Press, 1963.

Machel, Samora. *Mozambique: Sowing the Seeds of Revolution*. Harare: Zimbabwe Publishing House, 1981.

Mason, Philip. *The Birth of a Dilemma: Conquest and Settlement of Rhodesia*. London: Oxford University Press, 1956.

Memmi, Albert. *The Colonizer and the Colonized*. Boston: Beacon Press, 1965.

Meredith, Martin. *The First Dance of Freedom: Black Africa in the Post-War Era*. New York: Harper and Row, 1984.

Mondlane, Edwardo. *The Struggle for Mozambique*. Baltimore: Penguin Books, 1969.

Motala, Ziyad. *Constitutional Opinions for a Democratic South Africa: A Comparative Perspective*. Washington, D.C.: Howard University Press, 1994.

Mungazi, Dickson A. *The Cross Between Rhodesia and Zimbabwe: Racial Conflict in Rhodesia, 1962–1979*. New York: Vantage Press, 1981.

————— . *The Underdevelopment of African Education*. Washington, D.C.: University Press of America, 1981.

————— . *To Honor the Sacred Trust of Civilization: History, Politics, and Education in Southern Africa*. Cambridge, Mass.: Schenkman Publishers, 1983.

————. *The Struggle for Social Change in Southern Africa: Visions of Liberty.* New York: Taylor and Francis, 1989.

————. *Education and Government Control in Zimbabwe: A Study of the Commissions of Inquiry, 1908–1974.* New York: Praeger Publishers, 1991.

————. *The Honored Crusade: Ralph Dodge's Theology of Liberation and Initiative for Social Change in Zimbabwe.* Gweru: Mambo Press, 1990.

————. *The Fall of the Mantle: The Educational Policy of the Rhodesia Front Government and Conflict in Zimbabwe.* New York: Peter Lang Publishers, 1993.

————. *Gathering under the Mango Tree: Values in Traditional Culture in Africa.* New York: Peter Lang Publishing, 1996.

————. *The Mind of Black Africa.* Westport, CT: Praeger, 1996.

O'Callaghan, Marion. *Namibia: The Effects of Apartheid on Culture and Education.* Paris: UNESCO, 1977.

————. *Rhodesia: The Effects of Apartheid on Culture and Education.* Paris: UNESCO, 1979.

Oldham, James. *White and Black in Africa.* London: Longman, 1930, p. 11.

Parker, Franklin. *African Development and Education in Southern Rhodesia.* Columbus, Ohio: State University Press, 1960.

Phillips, Claude. *The African Political Dictionary.* Santa Barbara, Calif.: ABC-CLIO Information Service, 1985.

Piper, Alan. *South Africa in the American Mind.* New York: Carnegie, 1981.

Powers, B. A. *Religion and Education in Tswana Chiefdom.* London: Oxford University Press, 1961.

Psacharopoulos, George. *Higher Education in Developing Countries. A Cost Benefit Analysis.* Washington, D.C.: World Bank, 1980.

Psacharopoulos, George, and Maureen Woodhall. *Education for Development: An Analysis of Investment Choices.* New York: Oxford University Press, 1985.

Ranger, Terrence. *Revolt in Southern Rhodesia, 1896–1897.* Evanston, Ill.: Northwestern University Press, 1967.

Raphaeli, Nimroid. *Public Sector Management in Botswana.* Washington, D.C.: World Bank, 1984.

Raynor, William. *The Tribe and Its Successors: An Account of African Traditional Life After European Settlement in Southern Rhodesia.* New York: Frederick Praeger, 1962.

Riddell, Roger. *From Rhodesia to Zimbabwe: Education for Employment.* Gweru: Mambo Press, 1980.

Samkange, Stanlake. *What Rhodes Really Said About Africa.* Harare: Harare Publishing House, 1982.

Segai, Ronald, and Ruth First. *Southwest Africa: Travesty of Trust.* London: Deutsch, 1967.

Smith, C. William. *Nyerere of Tanzania.* Harare: Zimbabwe Publishing House, 1981.

Smuts, J. C. *The League of Nations: A Practical Suggestion.* New York: UN, 1918.

Southall, Aldon. *The Illusion of Tribe.* The Netherlands: R. J. Brill, 1970.

Sparrow, George. *The Rhodesian Rebellion*. London: Brighton, 1966.

Thompson, A. R. *Education and Development in Africa*. New York: St. Martin's Press, 1981.

Turner, V. W. *Schism and Continuity in an African Society*. Manchester: Manchester University Press, 1957.

Tutu, Desmond. *Crying in the Wilderness: The Struggle for Justice in South Africa*. Grand Rapids, Mich.: William Eerdmans Publishers, 1982.

Vambe, Lawrence. *An Ill-Fated People: Zimbabwe Before and After Rhodes*. Pittsburgh: Pittsburgh University Press, 1957.

Van Til, William. *Education: A Beginning*. Boston: Houghton Mifflin Company, 1974.

Watson, George. *Change in School System*. Washington, D.C.: National Training Laboratories, NEA, 1967.

Weaver, Thomas [ed.]. *To See Ourselves: Anthropology and Modern Social Issues*. Glenview, Ill.: Scott, Foreman and Company, 1973.

Wills, A. J. *An Introduction to the History of Central Africa*. London: Oxford University Press, 1964.

GOVERNMENT DOCUMENTS AND MATERIALS

Botswana. *Ten Years of Independence*. Gaberone: Government Printer, 1976.

——— . *Report of the National Commission on Education*. Gaberone: Government Printer, April 1977.

——— . *Education Statistics*. Gaberone: Government Printer, 1979.

——— . *Education for Kagisano: Supplementary Report of the National Commission on Education*. Gaberone: Government Printer, July 1979.

——— . *Botswana Update*. Gaberone: Government Printer, 1982.

British South Africa Company Records. Earl Grey, 1896–1898: Folio: AV/1/11/1/11:547–548. Zimbabwe National Archives.

Huggins, Godfrey. "Rhodesia Leads the Way: Education for Europeans in Southern Rhodesia." *Times Educational Supplement*, February 14, 1931.

——— . "Partnership in Rhodesia and Nyasaland," a speech given during a campaign for the establishment of the Federation of Rhodesia and Nyasaland, May 1950.

——— . "Partnership in Building a Country," a political speech, December 21, 1950.

——— . "Taking Stock of African Education," an address to the Southern Rhodesia Missionary Conference, Goromonzi, August 26, 1954.

Mozambique. Samora Machel. "The Liberation of Women as a Fundamental Necessity for Revolution," an address given at the opening of the First Conference of Mozambique Women, March 4, 1973.

——— . Samora Machel. "Leadership Zimbabwe: Prime Minister. *Address to the Organization of African Unity*, Document No. 2. Freetown, Sierra Leone, July 4, 1980.

————. Ministry of Information: *Education in Mozambique. Maputo: Government Printer, 1982.*

Rhodesia. *African Education*, Ref. 738, 1973.

————. *Parliamentary Debates*, August 26, 1977, August 27, 1974, August 30, 1974.

————. *Report of the Commission of Inquiry into Racial Discrimination* [Vincent Quenet, Chairman], Ref. 27015/36050, April 23, 1976.

————. *Education: An Act*, No. 8, 1979.

South Africa. *Proclamation over Southwest Africa*, November 27, 1918.

Southern Rhodesia. *Education Ordinance Number 18: The Appointment of Inspector of Schools*, 1899.

————. *Ordinance Number 1*, 1903.

————. *Legislative Debates*, 1923–1961.

————. *Annual Reports of the Director of Native Education, 1927–1960.*

————. *Legislative Assembly Debates*, April 2, 1937.

————. *Annual Reports of the Director of Native Education, 1927–1960.*

Tanzania. *Education for Self-Reliance.* Dar es Salaam: Government Printer, 1967.

Zambia. Zambia Information Service: *Zambia in Brief.* Lusaka: Government Printer, 1975.

————. *Educational Reform: Proposals and Recommendations*, Lusaka, October 1977.

————. K. D. Kaunda: *Blueprint for Economic Development: A Guide on How to Clear Obstacles*, Lusaka, October 8, 1979.

Zimbabwe. ZAPU. *Zimbabwe Primary Syllabus*, August, 1978.

————. *Prime Minister Opens Economic Conference*, Harare, September 5, 1980.

————. *The Prime Minister Opens an Economic Symposium*, Harare: Government Printer, September 11, 1980.

————. *Prime Minister's New Year's Message to the Nation*, December 31, 1980.

————. *Not in a Thousand Years: From Rhodesia to Zimbabwe*, a documentary film, PBS, 1981.

————. Mugabe, Robert. "Literacy for All in Five Years," a speech given in launching a national literacy campaign, July 18, 1983.

————. *The Constitution of Zimbabwe.* Harare: Government Printer, 1985.

————. *Constitutional Amendment No. 23*, Harare, Government Printer, 1987.

————. *Annual Digest of Statistics.* Harare: Government Printer, 1988.

————. *Annual Report of the Secretary for Education, 1980–1989.* Harare: Government Printer, 1989.

————. B. T. Chidzero, Minister of Finance and Planning, *Budget Statement*, July 27, 1989.

NEWSPAPERS, JOURNALS AND MAGAZINES

Chicago Tribune. October 1, 1981.

Christian Science Monitor. "Future Leaders Learn Next-door: Namibians Study at U.N. School in Zambia." September 7, 1989.

Economist. September 30, 1989.

Herald (Zimbabwe). July 4, 1983–August 8, 1989.

————. "Mozambique Looks to the World for $450 Million Aid." April 13, 1989.

————. "Secondary Schools Hit by Shortage of Qualified Teachers." July 15, 1989.

————. "Apartheid Cannot be Condoned." July 10, 1989.

————. "Worry over Schools Zoning." July 17, 1989.

————. "Mozambique Peace Drive a Concern." July 20, 1989.

————. "Concept of Education with Production Explained." July 24, 1989.

————. "University of Zimbabwe gets $400 million from Federal Republic of Germany for Developing Equipment." July 28, 1989.

————. "Nkomo's Economic Objectives Are a Priority in Resettlement." July 28, 1989.

————. "Sanctions that Would Bite." August 11, 1989.

————. "Nkomo Lectures University Students." August 11, 1989.

————. "President Calls for Revolutionary Land Reform Programs." August 12, 1989.

————. "Compensation for Teachers who Joined Freedom Struggle." August 17, 1989.

Los Angeles Times. "Africa's Future Riding the Train to Nowhere." July 17, 1990.

Moto (Gweru). August 1983–August 1989.

New York Times. "Students Fail Zimbabwe and Pay Heavy Price." November 16, 1989.

————. "Higher Controls Seen in Zimbabwe." December 10, 1989.

————. "The Old Men versus the Public: Africa's Iron Hands Struggle to Hang On." July 15, 1990.

South Africa Scan. "Facts and Reports." 1989.

Sunday Mail (Zimbabwe). "Teachers Form Union." August, 1989.

Time. March 5, 1990.

————. July 9, 1990.

Washington Post. August 1, 1989.

The World Almanac and Book of Facts. New York: Pharos Books, 1990.

ZIMBABWE, MINISTRY OF INFORMATION. PRESS STATEMENTS AND SPEECHES BY GOVERNMENT OFFICIALS ON EDUCATION

Culverwell, Joseph, Minister of State for National Scholarship. "Take Education Seriously." Ref. 59/88/SL/BC, February 23, 1989.

Chung, Faye, Minister of Primary and Secondary Education. "Pre-School Training Graduates." Ref. 317/88/GB/SD/BJ, July 25, 1988.

————. "The Importance of Local Production of Science Textbooks." Ref. 80/89/CB/MA, March 9, 1989.

————. "The Role of Booksellers in Educational Development." Ref. 223/89/CB/E/S, July 13, 1989.

————. "Women Are Educated Less than Men." Ref. 230/89/CB/SM/SR, July 25, 1989.

————. "U.S. Sponsored Students Graduate." Ref. 78/89/CB/MA, March 1, 1989.

Hughes, Aminia, Deputy Minister of Transport. "Be Selfless and Dedicated Teachers." Ref. 482/88/SM, October 28, 1988.

Jujuru, Joyce, Minister of Community and Cooperative Development. "Women's Role in Nation Building." Ref. 4/1/89/SG/SM, June 6, 1989.

Karimanzira, David, Minister of Social Services. "Educate the People on the Dangers of Agrochemicals." Ref. 399/88/EMM/CB, September 14, 1988.

————. "Educate Farmers on Better Livestock Production." Ref. 472/88/EMM/SM, October 25, 1988.

————. "Government to Provide More Extension Staff." Ref. 235/89/EMM/SM/SK, July 25, 1989.

Kay, Jack, Deputy Minister of Lands. "Agriculture, and Rural Settlement: Zimbabwe Is SADDC's Breadbasket." Ref. 384/EMM/SG, August 29, 1988.

Ministry of Higher Education. "Learner-Tutor Course Applications." Ref. 459/88/CB/SM, October 17, 1988.

Ministry of Information. "Vacancies for Zimbabwe-Cuba Teacher Education Course." Ref. 460/88/CB/SM, October 17, 1988.

Ministry of Public Construction and National Housing. "Three Hundred Million Dollars Boost Rural Housing." Ref. 19/89/BC/SK, January 23, 1989.

Muchemwa, Felix, Minister of Health. "State Certificated Nurses Graduate in Masvingo." Ref. 29/80/RN/SD/BJ, July 21, 1988.

Mutumbuka, Dzingai, Minister of Higher Education. "Marymount Teachers Graduate." Ref. 365/88/03/MM, August 20, 1988.

————. "The University of Zimbabwe Staff Development." Ref. 405/88/CB/ME, September 14, 1988.

————. "The Role of Professional Bodies in National Development." Ref. 427/88/CB/EMM, September 22, 1988.

————. "Training Institutions Play Vital Role in National Development." Ref. 447/88/CC/ES, October 7, 1988.

————. "The Importance of Revising History." Ref. 15/89/CB/SK, January 23, 1989.

Nkomo, John, Minister of Labor. "A Call for Educational Program." Ref. 356/88/SK/EM/SG, August 17, 1988.

Nyagumbo, Maurice, Minister of Political Affairs. "Zimbabwe Objects to Education of U.N. Transitional Assistance Group." Ref. 7/89/BC/SM, January 13, 1988.

OTHER MATERIALS AND DOCUMENTS

UN Documents on Namibia

UNESCO. *International Conference in Support of the Struggle of the Namibian People for Independence.* Paris, April 25–29, 1983.

United Nations. Decree Number 1: *For the Protection of the Natural Resources of Namibia.* New York: Author, September 1974.

————. *A Trust Betrayed: Namibia.* New York: Author, 1974.

————. Namibian Uranium. New York: Author, September 1974.

————. Objective: Justice: Walvis Bay, an Integral Part of Namibia. New York: Author, April 24, 1978.

————. *Nationhood Program for Namibia.* New York: Author, 1981.

————. *Namibia: A Unique UN Responsibility.* New York: Author, December 1981.

————. *United Nations Council for Namibia: What it Is, What it Does, How it Works.* New York: Author, March 1983.

————. *Program of Action Against Apartheid.* New York: Author, October 25, 1983.

United Nations Council for Namibia. *Meetings Held in Algeria.* New York: United Nations, May 28–June 1, 1980.

————. *Meetings Held in Panama City.* New York: United Nations, June 2–5, 1981.

————. *Arusha Declaration and Program of Action on Namibia.* New York: United Nations: May 14, 1982.

On Southern Africa in General

ABC-TV, *20/20* "The Agony of Mozambique." March 2, 1990.

Africa Action Committee. *Uhuru for Southern Africa.* Kinshasa, December 15, 1984.

Afro-American and African Studies. *Africana.* College Park, Md., Vol. 2, No. 1, 1985.

Anad, Mohamed. *Apartheid: A Form of Slavery.* No. 37. New York: U.N., 1971. Pamphlet.

The Anglo-Rhodesian Relationship. "Proposals for a Settlement." Ref. Cmd/RR/46, 1971.

Ayittey, George. "In Africa Independence Is a Far Cry from Freedom." *Wall Street Journal,* March 28, 1990.

Basson, S.P.N., Administrative Secretary to President F. W. de Klerk. Letter dated 12 March, 1990, addressed to Dickson a. Mungazi, Northern Arizona Unviersity, Flagstaff, in response to his dated February 15, 1990, addressed to President de Klerk.

British Council of Missionary Society. "Violence in Southern Africa: A Christian Assessment." A statement of policy on Southern Africa, October 28, 1970.

British Methodist Church in Zimbabwe. "The Waddilove Manifesto: The Educational Policy of the Methodist Church." A statement of policy and principles, February 9, 1946.

Carlson, Brian. "American Education: A South African Perspective in the Process of Desegregation." *Kappa Delta Phi*, Summer 1988.

Center for Applied Research. *Social Implications of the Lagos Plan of Action for Economic Development in Africa, 1980–2000*. Geneva: Author, November 1981.

Central Committee for SWAPO. *Swapo: Political Program of the Southwest Africa People's Organization*. Lusaka: Author, July 28–August 1, 1976.

Churchill, Winston, and Franklin Roosevelt. *The Atlantic Charter*, August 13, 1941.

Congolese National Liberation Front (CNLF). *The Struggle for Liberation*. New York, 1975.

Davidson, Basil. *Africa: New Nations and Problems*, a documentary film, Arts and Entertainment, 1988.

Dodge, Ralph. "The Church and Political Community." Unpublished essay, 1963.

Dodge, Ralph E. "A Political Community." Unpublished essay, May 1964.

Gordimer, Nadine. *Gold and the Gun: Crisis in Mozambique and South Africa*, a documentary film, Arts and Entertainment, 1900.

Hartzell, James C. "The Future of Africa." *African Advance*, Vol. 2, No. 1, October 8, 1975.

Landis, Elizabeth. *Apartheid and the Disabilities of Women in South Africa*. New York: United Nations Unit on Apartheid, 1975.

The League of Nations. *The Mandate of Southwest Africa*, May 7, 1920.

The League of Nations Covenant. *Article 22*, January 20, 1920.

Lewis, Anthony. "The Harsh Reality Is that Apartheid Is Still in Place." *New York Times*, April 6, 1990, sec. 2, p. 15.

Loveridge, F. G., Senior Education Officer in the Ministry of African Education, Zimbabwe. "Disturbing Realities of Western Education in Southern Africa." An address to the Rotary Club International, Harare, March 13, 1963.

Macmillan, Harold. "Commonwealth Independence and Interpendence." An address to the Joint Session of the South African Parliament, Cape Town, February 3, 1960.

Maier, Karl. "Opponent May Thwart Mugabe's Bid for a One-party system." *Washington Post*, March 29, 1990, sec. 2, p. 16.

Malianga, Morton, a spokesman for ZANU. "We shall Wage an all out war to Liberate Ourselves." A statement issued following a battle between the colonial forces and the African nationalist guerrillas on April 29, April 30, 1966.

Mandela, Nelson. A statement made in Cape Town soon after his release from Victor Verster Prison, SABC-TV, February 11, 1990.

———. Speech given in Soweto during a Reception held in his honor, February 12, 1990. On SABC-TV.

M'Bow, Amadou-Mahtar, UNESCO Director-General. "Unesco and the Promotion of Education for International Understanding." An address to the New York African Studies Association Conference, Albany, New York, October 29, 1982.

McHarg, James. "Influences Contributing to Education and Culture of Native People in Southern Rhodesia. A Ph.D. dissertation, Duke University, 1962.

McNamara, Robert. "The Challenge of Sub-Sahara Africa." John Crawford Lectures, Washington, D.C., November 1, 1985.

Mnegi wa Dikgang. *Education with Production*. Vol. 5, No. 2. Gaberone: Government Printer, June 1987.

Molotsi, Peter. "Educational Policy and South African Bantustans." A paper presented at the New York Association of African Studies, Albany, New York, October 29–30, 1981.

Morton, Donald. *Partners in Apartheid*. New York Center for Social Action: United Church of Christ, 1973. Pamphlet.

Mozambique. "Documento Informativo." Ref. Doc/Inf.01/22, Maputo, 1979.

Mungazi, Dickson A. "Educational Innovation in Zimbabwe: Possibilities and Problems." *Journal of Negro Education*, Vol. 54, No. 4, 1985.

———. "The Application of Memmi's theory of the Colonizer and the Colonized." *Journal of Negro Education*, Vol. 55, No. 4, 1986.

———. "The Educational Policy of the British South Africa Company Towards Rural and Urban Africans in Zimbabwe: A Dilemma of Choice, 1899–1923." *African Urban Quarterly*, Vol. 2, No. 1, February 1987.

———. "A Strategy for Power: Commissions of Inquiry into Education and Government Control in Zimbabwe." *International Journal of African Historical Studies*, Vol. 22, No. 2, 1989.

———. "To Bind Ties Between the School and Tribal Life: Educational Policy for Africans under George Stark in Zimbabwe." *Journal of Negro Education*, Vol. 58, No. 4, 1989, p. 468.

———. Letter addressed to President F. W. de Klerk of South Africa, on the effect of apartheid on Southern Africa, February 15, 1990.

———. *Apartheid in South Africa: Origin, Meaning, and Effect*, a documentary film, Audio-Visual Services, Education, Northern Arizona University. Ref. AC/ECC/2/90, February 22, 1990.

———. "Educational Policy for Africans and Church-State Conflict During the Rhodesia Front Government in Zimbabwe." *National Social Science Journal*, Vol. 2, No. 3, June 1990.

Mutumbuka, Dzingai. "Zimbabwe's Educational Challenge." Paper presented at the World University Services Conference, London, December 1979.

New York Friends Group, Inc. *South Africa: Is Peaceful Change Possible?* New York: Author, 1984.

Office on Africa Educational Fund. *The Struggle for Justice in South Africa*. Washington, D.C.: Author, February 1984.

Organization of African Unity. *A Communique on Mozambique*. Nairobi, Kenya, August 8, 1989.

PBS. *Not in a Thousand Years: From Rhodesia to Zimbabwe*, a documentary film, 1981.

"Prospects of a Settlement in Angola and Namibia." A statement by the parties [Representatives of the Angola, SWAPO, Cuba]. New York: United Nations, 1988.

Rhodesia Front Government. "The Dynamic Expansion in African Education." A policy statement. Ref. INF/NE/Acc.40/2710, April 20, 1966.

Riddell, Roger. *From Rhodesia to Zimbabwe: Alternatives to Poverty, A Position Paper*. Gweru: Mambo Press, 1978.

Rubin, Leslie. *Bantustan Policy: A Fantasy and a Fraud*, No. 12/71. New York: United Nations, Unit on Apartheid, 1971.

Samuels, Machel. "The New Look in Angolan Education." *Africa Report*, November 1967.

Smith, Arthur. Minister of Education in Rhodesia. An interview with Geoffrey Atkins of the Rhodesia Broadcasting Service, Educational Policy for Africans, January 31, 1968.

Smuts, J. C. *The League of Nations: A Practical Suggestion*. Pretoria, South Africa: Government Printer, 1918.

South African Ministry of Information. "South Africa Stops Native Students from Territotirs from Attending its Schools." A press release, November 2, 1950.

Southern Rhodesia, United Federal Party. "Information Statement." Ref. UFP/SR/9, 1961.

Sullivan, Leon. "Meeting the Mandate for Change: A Progress Report on the Application of the Sullivan Principles on U.S. Companies in South Africa." New York, 1984. Pamphlet.

Tanzania. *Education for Self-Reliance*. Dar es Salaam: Government Printer, 1967.

Thompson Publications. *Parade*. Harare: Author, August 1989.

TransAfrica. *Namibia: The Crisis in U.S. Policy Toward Southern Africa*. Washington, D.C.: Author, 1983.

UNESCO. "Education in Africa in the Light of the Lagos Conference." Paper No. 25, Paris, France, 1976.

United Methodist Church. "Resolution Warning the Government of Southern Rhodesia Against Continued Policy of Discrimination." Harare, 1963.

United Methodist Church. *Southern Africa*. New York: Board of Global Ministries, 1986.

United Nations. *A Crime Against Humanity: Questions and Answers on Apartheid*. New York: Author, 1984.

University of Cape Town. "A Call for Postdoctoral Research Fellows, 1991." *Chronicle of Higher Education*, March 16, 1990, vol. 1, p. 7.

Walker, L. Kay. *Dickson A. Mungazi on Colonial Education for Africa: George Stark Policy in Zimbabwe*, documentary film, Northern Arizona University, 1995.

Washington Office on Africa. *Resources on Namibia*. Washington, D.C.: Author, March 1982.

Watson, P. *The Struggle for Democracy*. PBS, 1988. Film.

World Bank. "Alternatives to Formal Education: Unesco Conference on Education." Harare: Government Printer, June 18–July 3, 1982.

———. *Accelerate Development in Sub-Sahara Africa: An Agenda for Action*. Washington, D.C.: Author, 1983.

———. *Public Sector Management in Botswana*. Washington, D.C.: Author, 1984.

———. *Toward Sustained Development in Sub-Sahara Africa*. Washington, D.C.: Author, 1984.

World Council of Churches, Involvement in the Struggles Against Oppression in Southern Africa, 1966–1980. Pamphlet by World Council of Churches.

ZANU. *Zimbabwe: Election Manifesto*. Harare, 1979.

———. *Liberation Through Participation: Women in the Zimbabwean Revolution*. Harare: ZANU, 1981.

Zimbabwe Ministry of Education. *Arra Khris School Library News*. Harare. Vol. 6, No. 60, July 1986.

Zimbabwe, Conference of Catholic Bishops. *Our Mission To Teach: A Pastoral Statement on Education*. Gweru: Mambo Press, 1987.

Index

About the Authors

DICKSON A. MUNGAZI is Regents Professor of Education and History at Northern Arizona University.

L. KAY WALKER is Assistant Professor of Education at Northern Arizona University.

ISBN 0-275-95746-2

EAN

9 780275 957469

HARDCOVER BAR CODE

90000>